Coleridge

# Coleridge

Katharine Cooke

Routledge & Kegan Paul
London, Boston and Henley

First published in 1979
by Routledge & Kegan Paul Ltd
39 Store Street,
London WC1E 7DD,
Broadway House,
Newtown Road,
Henley-on-Thames,
Oxon RG9 1EN and
9 Park Street,
Boston, Mass. 02108, USA
Set in 11 on 12pt Latinesque
and printed in Great Britain by
Weatherby Woolnough, Wellingborough, Northants

©Katharine Cooke 1979

British Library Cataloguing in Publication Data

Cooke, Katharine

Coleridge.
1. Coleridge, Samuel Taylor – Criticism and interpretation
821'.7        PR4484        78-41237

ISBN 0 7100 0141 X

*For David, Gervase and Anna*

# Contents

# Acknowledgments

It is a pleasure to record my thanks to Professor Barbara Hardy for suggesting that I write this book, to Royal Holloway College Library for permission to borrow books, to my mother Mrs B. Lees for help with the typing and most of all to Dr P. M. Ball for much valued criticism and moral support.

# Abbreviations

| | |
|---|---|
| AR | *Aids to Reflection*, Bohn edition, 1884. |
| BL | *Biographia Literaria*, ed. with his aesthetical essays by J. Shawcross, 1907, in 2 vols. |
| C&S | *On the Constitution of Church and State*, ed. H. N. Coleridge, 1839. |
| CCF | *The Friend*, ed. B. Rooke, 1969, in 2 vols. |
| CCL | *Lectures 1795 On Politics and Religion*, ed. L. Patton and P. Mann, 1971. |
| CCLS | *Lay Sermons*, ed. R. J. White, 1972. |
| CCW | *The Watchman*, ed. L. Patton, 1970. |
| CL | *Collected Letters*, ed. E. L. Griggs, volumes 1-6, Oxford, 1956, 1959, and 1971. |
| CP | *The Poetical Works*, ed. E. H. Coleridge, 1912, in 2 vols. |
| CN | *Collected Notebooks*, ed. K. Coburn, 1957, 1962, 1973. |
| CIS | *Confessions of an Inquiring Spirit*, reprinted from the third edition of 1853, ed. H. St J. Hart, 1956. |
| EOT | *Essays on his own Times*, ed. S. Coleridge, 1850, in 3 vols. |
| JDC | *Poetical Works*, ed. J. D. Campbell, 1901. |
| LR | *Literary Remains*, ed. H. N. Coleridge, 1836-9, in 4 vols. |
| MC | *Miscellaneous Criticism*, ed. T. M. Raysor, 1936. |
| PhL | *Philosophical Lectures*, ed. K. Coburn, 1949. |
| ShC | *Shakespearean Criticism*, ed. T. M. Raysor, 1930, in 2 vols. |
| TL | *Hints towards the Formation of a More Comprehensive Theory of Life*, ed. S. B. Watson, 1848. |
| TT | *Table Talk and Omniana*, ed. T. Ashe, 1884. |

# Introduction

For many Coleridge's name means the 'Ancient Mariner', a few other poems, *Biographia Literaria* and *Shakespearean Criticism*. This has been enough to ensure a lasting reputation, but as I hope this book will show, it leaves a great deal out of consideration. Despite this narrow recognition of Coleridge's contribution to our culture, his influence has been deeply felt by those who have in their turn had a more general influence on our ways of thinking. Further, Coleridge, who lived from 1772 to 1834, speaks to us in the late twentieth century with a voice which we recognise for its concern with our concerns. Besides this, Coleridge offers us himself in a fashion peculiarly revealing and itself fascinating to the modern interest in personality. Coleridge as a whole as well as Coleridge on such-and-such a subject interests those who make his acquaintance in notebooks and letters as it did those who knew him in life.

Coleridge wrote so perceptively about himself that it seems impossible to say anything about him which he did not anticipate, which may be why so many books and articles contain so many extracts from his work; the present book is no exception. More than that, much as there is to be learnt from Coleridge, it has to be done the hard way, by reference to the works themselves. There can be no substitute for the experience of Coleridge's mind which comes from reading what he actually wrote; even where much seems to be dross, as in the more tortuous later prose, following the process of thought in a man like Coleridge has a unique value. It is therefore with genuine humility that I offer the following in the hope that it will serve not so much as a guide but as an invitation to the works themselves; in the hope that the reader will be able to echo the compliment quoted and cherished by Coleridge:[1]

1

Sir, I have never in the course of my life received so much and so valuable information from any man as from you. It is not this however that I shall most remember you by; but that every time, I have left you, I have felt myself a better man.

There is, however, another side to the issue. Not all students have found contact with Coleridge's mind an ennobling experience; for many he seems exasperatingly verbose, pretentious and over-rated. Among the earliest of those who were irritated by Coleridge's personal habits and felt that he achieved far less than he might have were the poets and critics who actually knew him: Southey, Wordsworth, De Quincey and above all Hazlitt at some time or other gave vent to such dissatisfaction. The following extract from a uniformly hostile review of the *Lay Sermon* by Hazlitt is quoted at length because it represents this sort of Coleridge criticism so aptly:[2]

The subtlety of his tact, the quickness and airiness of his invention, make him perceive every possible shade and view of a subject in its turn; but this readiness of lending his imagination to every thing, prevents him from weighing the force of any one, or retaining the most important in mind. It destroys the balance and *momentum* of his feelings; makes him unable to follow up a principle into its consequences, or maintain a truth in spite of opposition; it takes away all *will* to adhere to what is right, and reject what is wrong; and, with the will, the power to do it, at the expense of anything difficult in thought, or irksome in feeling. The consequence is, that the general character of Mr. Coleridge's intellect, is a restless and yet listless dissipation, that yields to every impulse, and is stopped by every obstacle; an indifference to the greatest trifles, or the most important truths: or rather, a preference of the vapid to the solid, of the possible to the actual, of the impossible to both; of theory to practice, of contradiction to reason, and of absurdity to common sense.

While this is very damaging it is by no means very inaccurate. It is damaging not so much because the critic misrepresents the writer, but because there is no sympathy for his point of view. This does lead to some inaccuracy, as Hazlitt, intent on a different set of principles, misses any coherence of idea in Coleridge, but as to the manner of the composition, neither Coleridge nor his defenders could deny that this is how it looks. It is the lack of sympathy which is important here, concentrating on what Coleridge does not do instead of looking for what he does. Critics who have been able to resist the pull of Coleridge's powerful personality have ever since been in a position to point out severe weaknesses in his work. One of the more notorious of the recent critics of this type is Norman Fruman, who displays also a frequent feature of such criticism, a sense of dismay that Coleridge has so easily pulled the wool over other critics' eyes. Here is an example:[3]

> If critics will not grant that the overall shape of Coleridge's Shakespeare criticism is crucially dependent upon Schlegel, how much less will the notion be entertained of still deeper and broader dependence!

Here Fruman raises one of the central problems of Coleridge criticism, his borrowings from the work of others. Again the question of sympathy is crucial. There is no disputing that in almost all Coleridge's work (poetry as well as prose) there is a heavy and frequently unacknowledged dependence on the ideas and even the words of other writers. Coleridge himself offers reasons for this, in public in the *Biographia* where he avows allegiance to 'truth as a divine ventriloquist', but more helpfully in the privacy of the notebooks:[4]

> In the Preface of my Metaphys. Works I should say – Once & all read Tetens, Kant, Fichte, &c – & there you will trace or if you are on the hunt, track me. Why then not acknowledge your obligations step by step? Because, I could not do so in a multitude of glaring resemblances without a lie / for they had been mine, formed, & full formed in my own mind, before I had ever heard of these Writers, because to have fixed on the partic. instances in which I have really been indebted to these Writers would have been very hard, if possible, to me who read for truth & self-satisfaction, not to make a book, & who always rejoiced and was jubilant when I found my own ideas well expressed already by others & would have looked like a *trick*, to skulk there not quoted, & lastly, let me say, because (I am proud perhaps but) I seem to know, that much of the matter remains my own, and that the Soul is *mine*. I fear not him for a Critic who can confound a Fellow-thinker with a Compiler.

This is convincing if it is looked at from Coleridge's position, if we identify with his attitude. If, however, the critic feels it is his duty not to accept such special pleading, then the list of borrowings remains formidable. It has proved well beyond the scope of these pages, where only occasional hints of Coleridge's sources will be found. In general, I have taken Coleridge at his word and considered the essential thought his own even when it is dressed in borrowed feathers.

Critics of Coleridge, then, seem to have fallen into two categories: those who find Coleridge's arguments convincing and interesting (not necessarily because they find them factually accurate) and those, like Hazlitt and Fruman and countless others, who see Coleridge as a writer who achieved little, deceived the world by an effect of learned thinking and so enjoys a reputation he does not deserve. This book belongs to the first category, partly because the Coleridge of Fruman and Hazlitt would not warrant a study of this kind, partly because as he himself said:[5]

> My experience tells me that little is taught or communicated
> by contest or dispute but everything by sympathy and love.
> Collision elicits truth only from the hardest heads.

Mainly it is because prolonged contact with Coleridge, both in formal publications and private utterances, has convinced me that there is in Coleridge something of such value that it more than compensates for his personal idiosyncracies and his deficiencies as a writer. Indeed, I am inclined to agree with T. McFarland, who considers that it is the whole of Coleridgean experience which is so valuable, for as he says:[6]

> Despite Coleridge's own frequent laments for his weakness, in a
> larger sense I do not find that term properly descriptive.
> Certainly the conception is a relative one. If we see legs buckle
> under a burden, we might ascribe the effect to weakness; but if
> the legs belong to Atlas, the ascription makes little sense.
> Coleridge, I have always felt, is in a special way a hero of
> existence: though life bore him down, he fought from his
> knees. ... If Coleridge's ruined existence thus contains elements
> of heroism, so too does his fragmentary work function
> culturally with no less power than work of more
> conventionally praised structure.

Coleridge was aware of this and instead of perfecting a technique to disguise any flaws, chose to display his workings in such a way that the reader could use them as a springboard from which to move forward, or as he said: 'If we are wrong, we yet wish to furnish at the same time a torch, which may assist the reader in the detection of our errors.'[7] It was a method which Coleridge had observed in Nature:[8]

> Observe, how graciously Nature instructs her human children. She cannot give us the knowledge derived from sight without occasioning us at first to mistake images of reflection for substances. But the very consequences of the delusion lead inevitably to its detection; and out of the ashes of the error rises a new flower of knowledge. We not only see, but are enabled to discover by what means we see.

This in turn leads Coleridge to include in published works what we should normally expect to be discarded as rough draft. Coleridge's knowledge was not an end result, a polished jewel; it was instead, a hard climb, a continuing process in which we must take what help we can get. It is a mark of the quality of Coleridge's mind that he should choose to offer his own false starts and his misapprehensions to act as such a help. It was a trait which Walter Pater remarked upon from his quite different standpoint. Of Coleridge's prose, he says:[9]

> the whole, just that mere preparation for an artistic effect which the finished literary artist would be careful one day to destroy.

This tells us quite clearly what Coleridge does not offer; instead, as he said answering criticisms of *The Friend* in a letter to Poole, he chose a style which suited his purpose:[10]

> Of Parentheses I may be too fond – and will be on my guard in this respect –. But I am certain that no work of empassioned & eloquent reasoning ever did or could subsist without them – They are the *drama* of Reason – & present the thought growing, instead of a mere Hortus siccus.

In Coleridge we are able, as George Whalley said: 'To study the mind of genius in its activity rather than in its products.'[11]

All this requires a patience and sympathy from the reader which

Coleridge strains to the limit in some of his published work. In the notebooks and letters, the reader is able to make a more direct contact with Coleridge's mind:[12]

> The soil that fell from the Hawk poised at the extreme
> boundary of Sight thro' a column of sunshine – a falling star,
> a gem, the fixation, & chrystal, of substantial light, again
> dissolving and elongating like a liquid Drop – how altogether
> lovely this to the Eye, and to the Mind too while it remained
> its own self, all & only its very Self –. What a wretched
> Frenchman would not he be, who could shout out – charming
> Hawk's *Turd*! – O many, many are the seeing, hearings, &
> tactual Impressions of pure Love, that have a Being of their
> own – & to call them by the names of things unsouled and
> debased below even their own lowest nature by Associations
> accidental, and of vicious accidents, is *blasphemy* –

Here Coleridge demonstrates the ease with which he can pass from observation to philosophy. It is a neat example of what he called active thought; Coleridge is not content merely to see the phenomenon, his mind reaches out to it, enlarging the significance of the experience.

I hope that the reader will feel encouraged by this brief introduction to further his acquaintance with Coleridge. What is now necessary is that I should say something of the nature of the book which follows. As the table of contents shows, various chapters have been set aside for different aspects of Coleridge's work. To a certain extent, such a division may seem a travesty of the organic whole of Coleridge's thought. When we read Coleridge's own description of 'Biographical Sketches of my own literary Life and Opinions on Politics, Religion, Philosophy and the Theory of Poetry –'[13] or the subtitle of *The Friend*, 'A series of essays in three volumes to aid in the formation of fixed principles in politics, morals, and religion with literary amusements interspersed',[14] the attempt to classify these works under any one head seems a mere impertinence, but if we are to perceive any order in Coleridge's work, it must be done. A certain amount of cross-referencing should prevent the reader from assuming that *The Friend* is merely political, the *Biographia* only literary critical. Furthermore, I hope that by concentrating attention on one aspect of each work the multifarious thoughts of Coleridge can be seen in an organised way. The accumulation of the various aspects of Coleridge's writings should enable the reader to see not only the overlap between them but also the central unity of Coleridge's thought, to which the conclusion further directs the attention.

There is, however, another way in which this categorisation of Coleridge's genius belies its nature. In order to concentrate on those aspects of Coleridge's work which seem central, I have had to overlook other areas in the chapter titles. Coleridge on science, Coleridge on language (his own and other languages he studied), Coleridge on education and child-development are all important aspects of his work which only receive a passing mention. They have been relegated to a subordinate position because I felt that the other categories more accurately reflect major preoccupations. To allow more prominence to minor classifications would cause a fragmentation which does not do justice to Coleridge's stature as a coherent thinker. On the other hand, I am aware that students of Coleridge who are particularly interested in these aspects will justifiably feel disappointed that there is so little here for them.[15]

Letters, marginalia and notebooks are referred to only as they illuminate the study of other works. Editions of all three are available or in progress and all are worth study in their own right. However, I wanted in this book to show that Coleridge the polymath, the disorganised giant of English romanticism could and did produce works which merit consideration as separate entities. This is why, with the exception of the inclusion of the *Biographia* and *The Friend* in two chapters, the various works are considered as units within each chapter. To further concentration on the published works, the occasional utterances of notebook and letter have been kept in a subordinate position. They can make no claim to unity, though they give wonderful instances of thought growing, and there is no finer commentary on Coleridge's work than these private remarks, whether they were made to friends or to his 'dear Book! Sole Confidant of a breaking Heart, whose social nature compels *some* outlet'.[16] It does not help us to see Coleridge's achievement as a writer if we concentrate too much on these incidental writings at the expense of works intended for the public.

Within each chapter I have first given a historical survey of the development of Coleridge's thought in each aspect and for this I have had recourse to letters and notebooks. This is followed by a more detailed study of the main ideas embodied in the works. For some chapters the introductory material has also included a more detailed historical background; this is primarily the case in the chapters on drama and journalism, which may make these chapters seem disproportionately long. While it is true that I have concentrated on aspects of Coleridge which have received less attention elsewhere, this is not meant to suggest that his work for the stage or for the newpapers is in any way more valuable than his poetry or his criticism, for example. Frequently, I have felt that the best advice I could offer the reader was the title of a book which gives more detailed treatment of a particular work than is possible in a general study. But this brings me back to what I said at the beginning: there can be no better way of studying Coleridge than to read the works themselves. Not what Coleridge thought but how Coleridge thought is what really matters.

# 1

# Life

He has been treated sufficiently often as a human contradiction
and as a biographer's puzzle. He has been pitied and
patronized, condemned and defended enough. The literature on
his 'case' must be now nearly as voluminous as his own
writings.[1]

That was over forty years ago; but the picture has altered little,
although the accumulation of studies is now considerably greater.
D. P. Calleo summed up the position tersely: 'No man ever had
more condescending biographers.'[2] It is wonderfully easy to 'tut-tut'
at Coleridge. It was done in his lifetime and has been done ever
since. He should not have married Sara Fricker, he should not have
left her; he should not have become addicted to opium; he should
not have become so involved with Wordsworth, much less with
Sara Hutchinson; he ought not to have deceived his friends,
borrowed from the writings of others, wallowed in ill-health,
wasted so much time on abstruse books – the list of charges could
go on. But to say all this is to say that he should not have been
Coleridge. Nor, if a moral tone is to be adopted, can Coleridge's
shortcomings be considered as really vicious; after all, he did not
father and abandon an illegitimate daughter as did Wordsworth, he
did not divorce his wife to marry a common maid who would not
have him, as did Hazlitt, and his sins do not bear mention beside
those of Byron and Shelley. Yet these men are recognised rightly for
what they are, without irrelevant moral opprobrium. The answer
cannot be that Coleridge setting great store in his work by a moral
life is found wanting by his own standards (though he would have
been the first to admit the truth of this), because Wordsworth even
more set himself up as a figure of moral rectitude. Coleridge's
trouble is that he is so open about his faults and failures. It is all

there for the prying eyes of posterity; his bowels, his skin complaints, his prescriptions for cures, his sufferings and his longings, all this as well as, on the lighter side, his recipes for ginger beer, his walking holidays, his recommendations for his children's diet, make Coleridge an intimate acquaintance. When in addition he records his sense of guilt and failure, it is difficult to resist the temptation to feel an easy superiority.

Coleridge's life was not an extraordinarily eventful one, but to all his life's events he responded in full. He was, too, alive in eventful times, and these affairs of the world at large had an influence on him which cannot be overlooked. All this makes a survey of his life in one chapter a difficult task. I have tried here to give an outline, referring the reader, where appropriate, to more detailed coverage in later chapters. The narrative has been interrupted from time to time to discuss various aspects of Coleridge's life which seem to warrant separate treatment. I have tried not to judge and to keep comment to a minimum, and there is no attempt to delve into Coleridge's personality – that, in the only way in which it concerns us, should emerge from the study of his writings in later chapters. Coleridge's life and character had such an influence on his work that it is difficult to discuss one apart from the other, and references perhaps not easily understandable at this stage have been inevitable. On the other hand, reading the rest of the book should help to fill out the picture of Coleridge which is only sketched here.

Samuel Taylor Coleridge was born on 21 October 1772 (he always thought his birthday was on the 20th). His childhood, in the small country town of Ottery St Mary where his father was schoolmaster, seems to have been uneventful enough. As the youngest of ten children, nine of them boys, he remembered being spoilt by both mother and father and being the object of his brothers' jealousy, as might be expected in the youngest of such a large brood. One incident Coleridge recounts in detail is his running away from home. This followed a scrap with his brother Francis, the next youngest, over a piece of cheese and resulted in Samuel's staying all night in the open. A great to-do was the result of this incident when it happened and critics since have explored the happening for seeds of Coleridge's future problems.[3] Coleridge himself laconically observed:[4]

I was put to bed – & recovered in a day or so – but I was

certainly injured – For I was weakly, & subject to the ague for
many years after –

It seems likely that a tendency to rheumatic pains (and possibly to
hypochondria) date from this incident.

Coleridge's childhood was abruptly and prematurely ended by
his father's death in 1781. His family was obliged to leave the
school-house and in the spring of 1782 arrangements were made for
Coleridge to attend Christ's Hospital School. From this time until
he enjoyed the different freedom of Cambridge undergraduate life,
Coleridge lost the carefree ways of a country upbringing. Coleridge
has many harsh things to say of his schooldays: 'our diet was very
scanty', 'The boys were ... under excessive subordination to each
other'.[5] The picture in 'Frost at Midnight' has been thought to owe
something to Wordsworth's belief in the value of nature, when it
recalls:[6]

> I was reared
> In the great city, pent 'mid cloisters dim
> And saw nought lovely but the sky and stars.

but the word 'pent' probably reflects accurately the feelings of the
young Coleridge in the restricted atmosphere of his school. Certain
free days were allowed, but Coleridge had few connections in
London until, towards the end of his schooldays, he was befriended
by the Evans family and treated as one of their own. The combination of being adrift from the large society of Ottery, where he
could count on being known and respected as his father's son, and
the sense of being restricted by high walls and rigid discipline in a
city school probably accounts for Coleridge's unhappiness at school.
Intellectually, he seems to have been more fortunate; the 'very
sensible, though at the same time, ... very severe master',[7] the
Reverend James Bowyer encouraged Coleridge's interest in literature. This was an interest which Coleridge had developed in his
solitary hours at home and his schoolmasters deepened his
knowledge not only of the classics but also of the great English
writers, notably Milton and Shakespeare. He seems at this time also
to have begun to take an interest in metaphysics, profiting from the
city's library resources to explore works of philosophy, so that
Charles Lamb, a year or two younger than Coleridge, was highly
impressed by his fluent learning.[8]

Altogether, it was not the stable childhood that would foster emotional self-sufficiency or self-confidence even in someone less easily influenced by life's vicissitudes than Coleridge. It is hardly surprising that troubles should throng quickly upon him when he was installed at Cambridge. His arrival at Jesus College in October 1791 was unfortunate (some confusion caused him to be penniless and without permanent rooms) and he was lonely:[9]

> I sit down to dinner in the Hall in silence – except the noise of suction, which accompanies my eating – and rise-up ditto.

In his next letter he remarks: 'There is no such thing as *discipline* at our college'[10] and it was not long before Coleridge, without the support of an organised routine displayed his incapacity for self-discipline. Rheumatism and opium are an ominous conjunction but at first, Coleridge's problems were primarily financial. Nearly thirty years later Coleridge wrote to his son, Derwent, as he entered his Cambridge career, not to incur:[11]

> any Cambridge Debt – the very thought of which agitates me, who can never forget the stupifying effect of my first Term Bill ... affected and infected my whole life following –

He was at this time in close correspondence with the Evans family and this recourse to old London friends suggests a loneliness at Cambridge which he was unable to alleviate by ordinary under-graduate friendships. Oxford and Cambridge in those days were not primarily educational establishments but a step on the road from country society to ordination, thence back to country life. Those whose roots were unthinkingly established in this system, as for instance Parson Woodforde,[12] adjusted well to the lax discipline, excessive consumption of food and drink and leisurely study. Coleridge was not of that type (nor was Wordsworth, who could not settle at Cambridge either); he was an orphan and a scholar whose mind had already been opened to worlds beyond the ken of country parsons' sons. At this time rejecting his own background in the established church, Coleridge entered into the political life of the university under the influence of William Frend, a Unitarian and supporter of the French Revolution whose following among under-graduates was frowned upon by his fellow dons.

This introduction to Unitarianism was to have important con-sequences for Coleridge. Unitarian circles at this time offered an opportunity for sociable study which must have been very attractive to Coleridge. The atmosphere of a small group of dissenters banded together in the face of general social opprobrium had the added advantage of being open to intellectual enquiry. The desire to justify their own view of Christianity led Unitarians to the study of philosophy as well as of Bible criticism. E. S. Shaffer[13] suggests that it was through Unitarian contacts both at Bristol and at Cambridge that Coleridge first became interested in German thinkers, and undoubtedly the Unitarian influence fostered his interest in David Hartley. Unitarianism had a political dimension too. The storming of the Bastille while Coleridge was at school had been welcomed in England as a manifestation of the spirit of freedom. Later, fears for British institutions led the establishment in England to repressive measures; unorthodoxy of thought was suspect, meetings were watched and restrictive legislation was brought in. Dissenters in England who had not wavered in their support of revolutionary ideals were now stimulated by oppression to oppose the government. Hartley's 'necessarianism', especially as it was espoused by the prominent Unitarian, Priestley, formed an important part of Unitarian political thinking. Man, who had little control over his own destiny, was capable of the greatest good if only his environment were made more favourable. In political terms, this emerged in Coleridge's Bristol lectures, for instance, as an indictment of a war-mongering government exploiting the poverty of the people. Necessarianism could not for long satisfy Coleridge, who seems always to have felt a repugnance for any theology or philosophy which denied him some hand in his own fate. The neo-platonists whom he had read at school and whom he further studied at Cambridge soon began to modify his necessarianism. The evolution of Coleridge's thought was slow but steady from this time forward, and it involved him in a critical appraisal of many of his fellow thinkers. Hartley was in the ascendent still when his first son was born in 1796, but by 1798 he was to have changed sufficiently to name his second son for Berkeley, the platonist Anglican Bishop. Some ten years later Southey was to report on Coleridge's progress:[14.]

Hartley was ousted by Berkeley, Berkeley by Spinoza, & Spinoza by Plato. When last I saw him Jacob Behmen had some chance of coming in.

Not until after this did Coleridge really develop his own thought

13

fully, demonstrating how he had used his earlier reading to enrich his understanding of his own mind and experience. The *Biographia* is the mature fruit of his study and in that book the reaction against Hartley is best studied. Godwin, although he never had the same influence over Coleridge as Hartley, deserves a mention here. The reason why Coleridge never fell under Godwin's sway was that he could not accept the older man's rejection of emotion. His reaction to this aspect of Godwinianism provided an important impetus in the early political prose and in the poetry.

At Cambridge Coleridge's reading seems to have been unorthodox and spasmodic, his studying pursued in fits and starts, his way of life most irregular. Coleridge wrote a confessional letter to his brother:[15]

> My Affairs became more and more involved – I fled to Debauchery – fled from the silent and solitary Anguish to all the uproar of senseless Mirth! Having, or imagining that I had, no *stock* of Happiness, to which I could look forwards, I seized the empty gratifications of the moment, and snatched at the Foam as the Wave passed by me. – I feel a painful blush on my cheek, while I write it – but even for the University Scholarship, for which I affected to have read so severely, I did not read three days uninterruptedly – for the whole six weeks, that preceded the examination, I was almost constantly intoxicated!

Desperate remedies were sought: Coleridge enlisted in the Dragoons. He took a pseudonym, Silas Tomkyn Comberbache, but it seems very likely that he was not sorry to be recognised by an old school acquaintance who made his plight known. Recriminations and profound apologies over, Coleridge was returned to Cambridge, though with only a meagre supply of funds. By June 1794 Coleridge's spirits were sufficiently recovered for a walking tour of Wales with a fellow undergraduate. The first major stop was at Oxford, where Coleridge was introduced to Southey, and the first of an important series of friendships was begun. Southey too was an impecunious orphan, and his expulsion for disruptive behaviour from Westminster School seemed to indicate a fellow non-conformist, but in the summer when Habeas Corpus was suspended and prominent English radicals like Horne Tooke, Thelwall and Hardy were arrested, it was political sympathy which carried the two men into a friendship which was to last in spite of fundamental differences in character, reflected in several prolonged quarrels, until Coleridge's death.

This raises two issues which need further comment. One is the impact of the French Revolution on Coleridge's developing thought, and for a detailed discussion of this the reader should consult the chapters on Coleridge's political writing. The other is the importance throughout Coleridge's life of a succession of friendships. This is not an easy subject to discuss briefly,[16] and the strength of friendships with Southey, Wordsworth, Poole and finally the Gillmans as well as lesser but equally revealing friendships with Cottle, Humphry Davy, Morgan, Allsop and Green among others does not emerge clearly from the story of his life. After all, other men have friends and quarrel with them; but in Coleridge's case there was something more. Students of Coleridge with psychiatric training have seen in these relationships a reflection of Coleridge's inadequate relations with his parents, and it seems fairly obvious that in these friendships Coleridge was trying to create a bond like that of family between himself and men who showed themselves sympathetic to his position. The friendship with Wordsworth is something of a special case, on account of its importance to the development of the genius of both writers, but the friendship with Southey, begun only three months after his humiliating return to Cambridge, may perhaps serve as an illustration of some of the common features of these friendships. After three weeks stay at Oxford, Coleridge was writing to Southey:[17]

> When the pure System of Pantocracy shall have aspheterized
> the Bounties of Nature, these things will not be so – ! I trust,
> you admire the word 'aspheterized' from α non, σφέτερος
> proprius! We really *wanted* such a word – instead of travelling
> across the circuitous, dusty, beaten high-Road of Diction you
> thus cut across the soft, green pathless Field of Novelty! –

The enthusiasm displayed in a Coleridgean love of new words and word play is evident, a hall-mark of Coleridge's friendships in their early stages. That Southey and Coleridge should, on such a slight acquaintance, embark on an ambitious scheme like Pantisocracy (as it was later called) is typical of the way in which this friendship set alight the ideals of the two young men. The plan was that Southey, Coleridge and a few well-chosen friends should emigrate to start a colony where all property and all labour would be shared. A few months later, in Bristol, the plan was enlarged to include a number of women – notably, the three Fricker sisters, Edith, who was to marry Southey, Mary, the wife of Robert Lovell, already a Pantisocrat, and Sara, who was to marry Coleridge. The women were to help with the children, the washing and cooking; the men were to till the fields and study in the evening. As the plan developed, the practicalities of the scheme caused bitter disagreement between the friends, but at first all was unalloyed enthusiasm. Partly to raise funds for the scheme, *The Fall of Robespierre* was published in 1794 after Coleridge's return to Cambridge and his engagement to Sara. The engagement seems to have been embarked upon in an impulse of enthusiasm for Southey and the pantisocratic venture, which had now fixed on the valley of the Susquehanna as its setting, though Sara Fricker was by no means an unattractive girl. At all events, it was not long before Coleridge was recalling the more congenial nature of Mary Evans and regretting his hasty step. He retreated to London and Cambridge, and displeased both new friends and prospective bride by his failure to send letters to Sara. Coleridge was maturing. Ideas, aspirations, beliefs were to undergo profound change, but the letters of this period reveal something essentially Coleridgean:[18]

> I am so habituated to philosophizing, that I cannot divest myself of it even when my own Wretchedness is the subject. I appear to myself like a sick Physician, feeling the pang acutely, yet deriving a wonted pleasure from examining it's progress and developing it's causes.

At about this time Coleridge began his first notebook, one of the earliest entries being a draft sermon which includes the following:[19]

> That Scripture no where has it [Faith] in contradistinction to Reason

This in one short sentence anticipates much of Coleridge's later thought on the relationship of Faith to Reason. It indicates a core of constant thinking in Coleridge which seems not to have been affected by the turbulences of his life and changes in less fundamental thinking.

In December 1794 he wrote a farewell letter to Mary Evans and wrote to Southey 'I *will do my Duty*'.[20] Even so, Southey had to fetch him from London and the convivial society of Charles Lamb. Lamb was not mentioned in the list of friends above because his relationship with Coleridge was unlike the more fervent but less stable relationships mentioned there. Lamb was a school friend and the friendship endured all through the lives of both men (they died within a year of each other) uninterrupted by quarrel except for one brief if bitter dispute which was probably helped along by Southey and Charles Lloyd. Lamb and his sister Mary were unique among Coleridge's friends for the way in which they accepted him as he was and, without ever seeking to correct his failings, remained always aware of his good points. It is an indication of the sort of friend that Lamb was that in his company, with a pipe in the 'Salutation and Cat', Coleridge was engrossed in lengthy conversation, while in Bristol Southey was rightly if self-righteously fretting over his more weighty joint undertakings with Coleridge.

But it is to Southey that we owe the first publications by Coleridge. Like their combined dramatic work, the series of lectures on political and religious topics given in 1795 was designed to raise funds for the pantisocratic scheme now modified to a trial-run in Wales. More poetry was written, some of which appeared in the national *Morning Chronicle*, and Joseph Cottle, a local printer, extended his patronage and published volumes of poems in 1796 and 1797. Cottle paid for the poems in advance even of their being written and the culmination of his friendship was the publication in 1798 of *Lyrical Ballads*. To Cottle Coleridge also owed gratitude for help with domestic matters, not least the wall-papering of his first home at Clevedon. The bitter *Early Reminiscences* published after Coleridge's death have clouded over posterity's attitude to Cottle's patronage, but nothing should detract from the moral as well as the financial support which he generously gave during this early period.

The year 1795 was an important one for Coleridge; lectures and other publications must have given him a sense of potential in the public field, and the appearance of his poems added confidence in his ability. He made the final break with Mary Evans and hopeless passion and after an October wedding settled down to a period of unexpected domestic happiness. Also during 1795 came the end of the pantisocratic dream and the break with Southey. They were, as men married to sisters, to resume their friendship later on, but never on the same footing. The pantisocratic ideal caused the split. Southey, realising that it was a great gamble and unwilling to take

the risk, opted for law studies and family patronage. Coleridge, who
researched the American scene carefully, to the end of his life
maintained that the scheme was feasible, a view which numbers of
communes flourishing today seem to support. Southey thought
otherwise and, as a long recriminatory letter from Coleridge makes
clear, had long been trimming the original whole-heartedly com-
munistical venture. Wales had been substituted for America, family
connections and servants were to be included and finally:[21]

> Your private resources were to remain your individual
> property, and every thing to be separate except on five or six
> acres. In short, we were to commence Partners in a petty
> Farming Trade. This was the Mouse of which the Mountain
> Pantisocracy was at last safely delivered!

Coleridge loftily concludes:[22]

> FRIEND is a very sacred appellation – You were become an
> Acquaintance, yet one for whom I felt no common tenderness.
> I could not forget what you had been.

The real rupture came when Southey cut Coleridge in the street and
despite the sustained self-righteousness of this long letter, it appears
that Southey too felt aggrieved, that Coleridge had not pulled his
weight in joint literary ventures. It seems likely, furthermore, that
Southey had not been unaffected by Coleridge's reluctant return
from London. In truth, the two men were not suited to the sort of
friendship which both of them seem to have craved. They got on
much better in later years as brothers-in-law; Coleridge feeling
superior to Southey's more calculated way of life, Southey to
Coleridge's impulsive and chaotic existence. Southey married Edith
Fricker secretly and sailed to Portugal, and Coleridge began to
tackle his problems single-handed.

His first venture was the *Watchman*, an eight-daily newspaper (to
avoid tax incurred by weeklies – on grounds of economy and
principle) in which Coleridge hoped to put forward the Whig point
of view on the curtailment of citizens' liberties. The paper was also
intended to keep Coleridge and his wife and help to keep his wife's
dependants. (Although Coleridge was all his life short of money, he
never regarded the support of relatives or friends in need as other
than a first claim on his resources.) The paper did not pay; public
sympathy shifted during the year and events caused Coleridge to

think again about his sympathy for the French cause. Not all was loss – the *Watchman* tour, immortalised in the *Biographia*, must have made Coleridge's name familiar in provincial England and the practical experience of editing a paper was invaluable to the young idealist. His ideals, though, were to be hit hard during 1796, as France rejected English peace moves and formed an alliance with Spain to make war on England. Buonaparte's brilliant Italian campaign of that year demonstrated that under the Directorate France was no longer simply an embodiment of new political ideals but also a military power which threatened the freedom of Europe. Coleridge was not to become a supporter of the war against France until after the Peace of Amiens in 1802, but his sympathy for the French cause disappeared long before that, and his poem 'France, an Ode', published in 1798, records this change of heart. It was the cost to English society which caused Coleridge's antipathy to the war. Bad weather aggravated the effect of war on corn prices and the poor, whose staple was bread, suffered more than the rich, whose diet was more varied. Not until the second phase of the war, when Napoleon's command of most of Europe further damaged English commerce by affecting the supply and transport of imported luxury goods, were the middle and upper classes really affected. The industrial revolution was already shaking the foundations of the old rural agricultural economy and the requisites of war, in terms of both men and manufactured goods (the textile industry of the North of England provided French as well as English uniforms), further disrupted the established pattern of society, offering nothing in its place except, for many years, defeat and deprivation. It is difficult to over-estimate the importance of the combined phenomenon of the French Revolution and the Napoleonic War on the political thinking of Coleridge, and I have tried to speak more specifically of this in the chapters dealing with the political writings.

Before the end of 1796, Coleridge withdrew from the bustle of provincial society to his own rural retreat at Nether Stowey. A plan that he should go as tutor to a Derbyshire family never materialised, and at Stowey he could enjoy the society of his new friend Thomas Poole, tanner and prominent West-country radical. In the mean-time, during Coleridge's absence from home, Mrs Coleridge had given birth to a son, David Hartley (in honour of the philosopher); both were well and when Coleridge saw them together on his return, he tells Poole:[23]

I saw it at the bosom of it's Mother; on her arm; and her eye tearful & watching it's little features, then I was thrilled & melted, & gave it the Kiss of a FATHER. –

The birth of his children, Berkeley, born in May 1798 (he died the following February), Derwent, born in September 1800, and Sara, born in December 1802, was to provide a bond between man and wife of which both were equally aware, even when to Coleridge it seemed more like bondage. Hartley was to be an especial joy, featuring in notebooks, letters and poems, and all the time adding to his father's store of experience of the working of human perception.

Nether Stowey was not an altogether happy house for the Coleridge family. Its cramped conditions must have made life difficult for all its inhabitants, but especially for the young mother, now removed from the support of her family. The addition to the household of Charles Lloyd, who came as a pupil and paying guest, must have increased the problems, especially as he was subject to frequent epileptic fits. For Coleridge the genius, Nether Stowey was the base from which many important poems sprang. The friendship of Poole was invaluable. Level-headed in business matters, he had also a lively awareness of his friend's great gifts. In his early years Coleridge had no better supporter and with Poole he discussed his chief interests of the time, poetry and politics. From Stowey Coleridge supervised the publication of his poems while he tried to implement pantisocratic self-sufficiency – although his efforts, confined to a vegetable garden, a pig and some poultry, did not last long. On one of his frequent trips to Bristol, he met Wordsworth, staying with his sister at Racedown near Crewkerne, where Coleridge was soon a visitor. Both Coleridge and Wordsworth were engaged on poetic tragedies as well as on poetry in its more common forms and had a great deal to talk of. Politics, too, brought the two men together, for both had felt a great enthusiasm for revolutionary ideals and both were now undergoing a change of heart. The consequences of this friendship are greater than can be easily summarised. *Lyrical Ballads* and its preface, first published in 1798, have long been recognised as a milestone in the development of English poetry but other major works also reflect the interaction of two poetic minds so different in intention and achievement. *The Prelude* and the *Biographia* are both the fruit of this cross-pollination. Coleridge, too, used his insight into a creative genius of whose stature he was never in doubt to further his developing knowledge of the processes of the creative and hence the common mind of man.

Time was to corrode this friendship too, and it ended bitterly, but for a long time it was to impart an especial strength to Coleridge. Also, unfortunately, it made apparent the unsuitability of Sara Fricker as wife to Coleridge. She resented her husband's intimacy with Wordsworth and his sister and she probably felt that their influence was furthering his interest in unprofitable poetry, while she was more mindful of the need to find an occupation which would pay the domestic bills. While in Nether Stowey the friendship of Poole helped the young married couple to co-exist peacefully; Sara had her friends in the neighbourhood, Coleridge had his. But life at Nether Stowey was precarious because of a lack of funds, and when Coleridge's Unitarian friends at Bristol recommended him to the vacant ministry at Shrewsbury, he set off despite misgivings. His triumph there, and his meeting with Hazlitt almost won him over to a life which, while it would have suited Sara, would have stultified Coleridge's genius in the civilities of provincial dissenting circles. Rescue came from the £150 annuity offered by the Wedgwood brothers, Josiah and Thomas, who had met Coleridge in Bristol society. The connections Coleridge made in this way were important to him; it should perhaps be emphasised, to redress the balance of opinion that Coleridge wasted his intellectual resources in talk, that it was in all probability his gift for conversation which brought him the Wedgwood annuity and also the opportunity to work for the *Morning Post*, whose proprietor, Daniel Stuart, was one of the Wedgwood circle. In opting for the annuity Coleridge was choosing intellectual as well as social freedom. This is an important indication of how, throughout Coleridge's life, truth was not to be fixed and immutable (as it would have to be if he were to propound Unitarian dogma for the rest of his days) but to be embodied in a continuous enquiry.

Coleridge returned to Stowey, the society of the Wordsworths, now living at nearby Alfoxden, and a crowd of summer visitors, including the Lambs and John Thelwall, the prominent Radical. Many of his finest poems date from this time and the *Lyrical Ballads*, planned to defray the expenses of a walking tour, made their appearance. By the end of 1798, however, the poet was with the Wordsworths in Germany on a journey that was to have serious consequences. To undertake it with his new friends, benefiting from his new financial independence, he left his wife, now with two small babies, behind in Nether Stowey. For practical reasons, she could hardly have accompanied them, but in all probability the trip would have lost half its charm if domestic ties had not been left behind. As it was, Berkeley was very ill during Coleridge's absence and in March 1799 Poole wrote to Coleridge of his younger son's death. Coleridge's letter to his wife is stunning in its cold formality:[24]

> To look back on the life of my Baby, how short it seems! – but consider it referently to non-existence, and what a manifold and majestic Thing does it not become?

Coleridge felt the death of his baby deeply, as the conclusion to a letter to Poole reveals:[25]

> My dear Poole! don't let little Hartley die before I come home. – That's silly – true – & I burst into tears as I wrote it.

but he could not or did not reveal his feelings to his wife and towards the end of his letter to her expresses the hope that:[26]

> this event which has forced us to think of the Death of what is most dear to us, as at all times probable, will in many and various ways be good for us ... When in Moments of fretfulness and Imbecillity I am disposed to anger or reproach, it will, I trust, be always a restoring thought – 'We have wept over the same little one – '

The recipient of this letter, a young mother who had long nursed the sick infant before his death, must have felt very remote from the sender, her husband. Coleridge later often accused Sara of coldness, though she was an affectionate mother; one wonders whether her heart was hardened by her experiences while the poet was in Germany. She turned to Poole and the Southeys, whose solicitude and care must have provided a bitter contrast with her absent husband.

Meanwhile, Coleridge was working hard. He and Wordsworth had split up, in accordance with their different aims, and Coleridge learned German, studying at the University of Göttingen under the most recent of a long line of professors, whom Coleridge listed for his wife:[27]

> Mosheim, Gesner, Haller, Michaelis, Pütter, Kästner, Heyne,
> Letz or Less, Blumenbach, Lichtenburg, Plank, Eichorn,
> Meiners, and Jacobi

The frequency with which Coleridge later referred to the writings of men whose names appeared on this list indicates how deeply the German trip improved Coleridge's education. Detailed study was to come later, but the interest in and sympathy for German thinking unquestionably owes its extent to Coleridge's stay in the country. Coleridge's journal letters home, which were later to appear in *The Friend* and again as Satyrane's Letters in the *Biographia* reveal a full experience of German life and Coleridge was to further an increasing awareness of the new German thinking in England.

Coleridge wrote of being homesick and lonely, but his letters display a full social life and he was in no hurry to be home. He was expected in June, but arrived late in July. One of his first acts was a letter to Southey, suggesting that they let bygones be bygones. Southey responded unfavourably at first, but Poole's good offices finally effected a reconciliation and both families went on a short holiday to Devon. Coleridge was to spend little more time at Stowey. In October, he went to Bristol, thence with Cottle to meet the Wordsworths in the North, where they were staying with the Hutchinson family. A walking tour which introduced Coleridge to the Lake District was included in the holiday and while at Keswick Coleridge received an offer of regular work on the *Morning Post*. Before going home to pack up for the move to London, Coleridge returned alone to Sockburn, attracted by that happy family circle among whom was that other Sara, who was to dominate his emotional life for the next decade. Coleridge's love for Sara Hutchinson (Asra as he conveniently called her) was always tinged with the sadness of her inaccessibility. Although in the end Coleridge left his wife, he knew that Asra could not take her place. There was too much else involved. Wordsworth was to marry Asra's sister Mary in 1802 and a liaison with Asra would have meant the loss of the Wordsworths. To Coleridge, Asra was an embodiment of what might have been – a woman of his own who shared his life as a poet in the Wordsworth circle, in marked contrast to his wife, whose family were a burden and not a support to her husband and who mistrusted the Wordsworths deeply. As the years went on, and after Coleridge had left Greta Hall to live with the Wordsworths, Coleridge's sadness was increased by a fear that Asra, like the other women in that household, was more impressed by Wordsworth than by himself. She helped Coleridge by taking down much of *The Friend* as late as 1810, but significantly, the break with Wordsworth, later that year, was also a break with her.

From the end of 1799 to the end of March 1800, Coleridge was dedicated to profitable literary labour in London. He wrote regularly for the *Morning Post*, then an independent newspaper, ready to criticise the government even in war-time, though later to become a mouthpiece of the ministers, to Coleridge's outspoken horror. At the same time, he was busy on a commissioned translation of Schiller's *Wallenstein* plays. Despite an offer from Stuart to join him as editor of the *Morning Post*, Coleridge was still planning to return to the country but the problem was where to go. The Wordsworths had taken Dove Cottage in Grasmere and Coleridge was torn between joining them and returning to Somerset and Poole, which was Mrs Coleridge's preference. Coleridge chose to go north, disregarding Poole's warning about prostration before Wordsworth and answering with great confidence:[28]

> What if you had known Milton at the age of thirty, and
> believed all you now know of him – What if you should
> meet in the letters of any then living man, expressions
> concerning the young Milton *totidem verbis* the same as mine of
> Wordsworth, would it not convey to you a most delicious
> sensation?

By July Coleridge was resident at Greta Hall, Keswick; the situation of the house was charming, the landlord was friendly, garden and fields were a delight to Hartley, and Wordsworth was less than ten miles away. On the other hand, and ominously, Coleridge was soon ill; he had been working hard in London, and prone as he was to rheumatic complaints, the damp of the Lake District did not suit him. He was seldom well all the time he lived there. Money was still a worry and the birth in September of Derwent (named after the nearby lake), who was seriously ill for a while when very small, probably exacerbated the problems. By the beginning of 1801

Coleridge was really unwell and wrote to Davy of 'a succession of Indispositions, inflamed eyes, swoln eyelids, boils behind my ear, &c &c'.[29] These were followed by three weeks rheumatic fever while he was at Grasmere and a swelling of the left testicle. In all he was bedridden for five weeks.

He was not idle, however, and began to study the philosophical works which were to colour so much of his mature thought. The German writers whose acquaintance Coleridge had made at Göttingen were now studied in detail, together with other philosophers who could help Coleridge in his refutation of the Lockian enlightenment. The materialism inherent in the exaltation of reason which was heralded as an enlightenment in eighteenth-century England, and more especially in France, was abhorrent to Coleridge for its tendency to atheism and a denial of the religious in man. Instead, Coleridge turned to the German idealists, Kant, Fichte, Schelling and others – the list was to be extended throughout Coleridge's later years. At the same time, he returned to the mediaeval schoolmen whom he had first read at school and University. Coleridge began the attempt to find a new philosophy of his own which would blend in harmony all of man's faculties. The difficulties of the task are apparent but research brought other rewards for Coleridge, who never lost his sense of fun. A visit to Durham to study philosophy was only a partial success because the librarian, ignorant of continental scholarship, mistook a request for Leibnitz for an interest in live nits and directed the amused Coleridge to a purveyor of natural curiosities. As Coleridge was still sending articles occasionally to the *Morning Post*, his contact with the world at large was to continue to have an effect on the development of his philosophy, correcting any tendency to become self-absorbed.

Even when Coleridge was able to leave his bed, his health did not recover totally and he developed a condition which he called 'irregular gout'. To alleviate this, which lodged in his knee, with other symptoms in his back and stomach, Coleridge tried the application of laudanum, which in later years he was wont to say had caused his opium addiction.

Opium, then usually taken in alcohol as laudanum, had featured in Coleridge's life before this. Reference to school and college medicinal doses are supplemented by the later attribution of the writing of 'Kubla Khan' to the influence of the drug in Somerset days. It seems likely that Coleridge took laudanum not only for the physical ills but also for the mental pressures of life whenever they threatened to become too great for him. At Greta Hall, both genuine ill-health and increasing mental turmoil meant frequent recourse to the drug, but it was probably his sojourn in Malta which confirmed him in the habit. Laudanum was frequently prescribed medically at this period, often for such a slight complaint as tooth-ache, and the dangers of its addictive character were not appreciated, so that addiction was widespread. De Quincey was a well-known case, and Coleridge was fond of citing another fellow-addict, Wilberforce, the strictly evangelical abolitionist. The absorption of the addictive element in laudanum was slow, however, and only frequent use of increasingly heavy doses could have created the heavy reliance which Coleridge developed. Coleridge's loneliness in Malta resulted in the use of such heavy doses that he returned from his foreign journey an irretrievable addict. The Wordsworths noticed the change in him immediately but thought, such was the ignorance about drugs at this time, that he could break the habit if he would only make the effort. Coleridge was, unsurprisingly, incapable of such an effort and no doubt the sense of failure communicated to him by the Wordsworths at this period strengthened the drug's hold on him. When he left the Lakes in 1810, his use of the drug increased to such an extent that his life was endangered. He considered an asylum and the best medical advice, recognising the hopelessness of his case. Finally he accepted a place with Dr. Gillman in Highgate, in the hope that a cure could be effected under constant medical supervision. So indeed it proved, for although Coleridge frequently supplemented the allowed dose by clandestine imports from the local chemist, his addiction was now largely controlled.

It had by this time shaped Coleridge's life and character to a considerable degree. Addiction was, as he came to realise: 'for more than 30 years ... the guilt, debasement, and misery of my Existence'.[30] It caused him considerable physical suffering and immense anguish of soul. To posterity, and to Coleridge himself, the loss was not total. Long before his addiction he noted, in a letter to Poole, a pronounced difference between himself and Wordsworth:[31]

My many weaknesses are of some advantage to me; they unite me more with the great mass of my fellow-beings -

An instance of this shows in his criticism of Socrates' theory that 'ignorance was the ground of all vice and therein of all misery':[32]

> Every drunkard that lifts with trembling hands his glass to his lips and even sheds tears over it, knowing the anguish it will occasion, is a proof against it. No, it is impossible as the whole experience of the world shews. It is not an ignorance of the effects that will arise from it, but to get rid of the pain arising from the want of it, and that just in proportion as the pleasure declines, so the temptation, as it is called, becomes equal; then does the good, become most tremendous. Not a single ray of pleasure beforehand, but the daily round of habit from behind, *that* presses on the human mind.

Not often are references to his own life so transparent, but in all Coleridge's later work there is a sense in which all his experience deepened his thinking.

In 1801, when he began to take frequent doses of opium, there was no inkling of this. Coleridge had no real knowledge of the side-effects of the drug which his medical half-knowledge had seduced him into using. Life at Greta Hall soon settled into a pattern. Coleridge and his wife quarrelled frequently and bitterly. His children were a source of joy but his chief pleasure was in the company of Wordsworth and his sister and, after Wordsworth's marriage, with the Hutchinson sisters. Visits to Dove Cottage were frequent, especially when a new edition of the *Lyrical Ballads* was planned, for though Coleridge contributed nothing new, he took a hand in the editing and proof reading. In 1801, a journey to consult books at Durham included a stay with the Hutchinsons; in November of that year Coleridge visited London, in connection with the *Lyrical Ballads*, and stayed with Southey, as well as making the trip to Somerset to stay with Poole, postponing his return to Keswick until the following Spring. His 'Dejection' ode, first written as a letter in April of 1802, reveals the depths of misery which he now felt, 'a stifling, drowsy unimpassion'd Grief' to Coleridge far worse than active hardship. In the summer of 1802 Coleridge undertook a walking trip to St Bees, taking in Scafell Pike en route. Significantly, the letters which so magnificently describe this walk were sent to Asra. In November Coleridge was back in London, thence to Wales with Tom Wedgwood, writing letters to his wife which, with a mixture of tenderness and reproach, outline plans for more peaceful co-existence in the future. The birth of his daughter, Sara, followed in December just a day or two before Coleridge returned home in the company of Wedgwood. By February Coleridge wrote truthfully if playfully:[33]

> For the last 5 months of my Life I seem to have annihilated the present Tense with regard to place – you can never say, where *is* he? – but only – where *was he*? where *will* he be? – From Keswick – to London – Bristol – Pembroke
> – Birmingham – Manchester/Keswick – Etruria – Bristol – & in a few days to Blandford – probably, Stowey, Exeter – possibly, the Land's End.

In April 1803 Coleridge was back in Keswick, only to set off again in August with the Wordsworths to Scotland. This was not a successful excursion for Coleridge; he was irritable with Wordsworth, the open jaunting car was uncomfortable and wet, and he was without opium. Wordsworth's silence only made matters worse and at Arrochar they split. Coleridge continued on foot, walking prodigious distances. While he was in Edinburgh, he wrote 'Pains of Sleep', recounting the horrors caused by and causing his continuing use of laudanum, especially at night (though, as he later said, he was at the time unaware of the real cause of his nightmares). While in Edinburgh he heard of the death of the Southeys' only, and much awaited baby. The Southeys had gone to Greta Hall, where they were to stay for the rest of their lives, and Coleridge hurried home to comfort his friend. Despite the attempt on both sides to make a success of the Coleridge marriage, Coleridge's absence was clearly the best hope, especially once there were three Fricker sisters to contend with (Southey had also brought Lovell's widow). Early in 1804 Coleridge was off again; he stayed a while in London and then set sail for Malta.

Coleridge's letters home from Malta suffered losses typical of war-time mail, but research into the Maltese records gives us some idea of his life there.[34] Coleridge the poet quickly became a civil servant. The pay was a necessity but the work was not congenial, nor despite the friendship of the governor, Sir Alexander Ball, and his wife, did Coleridge much like Malta. The experience of public service must have deepened his political awareness, and he discharged his duties well enough to be asked to stay on. He made a brief trip to Sicily and was considered for a grain buying mission to Russia, as part of the war-time effort to avoid Napoleon's blockade of supplies to Britain. Coleridge was responsible for many minor acts of government, settling disputes and generally keeping the peace. He learnt Italian and studied works in that language and might have felt a release from his inward sorrow in all this activity but he missed the intellectual stimulus of congenial company. After eighteen months, despite an offer of continued employment from Sir Alexander Ball, Coleridge set off home. War-time exigencies made him choose the overland route but he got no further than Rome, where a rumour that Napoleon, who had been displeased by a Coleridge article predicting his downfall, was out for his life, caused him to take to the sea. After a journey in which Coleridge suffered greatly, he was in London by 17 August 1806. On 29 September he wrote to his wife, fretting at the delays which kept him in London. In fact, Coleridge was renewing business contacts; Stuart was approached, a plan for a series of lectures was put forward and it was not till the end of October that he was finally back in Keswick. He missed Asra at Penrith though he was in time to see the Wordsworths at Kendal on their way south to spend the winter with the Beaumonts. After a fortnight at home Coleridge recorded in his notebook: 'Keswick; finally resolved Wēsday, 15 Nov, 1806'.[35] He meant to leave Mrs Coleridge; he followed the Wordsworths south taking Hartley with him. Coleridge's plans were uncertain. Mrs Coleridge was aghast at the social opprobrium of a separation and wanted to visit Coleridge's family at Ottery to improve appearances. Coleridge's brother, hearing of the matrimonial split, would not receive them and they were stranded on their way. They spent some time with Bristol friends and met De Quincey, who was captivated and made Coleridge an anonymous and welcome gift of £300. De Quincey accompanied Mrs Coleridge back north and Coleridge stayed a while before going to London. All this upheaval increased the opium taking and Coleridge, who was often very unwell, considered consulting the famous surgeon Abernethy, who had helped De Quincey. Meanwhile, he renewed contact with Lamb and gave his first course of lectures, on Shakespeare.

By September 1808, Coleridge was back in the Lakes. The Wordsworths were now at Allan Bank and there Coleridge went, having fetched his small daughter from Keswick. The move seems to have invigorated him; a letter to his wife shows that her reception of him had encouraged him to work for their children in better heart and he wrote to T. G. Street, co-proprietor with Stuart of the *Courier*:[36]

> I am hard at work – and feel a pleasure and eagerness in it, which I had not known for years –

Coleridge seems to attribute this to a reduction in his consumption of opium:

> I left if off *all at once;* & drink nothing but Toast and Water, or Lemonade made with Creme of Tartar. If I entirely recover, I shall deem it a sacred Duty to publish my Case, tho' without my name – for the practice of taking Opium is dreadfully spread. – Throughout Lancashire & Yorkshire it is the common Dram of the lower orders of People – . . . surely this demands legislative Interference –

This shows a growing awareness of the real nature of drug addiction and a characteristically Coleridgean impulse to share his experience with others, especially if by doing so he could help them to avoid the mistakes he had made.

With the help of Stuart, the professional newspaperman, in London and of Sara Hutchinson in Grasmere, Coleridge surmounted his early problems with *The Friend* but finally the work of which Coleridge hoped so much was to bring about the end of his friendship with Asra and the Wordsworths. They never shared Coleridge's hopes for the paper, and when the work began to oppress Coleridge, they were discouraging. In the end, Sara left Allan Bank for a much needed holiday. The labour of writing and publishing a periodical like *The Friend* was exhausting, and when finally it was a financial failure, Coleridge, disappointed and despairing, had recourse to opium, once more in heavy doses. In March 1810, *The Friend* ceased and by October Coleridge was so ill that he planned to leave for London with Basil Montagu (an old friend of the Wordsworths) to try to obtain medical help. Wordsworth, exasperated by the irregular life of an addict and disappointed in Coleridge's lack of will-power, advised Montagu against having Coleridge live with him. Montagu foolishly told Coleridge of this during the journey to London and a smouldering resentment, which had been kept under control on both sides, flared into a bitter row. In a letter of 1822 Coleridge listed the double break with Wordsworth and Asra as two of 'the four griping and grasping Sorrows' of his life,[37] and the bitterness of the experience is recorded in letters and notebooks, where Coleridge referred to:[38]

> a compressing and strangling Anguish, made up of Love, and
> Resentment and Sorrow – quarreling with all the Future &
> refusing to be consoled for the Past –

The immediate effect was cushioned by the friendship of the Morgans and the Lambs, by Stuart's help with work on the *Courier* and by a second series of Shakespeare lectures. Gradually the hours of solitude became intolerable and Coleridge turned again to opium to alleviate his anguish. In the long term, the rupture must have been good for Coleridge. He had wasted many of his hopes on Wordsworth, relying on his genius to produce the 'philosophical poem' which in his youth he had himself contemplated. The dissatisfactions of the affair with Asra, and the way in which being near her involved being near his wife, had furthered the corrosion of his never very strong resolve.

Coleridge was in London from October 1810 to February 1812. He stayed most of the time with the Morgan family and wrote for the papers, gave lectures and took part in London society as a literary figure. In February 1812, he set off north to fetch copies of *The Friend* for a bound edition. He was at Keswick until the end of March without seeing Wordsworth, who, in late April, anxious that gossip about the quarrel would damage his reputation, followed Coleridge to London to settle the business. Letters were exchanged, Lamb acting for Coleridge and Crabb Robinson for Wordsworth, the exact nature of remarks was discussed and by May Wordsworth was to be seen attending one of Coleridge's lectures. Coleridge's mental ease was sufficiently restored for him to bear with equanimity the loss of half his Wedgwood allowance in December 1812, and he wrote a loving letter to Wordsworth on the death of his son, Thomas, but significantly, he did not go north. The break once made, Coleridge was able to resist the temptation of being needed by Wordsworth, of whose genius he never failed to be aware, and he stayed in London to attend to the business of staging his play, *Remorse*.

The play, originally written in 1797, was revised and enjoyed a great success, which did much to restore Coleridge's self-confidence. The fuss kept him busy, brought him a letter from Poole, with whom there had been some coolness after the refusal of a loan, and earned Coleridge a larger sum than all his previous undertakings put together. In March Coleridge and Morgan took a week's holiday at Bexhill-on-Sea (Coleridge was all his life very fond of sea-bathing). But, just as Coleridge seemed to be in a position to make a success in financial terms of his literary work, disaster struck. Morgan, a tobacco merchant, had long been in financial trouble and in October 1813 he fled to Ireland to avoid imprisonment for debt. Coleridge worked energetically for his friends, especially for Mrs Morgan and her sister and when they removed to Bristol, followed them there to give a series of lectures to help the family's finances. He gave Mrs Morgan as much practical help as he could but the worry, the work and the loneliness in Bristol took their toll; opium once more became a serious problem. In December, as he was recovering, he wrote to Mrs Morgan:[39]

> The Terrors of the Almighty have been around & against me
> – and tho' driven up and down for seven dreadful Days by
> restless Pain, like a Leopard in a Den, yet the anguish &
> remorse of Mind was worse than the pain of the whole
> Body. –

By April 1814 he was well enough to give another course of lectures and to attend the socialising which seems to have been their necessary accompaniment. Before the course ended, Coleridge was suffering from an 'erysipelatous complaint' and it is likely that the drinking and dining out had had an unfavourable effect on his precarious health. Cottle, at this time discovering his friend's opium addiction, decided to help him, financially by raising a subscription and personally by an exhortation to make the effort to break the opium habit. Cottle tried to awaken Coleridge to a sense of his Christian duty and was rewarded by the review of his religious thinking sent by the poet in April 1814. The letter shows the way in which Coleridge was working towards the philosophical and religious position of his later years.[40] The Trinity is acknowledged as a revelation, the distinction between mind and matter re-iterated and the conclusion drawn:[41]

> if there be but ONE directing MIND, that Mind is GOD! –
> operating, however, in Three Persons, according to the direct
> and uniform declarations of that inspiration which 'brought
> life and immortality to light'.

Other letters also show Coleridge turning to religion in his trouble; superficially, though, his life was unaltered. There was dining out, lecturing and unrestrained opium-taking. In March 1816, Coleridge was in London, probably to see about the staging of *Zapolya*, when he was again ill. The doctor who treated him introduced him to Gillman, saying that Coleridge wished to live with a medical gentleman that his drug intake might be controlled. Gillman met Coleridge, and on 15 April, Coleridge moved to Highgate. His troubles were by no means over, his drug-taking did not miraculously cease, nor did his health make a rapid recovery, but in Gillman and his wife Coleridge found friends who were able to unite the necessary sympathy with the equally necessary firmness.

The publication of 'Christabel' together with 'Kubla Khan' and 'Pains of Sleep' seems to indicate Coleridge's recognition of his inability to recapture the inspiration which began but could not finish 'Christabel'. John Murray brought out these poems (Byron had put in a good word with his publisher) and the following year published the unstaged *Zapolya*. Meanwhile another publisher was interested in Coleridge. This was Gale and Fenner, a house of a religious character. They commissioned the *Lay Sermons*, published the London edition of the *Biographia* and the 'rifacciamento' of *The Friend*. In 1818 they offered Coleridge the editorship of their proposed *Encyclopaedia Metropolitana*, but their treatment of Coleridge's preface, and their plans for regulated and supervised work caused considerable anxiety, before the bankruptcy in 1819 which involved Coleridge in grave financial loss.

In 1818 Coleridge wrote pamphlets and exerted his influence on behalf of the Cotton Factory Bill, which was to improve working conditions for mill children. The same year Coleridge gave his last courses of lectures, a series on literature, alternating with one on philosophy, but gradually his contact with the literary world of the capital was changing in character. Dining out had disastrous effects on Coleridge's health (his self-confessed inability to say 'no' would have been particularly dangerous in those days of generous imbibing), and in future people were to come to Highgate where the Gillmans could keep a watchful eye on him.

The friends of these later years are as varied as the interests which Coleridge fostered throughout his life. Among them were: H. F. Cary, whose translation of Dante Coleridge promoted in public; C. A. Tulk, a prominent Swedenborgian; Hyman Hurwitz, a Highgate neighbour and a prominent Jewish scholar with whom Coleridge worked on translations; Thomas Allsop, a young London businessman; J. H. Green, the prominent surgeon and thinker, who was to become Coleridge's literary executor; J. H. Frere, the diplomatist who translated Aristophanes; and Charles Aders and his wife, who held literary gatherings for London society. Old friends were not forgotten – Lamb, Montagu, Stuart, and Wordsworth, with whom in 1828 he was to make a short continental tour. Coleridge also renewed contact with his family and, especially after the marriage of his daughter Sara to her cousin, Henry Nelson Coleridge, with his nephews. Besides Henry, who helped with later publications, there was John Taylor Coleridge, a lawyer by profession, who for a while edited the *Quarterly Review*, and Edward, a clergyman and Eton housemaster. When Mrs Coleridge came to live with her daughter in nearby Hampstead, there was renewed friendship there too, and in 1832 Coleridge remarked in a letter to Green:[42]

> bating living in the same house with her there are few
> women, that I have a greater respect & *ratherish* liking for, than
> Mrs. C.

With his own children, with whom he had so little contact in their formative years, he took a new fatherly interest. This was to bring him much anxiety, especially over Hartley. In 1815, Hartley had gone as an undergraduate to Merton College, Oxford, his fees being paid by a subscription among Coleridge's friends. In 1819, when he graduated he was offered a probationary fellowship at Oriel, then one of the leading colleges. The restrictions of Oriel society sent Hartley to other company and a reputation for drunkenness meant that his fellowship was not renewed in 1820. Hartley and his father felt that insufficient allowance had been made for his youth and undisputed success as tutor. Coleridge went to Oxford, wrote letters, used his influence, all to no avail. Moreover, a year in London made it plain that Hartley had inherited in an aggravated form his father's weakness in the face of temptation and he was sent to the Lakes, where he spent most of the rest of his life. Derwent too caused a few qualms lest he should socialise too much and study too little, recalling Coleridge's own student days, but Derwent proved to be a credit to the family, a devoted son and a successful clergyman. The creative genius passed to Hartley but the intellectual inheritance seems to have gone to Sara. All reports stress her intelligence and industry, but her nervous temperament and the restricted outlets for intellectual women at the time confined her work to early translation and some children's fiction. She did, on her husband's death, continue his editing of her father's works, notably the only edition until 1978 of the journalism.

Coleridge's Highgate years were not unproductive. *Aids to Reflection*, published in 1823, earned him a reputation as a religious writer. In 1824 he was elected an Associate of the Royal Society of Literature. In return for £110 a year, each associate was expected to give an annual lecture. Coleridge only gave one, *On the Prometheus of Aeschylus* in 1825, but this was more than some associates achieved. The fund ceased on the accession of William IV, depriving Coleridge of his last hope of financial independence. In 1828, a three volume edition of the poems appeared, another followed in 1829 and a third in the year of Coleridge's death. *On the Constitution of Church and State* appeared in 1828 and established Coleridge as an influential figure in political and religious thinking in the next decades. The chief outlet of these later years was conversation, and H. N. Coleridge's record of this in *Table Talk* shows Coleridge's undimmed interest in politics and poetry as well as philosophy and religion. In 1822-3 Coleridge ran a small class for young gentlemen, to whom he dictated his philosophical ideas. In this way he hoped to produce them as a book and there is little doubt that dictation was Coleridge's favourite method of composition. Coleridge was at home to visiting literary figures on Thursday evenings and Thomas Carlyle, one of those who refused to be spellbound, leaves a clear insight into Coleridge's favourite activity of his later years:[43]

I have heard Coleridge talk, with eager musical energy, two stricken hours, his face radiant and moist, and communicate no meaning whatsoever to any individual of his hearers. ...
He began anywhere: you put some question to him, made some suggestive observation, instead of answering this, or decidedly setting out towards answer of it, he would accumulate formidable apparatus, logical swim-bladders, transcendental life-savers and other precautionary and vehiculatory gear, for setting out; perhaps did at last get under

way, – but was swiftly solicited, turned aside by the glance of
some radiant new game on this hand or that, into new
courses; and ever into new; and before long into all the
Universe, where it was uncertain what game you would catch
or whether any.

Carlyle regarded this as damning criticism, but Coleridge would no
doubt have ruefully accepted it as a necessary effect of his method
of thinking, exploring and expounding at the same time.

Coleridge's health was never good, despite annual autumn trips
to the sea at Ramsgate (paid for by Stuart), but he remained,
although physically weaker, in good mental health, for which he
was grateful. Although periods of ill-health kept him bedridden for
much of the day, his health stood up to the continental tour of
1828, and to a visit in 1833 to Cambridge, where he responded
whole-heartedly to the scene of his youthful ideals. He died on 25
July 1834, in a more peaceful frame of mind than he had spent
much of his life. He wrote himself a poetic epitaph during his last
months,[44] but a more fitting memorial is the earlier notebook
entry, surely intended for posterity:[45]

Take him on the whole – his head, his heart, his wishes, his
innocence of all selfish crime – & a hundred years hence what
will the balance be? – The good – were it but a single volume
that made Truth more visible, & goodness more lovely – &
pleasure at once more akin to virtue & self-doubled more
pleasurable – & the evil? While he lived it injured but himself
– & where is it now? In his grave & the writings, perhaps, of
vulgar wretches.

# 2

# Plays

Coleridge is unusual among Romantic poet-dramatists in that one of his plays, *Remorse,* was performed to considerable popular acclaim. Coleridge's letters during the play's twenty-performance run display his elation. To his wife he wrote:[1]

> I suppose, that no dramatic Author ever had so large a
> number of unsolicited, unknown, yet *predetermined* Plauditors
> in the Theatre, as I had on Saturday Night. ... You will have
> heard, that on my entering the Box on Saturday Night I was
> discovered by the Pit - & that they all turned their faces
> towards our Box, & gave a treble chear of Claps. I mention
> these things, because it will please Southey to hear that there is
> a large number of Persons in London, who hail with
> enthusiasm any prospect of the Stage's being purified &
> rendered classical. My success, *if* I succeed ... I succeed for
> others as well as for myself.

And to Poole later, when the extent of his success was plain, Coleridge confided:[2]

> It has been a good thing for the Theatre - They will get 8 or
> 10,000 £ - & I shall get more than all my literary Labors put
> together, nay, thrice as much, subtracting my heavy Losses in
> the Watchman & The Friend - 400 £: including the
> Copy-right.

Coleridge is not always the best guide to the success and failure of his own ventures but his comments can be supported with a few facts. R. M. Fletcher, in his book *English Romantic Drama 1795-1843,* provides some comparative figures:[3]

The play [*Remorse*] ran for twenty performances, an eminently respectable number. *Percy*, by Hannah More, was the single new tragedy (tragedy in the sense that leading characters are killed in the course of the action) that played in London for more than ten performances between 1777 and 1802. ... No other tragedy achieved even that number of performances until Coleridge's *Remorse*, but thereafter a significant increase took place in the frequency with which those surpassing the magic number ten were offered upon the stage.

Fletcher is quite certain of the truth of Coleridge's statement, 'if I succeed, I succeed for others as well as for myself' and asserts 'with Coleridge's *Remorse*, poetic drama in blank verse returned to the English stage.'[4] Of the rewards which success brought Coleridge himself, E. L. Griggs says 'W. Pople issued three editions of *Remorse* in 1813'.[5] It was from the sale of the texts of successfully produced plays that authors expected to make money.

Success had been a long time coming and Coleridge's earlier failure with the original of *Remorse*, *Osorio*, commissioned by Sheridan in 1797 for performance at Drury Lane, illustrates the difficulties in the way of the aspiring poet-dramatist. Sheridan evidently suggested a 'popular subject', which brought from Coleridge this puzzled enquiry:[6]

> The phrase 'popular subject' has a little puzzled me. ...
> whether you meant by it to recommend a fictitious and
> domestic subject, or one founded on well-known History. The
> four most popular Tragedies of Shakespear (Lear, Othello,
> Hamlet, and Romeo and Juliet) are either fictitious, or drawn
> from Histories and parts of History unknown to the Many:
> and the impression from Schiller's 'Fiesco' is weak compared to
> that produced by his 'Robbers'. There are however great
> advantages in the other scale. The Spectators come with a
> prepared Interest.

This reference to Shakespeare was not merely an academic one, reflecting the critical interest of Lamb, Hazlitt and Coleridge himself in the drama of the Elizabethan and Jacobean period. As Fletcher makes clear:[7]

> What [the audience] liked was, above all, Shakespeare ... they
> never seemed to grow weary of Kean as Hamlet or Macready
> as Macbeth

If it is true that the shadow of Shakespeare oppressed the Romantic attempt to revive poetic drama, this reflects not so much a remoteness from the contemporary theatre as a too slavish willingness to provide more of what was known to be popular.

The condition of the theatre in the Romantic era did not make matters any easier. There were only two London theatres licensed for the production of plays, Drury Lane and Covent Garden. Other theatres were restricted to musical plays and burlesques. The period known still for its great actors, the Kembles, Kean, Siddons, was in fact one in which the star system operated to the detriment of serious drama. Stars drew the crowds and in what was primarily a commercial venture, this gave those stars a tremendous power in the selection of plays, and in their production. The other big audience attraction was special effects. Poor illumination helped along mistaken identity plays and made even more startling the use of lighting effects. Trap doors, music, smoke, disguise were all essential ingredients in a successful play, and they are to be found in *Remorse*, but not in quite the exaggerated way in which they are offered in *Bertram*. This play by Maturin was immortalised by Coleridge in the critique published to fill up the second volume of the *Biographia*. It is worth a little attention here because it illustrates just what was wanted in the theatre of the time. Kean took the title role, and as the preface to Oxberry's 1827 edition of the play says:[8]

> To those who have witnessed the exertion of Mr. Kean's talent in the finest characters of the Drama, it is unnecessary to say, he in this tragedy had opportunities, of which the Public rapturously testified how well he knew to avail himself.

The play opens with a storm on which Coleridge cast his critical eye with high-spirited sarcasm:[9]

> But what is there to account for the prodigy of the tempest at *Bertram's* shipwreck? It is a mere supernatural effect, without even a hint of any supernatural agency; a prodigy, without any circumstance mentioned that it is prodigious; and a miracle introduced without a ground, and ending without a result. Every event and every scene of the play might have taken place as well if Bertram and his vessel had been driven in by a common hard gale, or from want of provisions. The first act would have indeed lost its greatest and most *sonorous*

39

picture; a scene for the sake of a scene, without a word spoken; as *such*, therefore (a rarity without a precedent) we must take it, and be thankful! In the opinion of not a few, it was, in every sense of the word, the best scene in the play. I am quite certain it was the most *innocent*: and the steady, quiet uprightness of the flame of the wax-candles, which the monks held over the roaring billows amid the storm of wind and rain, was *really* miraculous.

Moonlight, a monastery and a castle provide a proper setting for a robber band, an unhappy wife, a wronged husband and the desperado Bertram, as he cries:[10]

> Oh, that we were on the dark wave together,
> With but one plank between us and destruction,
> That I might grasp him in these desperate arms,
> And plunge with him amid the weltering blows –
> And view him gasp for life – and –
> Ha, ha, – I see him struggling –
> I see him – ha, ha, ha, (a frantic laugh)

In a world where this was acceptable, Coleridge's *Zapolya* was rejected, and it is hardly surprising that Coleridge should have taken the revenge open to a critic. It is not difficult to see why *Zapolya* was not acceptable to the management of the two patent houses. Charles Lamb, writing to Wordsworth, had a shrewd suspicion of the play's deficiency:[11]

> The Cov. Gard. Manager has declined accepting his Tragedy tho' (having read it) I see no reason upon earth why it might not have run a very fair chance tho' it certainly wants a prominent part for Miss O'Neil or a Mr. Kean.

There is no starring part in the play; Zapolya, Glycine and even Sarolta, vie for our sympathy among the women and among the men only Emerick the usurper has a really minor role. The relationships among characters are subtly varied and show interesting developments realistically presented, but the style of production and of acting then available could not portray subtly developing characters. Even the depiction of Shakespeare's characters on the stage was conveyed by 'points'; for instance, the high point of a delineation of Richard III was the delivery of the line 'Off with his head – so much for Buckingham'. In a theatre where such theatricality was the order of the day, *Zapolya* clearly could have little to offer despite its war-wolves and royalty in disguise. Where *Remorse* achieved a balance between the author's own creation and the demands of theatre audiences of the day, *Zapolya* on this count must be considered a failure.

Despite the inadequacies of theatrical production, there was great interest in drama in the Romantic period, which produced such fine dramatic critics as Hazlitt, Lamb and De Quincey, not to mention Coleridge himself. Byron was on the management committee at Drury Lane and encouraged Coleridge to follow up his triumph with *Remorse*. Significantly, though, his experience behind the scenes caused him to write in the preface to *Marino Falieri*, published in 1821:[12]

I have had no view to the stage; in its present state it is, perhaps, not a very exalted object of ambition.

The public, too, were enthusiastic for plays, published as well as produced. Amateur performances – such as that of *Lovers' Vows* by the fashionable German playwright, Kotzebue, in Jane Austen's *Mansfield Park* – show the popularity of dramatic entertainment, which may account for high sales of printed play texts.

Coleridge's first attempt at poetic drama was too politically volatile even to be offered for public performance and it seems equally unsuitable for private acting. As it was written as a money-making venture, we must assume that the authors considered there was a market for plays which were to be read, not acted.

*The Fall of Robespierre* was written for the pantisocratic movement by Southey and Coleridge. Originally, it was planned that they and Lovell should write an act each but Lovell's contribution was considered unsuitable so Southey rewrote the third act. Coleridge undertook to find a publisher, succeeding eventually in Cambridge, where he hoped his name might boost sales locally. In view of the author's avowed intention to raise money for their cause by writing of another cause with which they were in sympathy, perhaps the most interesting fact about the play is that it is a play, not a pamphlet. Coleridge clearly felt the limitations as well as the advantages of the form, as his dedicatory letter shows. He offers to H. Martin Esq. of Jesus College, Cambridge:[13]

the following Dramatic Poem, in which I have endeavoured to detail, in an interesting form, the fall of a man, whose great bad actions have cast a disastrous lustre on his name. In the execution of the work, as intricacy of plot could not have been attempted without a gross violation of recent facts, it has been my sole aim to imitate the empassioned and highly figurative language of the French orators, and to develope the characters of the chief actors on a vast stage of horrors

Coleridge speaks as though solely responsible for the work, which bore his name only on the title page. He explained to Southey:[14]

It would appear ridiculous to print two names to *such* a Work – But if you choose it, mention it – and it shall be done – To every man, who *praises* it, of course I give the *true* biography of it

Praise was not the likely outcome of publicity, but rather disapprobation, such as was shown by George Coleridge.[15] Southey, moreover, seems not to have requested the inclusion of his name, doubtless because he had a shrewd suspicion of how the play's reputation would affect his family and prospects.

The Dedicatory Letter clearly demonstrates Coleridge's interest in the dramatic form. The inherently tragic shape of Robespierre's rise and fall, the 'great, bad' aspects of the man and the restorative effect of his removal reflect the Hegelian view of tragedy, as exemplified in *Macbeth*. Furthermore, the dramatic form allowed the writers to display a general sympathy with the Revolution without requiring them to take sides. This was important since the two authors held different views, as a letter by Southey reveals:[16]

I believe him to have been sacrificed to the despair of fools and cow[ards]. Coleridge says 'he was a man whose great bad actions cast a dis[....] lustre over his name.' He is now inclined to think with me that ... Robespierre was the benefactor of mankind and that we should lament his death as the greatest misfortune Europe could have sustained – the situation of Europe is surely most melancholy –

Moreover, as the events depicted were still very recent, it was perhaps as well that the authors kept an open mind about the consequences; things were happening so fast that they could easily have made fools of themselves.

By the time Coleridge attempted his first full-length play, *Osorio*, his circumstances had changed. The pantisocratic dream was over and Coleridge, now a husband and father, was trying to make a living for his family by combining literary labours with domestic agriculture in the garden of the Nether Stowey cottage. When, early in 1797, Coleridge heard from his long-admired Bowles that Sheridan wished him to write a tragedy, he seized the opportunity to make financial gain from such congenial work. By the middle of March, the play was still in a chaotic condition though Coleridge had a clear conception of his tragedy:[17]

> It is 'romantic & wild & somewhat terrible' - & I shall have
> Siddons & Kemble in my mind

It was not until after meeting Wordsworth, then working on his tragedy *The Borderers*, that Coleridge finished the play. It was sent off to Sheridan via Bowles on 16 October. Whereas Southey influenced *The Fall of Robespierre* actively by sharing the writing, Wordsworth influenced *Osorio* indirectly, because he too was writing a tragedy at the same time. The effect is best shown in Coleridge's own words in a letter to Joseph Cottle:[18]

> Wordsworth admires my Tragedy - which gives me great
> hopes. Wordsworth has written a Tragedy himself. I speak
> with heart-felt sincerity & (I think) unblinded judgement,
> when I tell you, that I feel myself a *little man by his* side; &
> yet do not think myself the less man, than I formerly thought
> myself.

The play did not prosper in Sheridan's hands; by the following February Coleridge was writing laconically to his brother George:[19]

> I have received no answer from him, altho' I have written
> to him - & the only intelligence, I have received, was from
> Linley, Sheridan's brother-in-law, who told me that Sheridan
> spoke to him in extravagant terms of it's merits. - In all
> probability, Mrs Sheridan has made thread-papers with it.

Wordsworth and Coleridge considered publishing their tragedies together, but instead decided upon the *Lyrical Ballads*, in which two extracts from *Osorio* were published. Coleridge seems to have considered remoulding the piece at this time, but the German trip intervened. When he returned, his knowledge of German brought him a new experience of dramatic writing. Longmans, the publishers, approached Coleridge to translate Schiller's *Wallenstein* trilogy, of which they had acquired a copy expressly made for translation and attested by Schiller himself on 30 September 1799. Coleridge's translation, which was of two plays only, *The Piccolomini* and *The Death of Wallenstein,* was completed in a little over six months from that date, and Wordsworth later told Mr Justice Coleridge, 'there was nothing more astonishing than the ease and rapidity with which it was done'.[20] The version was not acted and, as Coleridge predicted, it was not a financial success as a published play.[21] It would, however, be a mistake to consider this a venture aimed at a small critical public, far-removed from the hurly burly of the theatrical world. A glance at the advertisements in the 1800 edition shows, that Longmans hoped that it would reach the same readership as works by such successfully performed playwrights as Holman and Reynolds. Schiller, too, clearly hoped the play would be performed in England[22] for, as J. L. Haney remarks:[23]

> Schiller wrote Wallenstein while the Kotzebue craze was
> at its height in London; there was consequently a good
> market in England for German plays.

The haste in translating the work may have been related to a desire to see the play performed in England as soon as possible after its production in Germany. Certainly, performance would have helped sales; *Remorse* went into publication and reached its third edition almost as soon as its successful run was over. There are signs, too, that Coleridge did not consider the play totally unperformable. A letter from Southey in 1823 refers to Coleridge's talk of 'adapting his translation of *Wallenstein* for the stage – Kean having taken a fancy to exhibit himself in it'.[24] One can imagine that Kean with his impassioned manner would have done well in the title role, but the problems involved in making an acting version are immense. These are demonstrated by a later attempt by Macready to condense the two plays into one.[25] The problem is not that the action is too involved nor that the play covers too great a time span (the action falls within the classically correct twenty-four hours) but that the characters develop in a way which cannot be abbreviated, because it is on these changing attitudes of the other characters to the hero-villain Wallenstein that the action turns.

Coleridge's German reading may have prompted another dramatic attempt shortly after *Wallenstein* was completed. The notebooks have two dramatic fragments, which Miss Coburn identifies as, first, Lessing's summary of a play of Spanish origin in Coleridge's own translation and, second, an adaption by Coleridge of the same Spanish play. A separate manuscript fragment opens with a whimsical frontispiece giving the name of the publishers, the date of a highly successful performance and a star-studded cast-list, but all that follows is the opening of the first Act.[26] This is entitled *The Triumph of Loyalty* and shows why the play attracted Coleridge. In the description of the hero's return to his native court, a conflict of loyalties between public duty and a private oath is suggested, as well as complex relations between the hero, his followers and his brother. There is much here to recall *Osorio* and *Wallenstein*, though the language (both prose and verse) is heavily Shakespearian.

Meanwhile, Coleridge had not forgotten *Osorio*. In April 1800 he had written to Southey of his intention to re-write the play, and a letter of July to Stuart shows that he was smarting under Sheridan's neglect:[27]

> I never blamed Mr Sheridan for not bringing my play on the stage. God knows my inmost heart, & knows that I never for an hour together thought it likely to succeed – I blamed Mr Sheridan solely for taking no kind of notice even of the receipt of my play, for returning me no answer whatever, & for withholding from me the copy of my play after repeated applications;

Sheridan did about this time approach Coleridge again:[28]

> wishing me to write for the stage, making all his old offers over again, & charging the non-representation of my play on my extreme obstinacy in refusing to have it at all altered!

Coleridge did not respond, and the following year was planning to re-write the play as a poem, but nothing came of this and *Osorio* seems to have disappeared from Coleridge's plans until in 1807 Godwin gave Coleridge a copy of the play found among his books. Coleridge was full of hopes once more:[29]

> with a few alterations which any person acquainted with the mechanism of the stage might easily suggest, it would *act* as

45

well as it reads. I certainly will correct it; & changing both the title, & the names of the Dramatis Personae, procure it to be presented to Covent Garden.

This is the beginning of the transformation of the unsuccessful *Osorio* into the highly profitable *Remorse*. Coleridge began rewriting and seems to have anticipated its performance in the winter season of 1807-8. Other troubles intervened (*The Friend* and its failure, the break with Wordsworth and the following opium misery) and the play was not offered to the theatre until the autumn of 1812. By this time, Coleridge had a certain London reputation; the play was accepted, went into rehearsal as *Remorse* in December 1812 and made its first rapturously received appearance on 23 January 1813.

This success was not pursued until the spring of 1815, when Coleridge once more made extensive plans for dramatic writing. This was probably in response to Byron's suggestion:[30]

> there never was such an opening for tragedy. In Kean, there is an actor worthy of expressing the thoughts of the characters which you have every power of embodying; ... We have had nothing to be mentioned in the same breath with *Remorse* for very many years; and I should think that the reception of that play was sufficient to encourage the highest hopes of author and audience.

Also at this time Coleridge was involved with a provincial production of *Remorse* in Calne, which further stimulated renewed dramatic efforts. Letters suggest a tragedy and Coleridge, writing to Byron, implies that immediate production was intended; various plans for plays were aired at this time, but if any of them materialised nothing has survived. The first positive reference to *Zapolya* comes in January 1816, when Coleridge wrote to Brabant:[31]

> this which I am now putting the last Hand to, is not the Tragedy, I promised to Drury Lane – while the present piece must depend almost for its fate, certainly for it's success, on the talents of the Actresses – in an equal, perhaps, in a greater degree than on those of the Actors. For there are three female Characters, each perfectly distinct from the other, and all prominent.

Despite this, Coleridge had no feeling that the play was not suited for the theatre:[32]

It will not be as interesting in the Closet, as the Remorse – I mean, that it is less a Poem – but I hope, it will be proportionately more so on the stage.

He must have been the more disappointed when the play was rejected by both the major theatres, for although the Drury Lane committee suggested a plan for its production as a melodrama, this too came to nothing. The play was published in 1817 and shortly after that produced at one of the unlicensed theatres, the Royal Circus and Surrey, as a melodrama, in which Coleridge had no hand and took no profit. This marks the end of Coleridge's dramatic career, but his interest in plays and acting continued. Occasionally, he visited the theatre with the Gillmans, and his acquaintance with the comedian Charles Mathews, now a neighbour in Highgate, kept him in touch with the acting profession. As late as 1823, when Southey reports talk of an adaptation of *Wallenstein* with Kean as hero, Coleridge gave his opinion on the actor to his nephew:[33]

To see him act, is like reading Shakespere by flashes of lightning

Other recorded comments show that his interest in Shakespeare never dwindled, even when, towards the end of his life, there can have been little opportunity to see plays in the theatre.

Something in Coleridge's character made him respond to the dramatic; even his best-known poem, the 'Ancient Mariner' is cast in dialogue form. Also, he had a genuine interest in the theatre; his account of the success of *Remorse* shows this, and reports of audience reaction to his lectures show a similar awareness of himself as performer. The theatre of his time was not conducive to great drama, and Coleridge's plays make no pretence to greatness. Even so, they have an importance which is often overlooked. They round out our appreciation of his practical literary craftsmanship and deepen our insight into his contemporary reputation as a literary genius.

*The Fall of Robespierre*, as a joint work, does not truly represent either of its authors except as a memorial to youthful enthusiasm. Of his short play, Coleridge wrote only the second act, which gives the speeches in the Tribune as Robespierre and his few followers try to talk their way out of execution. The intention to portray passion is evident throughout, but the speeches are perfunctory rather than passionate, like the following lines from the end of the Act:[34]

> *Billaud Varennes:* I demand
> The arrest of all the traitors. Memorable
> Will be this day for France.
> *Robespierre:*   Yes! Memorable
> This day will be for France – for villains triumph.
> *Lebas:*   I will not share in this day's damning guilt.
> Condemn me too./*Great cry – Down with the Tyrants!*

*Osorio,* completed at the same time as Wordsworth's *Borderers,* shares a common interest with that play. In both plays guilt and remorse have an important part and in both they are illuminated in the relation of two men, of the brothers Osorio and Albert in *Osorio* and of Oswald and Marmaduke in *The Borderers.* The plot of the latter is very complicated but its central core relates to the guilty Oswald's desire to re-create in Marmaduke the same sense of guilt which colours his life; in Coleridge's play the emphasis is reversed, the innocent Albert, whom Osorio assumes is dead at his instigation, having escaped death returns to try to bring his brother to a sense of remorse for what he intended and to a realisation that he was innocent of the actual deed. Here are themes which interested the poets deeply, and were to appear in the 'Ancient Mariner' and the unfinished 'Wanderings of Cain'. Although Coleridge's interest in the remorse theme stems from this period, it is in the revised version of 1813 that it receives its more perfect embodiment in the play which now bears that title.

The plot of the play hinges on the two brothers, Alvar and Ordonio. Alvar is supposed dead by the other main characters. Ordonio thinks he has been killed by Isidore, a Christianised Moor hired by himself as assassin; Teresa, once engaged to Alvar, whom she has loved since childhood, and Valdez, the brothers' father, assume that he has been killed by bandits. In fact Alvar talked Isidore out of the killing and escaped to the Netherlands, whence at the play's opening he has returned disguised as a Moor. The play's weakness really lies in providing convincing motives for the disguised return. Teresa refuses to accept the fact of Alvar's death and accordingly will not marry Ordonio despite pressure from Valdez as well as from Ordonio, who killed his brother to achieve this end, and in desperation to prove Alvar's death Ordonio plans a magic scene in which 'proof' of the death will be given. Alvar himself, still disguised, is to act the role of magician and he plans to use this opportunity to bring home to Ordonio his guilt. The effect of this is not what was intended: Alvar is arrested under the Inquistion and Ordonio, suspecting Isidore of treachery, decides to silence him with death. Both Ordonio and Teresa are disturbed by the scene, and while Ordonio sends Isidore to an undeserved and horrible death, Teresa visits Alvar, still thinking him the Moor-magician, in the dungeons. Now the action comes to its climax. The widow of Isidore, Alhadra, pursues Ordonio for revenge (a neat portrait of unheeding reaction to wrong and a contrast to Alvar's inactivity); meanwhile, Ordonio has gone to find his magician in the dungeons. There he discovers the reunited Teresa and Alvar, who are foiled in their attempt to rescue Ordonio from the sense of guilt which he now clearly feels because now he has actually committed a murder. Alhadra enters with her band of vengeful Moorish women and kills Ordonio who cries 'ATONEMENT!' (In the earlier version Ordonio is killed offstage and this important moment of tragic resolution is lost.) Finally, Alvar and Teresa reconcile Valdez to all that has happened.

As a plot this has much to recommend it. The relationship between the brothers allows dramatic use of misunderstanding and disguise and double meaning which enriches the play and also appealed to contemporary audiences. The characters are well differentiated by their active roles as well as by personality. At the same time the plot presents one fundamental problem. The early *Osorio* makes clear by its title that the play's tragic hero is its villain (nothing untoward here, the same could be said of *Macbeth*, *Tamburlaine* and many others) and the tragedy is his only. However, the figure of Alvar, and to a lesser extent that of Teresa, attract attention away from Ordonio, who even in the revised version remains an inadequate figure, partly because so little of his history before the attempted killing of Alvar is made known to us. We simply do not know what sort of man remorse is acting upon, and yet, as Zulimez' remarks which were used as a motto to the published version of the play show, this knowledge is essential to an understanding of the play's theme. Alvar, who in his hesitation has, like Coleridge, a 'smack of Hamlet', is a character with whom it is easier to identify ourselves and the audience's main concern is to discover whether the lovers will be reunited.

A comparison of the early *Osorio* and the revised *Remorse* demonstrates quite clearly the superiority of the latter. Themes, like the intention of the hero to bring the villain to remorse, are more fully explored in the latter, characters are better delineated, and the play is constructed in a tighter way. However, in the sixteen-year interval there has been no changing of the story, no deviation from the intentions of the original, and all the improvements create a better vehicle for the author's ideas, which remain unaltered. In fact, many of the improvements stem from the introduction of a new first scene in *Remorse* which introduces the hero Alvar and enables him to recount his story and discuss motives:[35]

> *Alvar:*   Remember, Zulimez! I am his brother,
> Injured indeed! O deeply injured! yet
> Ordonio's brother.
> *Zulimez:*   Nobly-minded Alvar!
> This sure but gives his guilt a blacker dye.
> *Alvar:*   The more behoves it I should rouse within him
> Remorse! that I should save him from himself.
> *Zulimez:*   Remorse is as the heart in which it grows:
> If that be gentle, it drops balmy dews
> Of true repentance; but if proud and gloomy,
> It is a poison-tree, that pierced to the inmost
> Weeps only tears of poison!
> *Alvar:*   And of a brother,
> Dare I hold this, unproved? nor make one effort
> To save him? - Hear me, friend! I have yet to tell thee,
> That this same life, which he conspired to take,
> Himself once rescued from the angry flood,
> And at the imminent hazard of his own.

This essential likeness of the revised to the original version is emphasised by Coleridge's remark in J. D. Campbell's notes to *Remorse:*[36]

> The growth of OSORIO's character is nowhere explained, and yet I had most clear and psychologically accurate ideas of the whole of it.

This shows quite clearly that the later play did not need any additional insight into the psychology of the theme, but merely a better dramatic form. This provides an interesting contrast to the seeming inability of the later Coleridge to find an imaginative form for his ideas. Here he is embodying old themes in a way which makes them more vital and new than they seemed originally.

The play comes to a climax of incense, fire and clashing music when the picture which should prove Ordonio's death is displayed. A note on the original manuscript shows Coleridge's awareness of the inadequacy here:[37]

> The scene is not wholly without *poetical* merit, but it is
> miserably undramatic, or rather untragic. A scene of magic is
> introduced in which no single person on the stage has the least
> faith - all, though in different ways, think or know it to be a
> *trick* -

In *Osorio* when the portrait of Teresa is displayed reactions are confused. Prominent among them is Alvar's comforting of Teresa, who asks:[38]

> Ha! who art thou?
> *Alvar:*   My heart bursts over thee!
> *Teresa:*   Didst thou murder him?
> And dost thou now repent? Poor troubled man!
> I do forgive thee, and may Heaven forgive thee!

This clearly has theatrical potential and an audience conditioned to the sentimental and pathetic would respond well to it, but it is hardly dramatic and does not further the plot as Alvar leaves the scene tamely arranging to meet Teresa at her foster-mother's. In *Remorse* Alvar substitutes a picture of his assassination by the Moor Isidore which will startle Ordonio but not their father and Teresa is not present when the picture is revealed. The response is brief. Ordonio cries out 'Duped! duped! duped! - the traitor Isidore!', the Inquisitor, encouraged by Ordonio, rushes in to take Alvar to the dungeons and the scene ends. In the following scene Coleridge gives Ordonio his chance to express the remorse which is the play's theme: He describes the grave of Alvar:[39]

> There, where Ordonio likewise fain would lie!
> In the sleep-compelling earth in unpierced darkness!
> For while we live -
> An inward day that never, never sets,

Glares round the soul and mocks the closing eyelids!
Over his rocky grave the fir-grove sighs
A lulling ceaseless dirge! 'Tis well with him.

This mood of passive misery did not make its full effect onstage 'from want of depth and volume of voice in Rae' until after the lines were published, although 'during rehearsals all the Actors and Actresses and even the mechanics on the stage [were] clustering round while these lines were repeating just as if it had been a favourite strain of Music.'

Comparison of the two plays shows a much improved grasp of structural dramatic skills, the ability to create from the various incidents and characters a dramatic unity without sacrificing – indeed, rather, enchancing – the characterisation. What makes this surprising is that *Osorio* is more or less contemporary with the 'Ancient Mariner', a work of controlled unity of vision, while *Remorse* comes between the unfinished (some thought unfinishable) *Friend* and the somewhat oddly conceived *Biographia*. However, our surprise should be lessened by remembering that it is critical opinion (both contemporary and recent) which has created an expectation that Coleridge's work should be lacking in structural finish, and created it partly by overlooking such works as *Remorse*. A partial explanation of Coleridge's greater mastery of dramatic technique in his later years (for *Zapolya* is another example) may be found in the work which Coleridge must have done to produce the translations of Schiller's *Wallenstein* and by his study of Shakespeare for the 1812 lectures.

The *Wallenstein* translations have enjoyed a varying reputation. By 1814 Coleridge was able to write to John Murray, the publisher:[40]

I have received testimonials from men not merely of genius according to *my* belief, but of the highest *accredited* reputation, that my Translation of the Wallenstein was in language & in metre superior to the original – & the parts most admired were substitutions of my own, on a principle of Compensation. – Yet the whole work went for waste paper.

Even allowing that Coleridge was here trying to get more favourable terms for a translation of Goethe's *Faust*, his statement

cannot be dismissed, especially as there is evidence to give substance
to Coleridge's shadowy 'men not merely of genius according to my
belief'. J. D. Campbell records the opinion of Walter Scott and
Thomas Carlyle.[41] Moreover, Murray would hardly have
approached Coleridge for this translation if *Wallenstein* had not been
well thought of. Later, there was a reaction; the *Westminster Review*,
reviewing the 1850 edition of the play, counters earlier favourable
reviews with:[42]

> Misconstructions, vapid paraphrases, omissions and spurious
> additions, abound in Mr Coleridge's translation to an
> extent which would not meet with the approbation of
> anyone who thoroughly understands the original.

P. Machule, who gives a much more extensive treatment of the
translation concludes, 'der übersetzer kein treues bild des originals
gegeben hat'.[43] But as B. Q. Morgan points out, some of these
criticisms are based on use of differing editions, either of Coleridge
or of Schiller. Certainly, G. H. E. in the *Westminster Review* opens
his attack on the line 'Spät kommt ihr' which he says is mis-
translated as 'You come too late', whereas the first edition and E.
H. Coleridge's text both give 'Ye have come late'.

This hasty translation done for profitable publication (and
possible performance) cannot be treated like a work of scholarly
accuracy done for the library reader. It is a good translation for its
purpose although it has too many inaccuracies to be considered
truly great. B. Q. Morgan sums up:[44]

> Though I stated at the outset that Coleridge's translation never
> merited the repute it actually enjoyed, I should be the first to
> acknowledge the fine qualities it does possess. Coleridge
> responded warmly and authentically to Schiller's dramatic
> fervor, and he adopted Schiller's drama, as it were, and made
> it his own. Whole passages have the sweep and fire of original
> creation, and any reader who could not follow Schiller's text,
> or who did not make detailed comparisons might easily be
> persuaded that here was one of the great translations.

When the play opens, the officers of Wallenstein's army are
whole-hearted in their support of their leader, but the second scene
shows Octavio Piccolomini's disaffection. As the play develops we
see Wallenstein planning to break away from the Emperor with

help from Protestant Sweden. Octavio convinces his son, Max, who had previously hero-worshipped Wallenstein, of his leader's duplicity and troubles to come. Plots are made, but the issue is complicated because of Max Piccolomini's love for Thekla, Wallenstein's daughter. Other officers desert Wallenstein, to join Octavio Piccolomini. Before the play ends Max Piccolomini, torn between rival loyalties, has been killed in the service of the Emperor; Thekla, hearing this, has run away to kill herself; various officers have been killed; Wallenstein assassinated and Octavio Piccolomini become General in his place. In all this, Wallenstein is more acted upon than active, a trait of character emphasised by his belief in the stars which betrays him into his fatal trust of Octavio Piccolomini.

The attention of readers of these two plays seems to have been confined to a concern for the quality of the translation. This should not eclipse an interest in the play itself. Despite Coleridge's complaints while working on the translation that it is a dull heavy play, the reader can sense Coleridge's interest in the themes which the historical action raises. The personal and the political aspects of the play have features in common with Coleridge's own work. The question of conflicting loyalties is raised again in the fragment, *The Triumph of Loyalty*, and more fully in *Zapolya*. The question of leadership and Coleridge's concern for the effect of loyalties divided by the creation of factions, which is fundamental to *Wallenstein*, occurs in Coleridge's later political prose. All of Coleridge's plays, except *The Fall of Robespierre*, but including these translations, are concerned with personal relations within a political framework. The *Wallenstein* plays are closest to *Zapolya* in this exploitation of the interaction between the two. These likenesses should make it clear that *Wallenstein* was not only a work of mechanical translation, but a real attempt to make a viable English play from the German original.

*Zapolya*, which Wilson Knight called Coleridge's 'greatest full-length work',[45] is the most neglected of all Coleridge's plays. It was never produced, enjoyed no contemporary success and is now almost forgotten, yet the features which made it unsuitable for performance in 1817 should make it more interesting to twentieth-century readers. Like *The Winter's Tale*, on which its structure is based, the play is a serious comedy and as such lacks the black-and-white portrayal of hero and villain which was so much a part of Romantic theatre. Instead, the foreground is given to the loyalty of a few and Emerick, the usurper king, the play's only true villain, is deliberately kept in the background. The play is divided into two parts, the Prelude, 'The Usurper's Fortune', and the Sequel, 'The Usurper's Fate'. In the Prelude, which is the equivalent of the first act in a five-act play, we see Emerick seize the throne on his brother Andreas' death, repudiating Queen Zapolya and her baby son, who escape with the loyal general, Raab Kiuprili, and an old soldier, Chef Ragozzi. The main action takes place twenty years later in the country surrounding the castle of Casimir, son of Kiuprili but in the service of Emerick. His wife Sarolta is there with Glycine her maid, when local troubles reveal that the two local foresters, Bathory and Bethlen, are not, as was supposed, father and son, but that Bethlen was found as a baby in the forest and entrusted into Bathory's care by his mother, who then disappeared. Hearing this, Bethlen sets off into the forest to search for traces of his parentage. Glycine, who loves him and is afraid for his safety in a forest where there are supposed to be war-wolves, follows and discovers Zapolya and Kiuprili, in hiding. When Bethlen appears he is re-united with his mother and, realising that he is the rightful king, returns to the castle to fetch Kiuprili's sword. There he surprises Emerick trying to seduce Sarolta in her chamber. They fight, and Casimir, who had heard rumours of Emerick's designs on Sarolta, returns during the struggle. Casimir and Bethlen plan the overthrow of Emerick which takes place the following day in the guise of a hunt. Two of Emerick's henchmen are killed, and Casimir, re-united with his father, slays the tyrant with his father's sword. The play ends with Bethlen pronounced king and, amid general rejoicing, betrothed to Glycine, who is discovered to be the daughter of Chef Ragozzi.

The prominence of the women adds an extra dimension to this story. Coleridge emphasises the domestic roots of good government, and Sarolta closes the play with a speech to this effect:[46]

> E'en women at the distaff hence may see,
> That bad men may rebel, but ne'er be free;
> May whisper, when the waves of faction foam,
> None love their country, but who love their home;

This is reinforced by the rural setting and by the importance of the goodness of Bathory and Sarolta. Coleridge called the play 'A

Christmas Tale' with an intended reference to *The Winter's Tale*, but the likeness consists chiefly in the two-part structure, which caused Coleridge some worry, as his advertisement makes clear:[47]

> The form of the following dramatic poem is in humble imitation of the *Winter's Tale* of Shakespeare, except that I have called the first part a Prelude instead of a first Act, as a somewhat nearer resemblance to the plan of the ancients, of which one specimen is left to us in the Aeschylean Trilogy of the *Agamemnon*, the *Orestes*, and the *Eumenides*. Though a matter of form merely, yet two plays, on different periods of the same tale, might seem less bold, than an interval of twenty years between a first and second act. This is, however, in mere obedience to custom. The effect does not, in reality, at all depend on the Time of the interval; but on a very different principle. There are cases in which an interval of twenty hours between the acts would have a worse effect (i.e. render the imagination less disposed to take the position required) than twenty years in other cases.

This gives an insight into Coleridge's idea of dramatic unity in contrast to the eighteenth century's adherence to the classical unities. When we consider that *The Winter's Tale* bridges the same time span quite unconcernedly, it seems remarkable that Coleridge should have thought the matter warranted such attention but here, as so often in Coleridge, eighteenth-century standards show their influence. Although ultimately and with far-reaching consequences, he was to reject them in his criticism of Shakespeare and in aesthetics generally, it is as a reaction to those standards that many of his ideas took shape.

Coleridge's reference to *The Winter's Tale* should not mislead us into thinking that this play is derivative; it is in fact as fresh a play in its handling of theme and character as any Romantic drama and far less dependent for its style and atmosphere on older dramatists than many. Moments of psychological truth – such as the meeting of the starving and frightened Kiuprili and Zapolya with the equally frightened Glycine outside the forest cave and in the first act the meeting between Chef Ragozzi and Zapolya – are convincing and not unmoving. The action, where Coleridge seems to be relying on standard contemporary 'blood and thunder', is not always so well-managed. The use of the henchman's corpse in the struggles leading to Emerick's death, which is not very convincing when read, would be difficult to stage. The story, however, develops well, Emerick's assault on Sarolta which causes his presence at the dénouement is a good device and the early offstage disclosure of Bethlen's true identity makes a fitting preparation for the reunion of mother and son. The play displays the same narrative skill which we find in 'The Ancient Mariner'; despite its lack of success on the stage, *Zapolya*, too, holds the attention by involving the reader in the characters' plight.

While this chapter has given prominence to Coleridge's successes in the dramatic art, there has been no intention to create a place for Coleridge the dramatist in the history of great literature. At the same time, I do think that Coleridge the dramatist ought to have a place along with Coleridge the critic, Coleridge the religious thinker and Coleridge the philosopher (to name but a few of the accepted labels) not only because an understanding of his achievement in the drama makes possible a more balanced view of his whole work. The plays are interesting enough to warrant more attention than they are usually accorded and a greater interest in the plays themselves might enable us to gain a different perspective on Coleridge as critic of Shakespeare and other dramatists. Just as we approach his criticism of Wordsworth as the work of a creative poet, so we should consider the Shakespeare criticism as the work of a practising playwright,[48] a writer who had a persisting interest in the technique of constructing plays as an applied art as well as a theoretical science. A. S. Downer in his book on Macready suggests[49] that it was hearing Coleridge's lectures of 1818, when he propounded the view of the unity of Shakespeare's idea of a play as contrasted with Beaumont and Fletcher's mere aggregations of detail, which helped Macready to formulate his aim to create a 'Harmonious and complete arrangement of parts' in his work as actor-director. Certainly Coleridge belongs closer to the theatre tradition than is commonly recognised and there are grounds for thinking that the interaction between Coleridge as critic and Coleridge as playwright was a complex and far-reaching one which affected the drama as well as the criticism of subsequent ages.

# 3
## Poetry

If Coleridge's first published book was a play, *The Fall of Robespierre*,
his earliest publications were poems; these appeared in the *Cambridge
Intelligencer*, whose editor, Benjamin Flower, was responsible for the
publication of *Robespierre*. It was a poetry volume which Coleridge
was preparing for the press when he died and all his life poetry was
an habitual form of utterance. His earliest contributions to the
papers were topical if not political, but they were in verse not prose.
To the end of his life, notebooks and letters illustrate how readily
Coleridge cast his thoughts in metrical form. That 'Dejection',
published as an ode, was first written as a verse-letter is commonly
known, but it is not often realised that this is but one of Coleridge's
well-known poems which were first sent in letters, as were many
lesser known poems. A version of 'This Lime-tree Bower' was sent
to Southey in a letter, as was 'Pains of Sleep' six years later, and his
'Epitaph' was written in the last year of his life in a letter to J. H.
Green. Metrical experiments and snatches of verse recur through the
notebooks, many of them to find publication as 'Fragments' in the
*Complete Poetical Works*.[1] Yet by late 1800, Coleridge was beginning
to consider that poetry was not his natural bent. He wrote to
Thelwall:

> As to Poetry, I have altogether abandoned it, being convinced
> that I never had the essentials of poetic Genius, & that I
> mistook a strong desire for original power.

The following March he wote to William Godwin:[2]

> The Poet is dead in me - my imagination (or rather the
> Somewhat that had been imaginative) lies, like a Cold Snuff
> on the circular Rim of a Brass Candle-stick, without even a
> stink of Tallow to remind you that it was once cloathed &

mitred with Flame. That is past by! – I was once a Volume of
Gold Leaf, rising & riding on every breath of Fancy – but I
have beaten myself back into weight & density, & now I sink
in quicksilver, yea, remain squat and square on the earth amid
the hurricane, that makes Oaks and Straws join in one Dance,
fifty yards high in the Element.... If I die, and the
Booksellers will give you any thing for my Life, be sure to say
– 'Wordsworth descended on him, like the Γνῶθι σεαυτόν
from Heaven; by shewing to him what true Poetry was, he
made him know, that he himself was no Poet.'

Posterity has accepted this verdict, though recognition of
'Dejection', which came two years after this professed abandonment
of poetry has modified the view somewhat. Moreover, with the
exception of 'Dejection', none of Coleridge's finest poems was
written after these letters.

Wordsworth the poet is the central, possibly the shaping, interest
in the *Biographia* and this reflects his importance to Coleridge as
man, as critic and as poet. Early in their friendship this provided a
stimulus, the happy excitement of meeting with new friends added
vitality to the conversation poems, with which Coleridge was
already experimenting. Joint ventures with Wordsworth and the
desire to do something which would complement his friend's work,
produced the poems which explore the supernatural, the 'Ancient
Mariner', 'Kubla Khan' and, finally, 'Christabel'. Coleridge's wide
reading in philosophy and anthropology and his abiding interest in
the recesses of the mind made him well suited to this type of
composition and the poems he produced are works of genius to set
beside any of his friend's achievements. Why, however, should there
have been so little in this vein, when what there is is so suggestive
of further riches? The unfinished 'Christabel' may provide a clue.

Coleridge was not a man to stand alone. He needed the support
of reassurance, friendship and criticism. Almost all his completed
works, prose as well as verse, have a secondary figure standing
behind their author: Southey for the early political works,
Wordsworth for the poetry of 1797-8, Sara Hutchinson for *The
Friend*, John Morgan for the *Biographia* and the Gillmans for later
prose. The 'Ancient Mariner', Coleridge's most sustained poetic
composition was completed for the *Lyrical Ballads* and 'Christabel'
was intended for the second edition, but Wordsworth had been

uneasy about the effect of the 'Ancient Mariner' on sales and was equally uncertain of Coleridge's new poem. On 18 December 1800 Wordsworth wrote to Longman and Rees, the publishers, sending a substitute for 'Christabel':[3]

> A Poem of Mr Coleridge's was to have concluded the Volumes: but upon mature deliberation I found that the Style of this Poem was so discordant from my own that it could not be printed along with my poems with any propriety.

As early as October, Coleridge had written to Humphry Davy:[4]

> The Christabel was running up to 1300 lines – and was so much admired by Wordsworth, that he thought it indelicate to print two Volumes with *his name* in which so much of another man's was included – & which was of more consequence – the poem was in direct opposition to the very purpose for which the Lyrical Ballads were published – viz – an experiment to see how far those passions, which alone give any value to extraordinary Incidents, were capable of interesting, in & for themselves, in the incidents of common Life.

Although there is a marked difference in tone between the two passages, one thing is clear: the original idea that there should be two sorts of poem, the commonplace and the supernatural, has been abandoned in favour of poems in the Wordsworthian manner. At the time, Coleridge bore this with equanimity, presumably because he agreed with Wordsworth's judgment. It was less than two months later that he wrote:[5]

> He is a great, a true Poet – I am only a kind of a Metaphysician. He has even now sent off the last sheet of a second Volume of his *Lyrical Ballads* –.

The reference to the second volume of *Lyrical Ballads* (the one which was originally intended to conclude with 'Christabel') so near to the deprecation of his poetic powers indicates how Coleridge received the Heaven-sent message that he was 'no Poet'. Only later, after their bitter quarrel, was Coleridge formally to state the idea of two sorts of poem. The years and Coleridge's habit of mind seem to have conflated editions but the same central factors emerge:[6]

> With this view [of providing supernatural poems] I wrote 'The Ancient Mariner', and was preparing among other poems,

'The Dark Ladie', and the 'Christabel', in which I should have more nearly realized my ideal, than I had done in my first attempt. But Mr Wordsworth's industry had proved so much more successful, and the number of his poems so much greater, that my compositions, instead of forming a balance, appeared rather an interpolation of heterogeneous matter. Mr Wordsworth added two or three poems written in his own character, in the impassioned, lofty, and sustained diction, which is characteristic of his genius.

Beneath the restraint and despite the exaggerated respect there is more than a hint of resentment, and significantly, this prefaces Coleridge's discussion of the disagreement between the poets on the subject of poetic diction and the preface to the second edition of *Lyrical Ballads*.

Coleridge, unable to stand alone, lost the support of the poet he so greatly and generously admired, and instead of extricating himself from this disagreement with a clearer knowledge of what he was as a poet, succumbed to Wordsworth's standards, and pronounced himself 'no Poet'. Other poems were written after this, but henceforward Coleridge was to consider himself firstly as a 'kind of a Metaphysician'. One of the results of this is that there is a long tradition which regards Coleridge as not really a great poet after all.

Coleridge the poet made an auspicious beginning, and several early poems appeared in the newspapers. His own periodical, the *Watchman*, included some of his verses and in December 1794 and January 1795 a series of sonnets on eminent characters appeared in the *Morning Chronicle*. In 1796 *Poems on Various Subjects*, including many of the poems which had originally appeared in the papers, was published by Joseph Cottle. Although some poems, like the 'Monody on the Death of Chatterton', were revised versions of earlier compositions, most were recently if not specifically composed. Coleridge thought 'Religious Musings' the finest poem in the volume and placed it last to provide a grand climax. A contemporary reviewer took the same attitude:[7]

> The longest piece in the volume, entitled 'Religious Musings, a desultory Poem written on Christmas Eve', is reserved for the conclusion; and properly so, since its subject, and the manner of treating it, place it on the top of the scale of sublimity.

61

Posterity has preferred those poems – 'Lines at Shurton Bars', 'Reflections on having left a place of retirement', and chiefly 'The Aeolian Harp' – which celebrate life with Sara in rural Somerset. Poems by Lamb and Lloyd were included to swell the volume, which was reissued the following year with some alterations and new poems. These included sonnets celebrating the birth of his son Hartley, a few poems addressed to friends and 'Ode to the Departing Year' commissioned by Flower to appear in the *Cambridge Intelligencer* on the last day of 1796, but also issued separately as a pamphlet. The volume opened with dedicatory lines to George Coleridge, but the dedicatee was 'displeased and thought his character endangered by the Dedication',[8] as Coleridge wished posterity to know.

*Poems on Various Subjects* appeared in a third edition in 1803 but not until 1817 did a new collection of poetry by Coleridge appear, though in the meantime poems published in the papers kept his name before the public. In November 1797 three sonnets signed Nehemiah Higginbottom were published in the *Monthly Magazine*. A subtitle stated that these were 'attempted in the manner of contemporary writers', but Lloyd, Lamb and Southey, deciding they were the objects of the satire, were not amused, and the incident caused the only breach in the lifelong friendship of Lamb and Coleridge. The *Cambridge Intelligencer* published occasional political squibs, but the *Morning Post* was chief publisher of Coleridge's poems. Initially the poems were political; 'Fire, Famine and Slaughter' appeared in January 1798, 'France' in April the same year and 'Recantation' in July. 'The Devil's Thoughts' published anonymously in September 1799 was composed jointly with Southey and soon earned considerable notoriety. Later, there were non-political contributions including translations or adaptations (not always acknowledged, as in the case of the infamous 'Hymn before Sunrise'). Some of the poems were mere trifles, but 'The Picture', a poem of some length, and 'Dejection' both appeared in autumn 1802. Even unsigned poems were often recognised by the cognoscenti, and the trickle of publications in the press must have helped maintain Coleridge's position as a literary figure during his long absences from London.

In 1798, *Lyrical Ballads* brought before the public the new techniques and interests which Coleridge and Wordsworth had been discussing at Racedown, Alfoxden and Nether Stowey. The poets' main aim in publishing the volume was to raise money; various plans had been considered before the poetry was chosen, and up to the last minute there seems to have been some doubt. Cottle, the publisher, remained uncertain even until publication day, possibly because Southey thought he should be warned against a venture which was bound to lose money. In the end the book was printed by Cottle in early September and published by J. & A. Arch of Gracechurch Street on 4 October 1798.[9] Although the poets freely admitted that financial gain was their original impulse, the Advertisement written by Wordsworth turned the book into a revolutionary gesture. Coleridge later dissented with some bitterness from the expanded Preface to the 1800 and 1802 editions but he acknowledged even then the value of Wordsworth's 'remonstrance in behalf of truth and nature'[10] and it is significant that the words which above all others aroused Coleridge's wrath, 'the real language of men', did not appear in 1798, where the phrase has a more Coleridgean cast:[11]

> The majority of the following poems are to be considered as
> experiments. They were written chiefly with a view to
> ascertain how far the language of conversation in the middle
> and lower classes of society is adapted to the purposes of poetic
> pleasure.

As Coleridge gave his 'Reflections on having left a place of retirement' the motto 'Sermoni propriora' and his 'Nightingale' the subtitle 'A conversational poem', it seems likely that this experiment not only had Coleridge's blessing but was in part the fruition of his own thinking. In fact, G. Watson traces back to *Poems on Various Subjects* the influence of Coleridge:[12]

> he is rather more likely than Wordsworth to have evolved the
> blank-verse monody which he came to call the conversation
> poem, and which, in Wordsworth's more industrious hand,
> became 'Tintern Abbey' and, in a vastly extended form, the
> *Prelude* of 1805.

Another of Coleridge's conversation poems, 'Frost at Midnight', appeared in a pamphlet in 1798 together with two of Coleridge's more sustained poems on contemporary events: 'France, an Ode' and 'Fears in Solitude'. These poems with the 'Ancient Mariner' represent some of Coleridge's finest and most finished work, but only 'France' seems to have excited much favourable interest. It

63

appeared in the *Morning Post* on 16 April 1798 with the following introduction:[13]

> It is very satisfactory to find so zealous and steady an Advocate for Freedom as Mr. COLERIDGE concur with us in condemning the conduct of France towards the Swiss Cantons. ... What we most admire is the *avowal* of his sentiments, and public censure of the unprincipled and atrocious conduct of France. The Poem itself is written with great energy. The second, third and fourth stanzas contain some of the most vigorous lines we have ever read.

The *Annual Anthology* edited by Southey in 1800 published other recent poems, most notably, 'This Lime-tree Bower'. The 1800 edition of *Lyrical Ballads* which did not include 'Christabel' did have another additional poem by Coleridge, 'Love', which is similarly Gothic but without any hint of the supernatural. Manuscript circulation gave Coleridge's work considerable currency so that both Scott and Byron were able to avail themselves of the metrical example of 'Christabel' before the poem was published. Coleridge had to insert a note to excuse himself from copying them when the poem appeared in 1816. Financial need was responsible for the eventual publication of 'Kubla Khan' and 'Christabel' so long after their composition, both still according to the poet unfinished. They appeared with 'Pains of Sleep' in a small pamphlet to which Coleridge sought to give some coherence by connecting 'Kubla Khan' with 'Pains of Sleep':[14]

> As a contrast to this vision, ['Kubla Khan'] I have annexed a fragment of a very different character, describing with equal fidelity the dream of pain and disease.

Coleridge maintained the separation of these poems from the main body of his work by omitting them from *Sibylline Leaves* (1817), which collected most of his previously published work (though only 'The Aeolian Harp' from *Poems on Various Subjects*) and a few poems hitherto unpublished. Among these was 'Recollections of Love', which looked back to Stowey days, and 'To William Wordsworth', written after hearing the *Prelude* and recalling the high point of the two poets' friendship. The remaining collections in which Coleridge had a hand were the three-volume edition of 1828, reissued in 1829 and the 1834 edition which, although published within days of the poet's death, was prepared by H. N. Coleridge with his uncle's help. These included the plays, *Remorse*, *Zapolya*, and the translated *Piccolomini* as well as a few unpublished poems, some of them newly written. By the last decade of his life Coleridge's reputation was beginning to be of interest to publishers and he made contributions to several of the literary annuals fashionable at that time. 'Work without Hope' appeared in *Bijou* in 1828, 'The Garden of Boccaccio' accompanied a plate by Stothard in the *Keepsake* for 1829 and in 1834 *Friendship's Offering* published four 'Lightheartednesses in Rhyme' by Coleridge.

This brief bibliographical summary indicates the way in which Coleridge's poetic career developed. There was a crescendo towards the end of the eighteenth century, followed by a gradual lessening of poetic production and, apart from a trickle of newspaper appearances, a long silence. The publications of 1816 and 1817 mark a revival chiefly reflected in prose but towards the end of the 1820s there was a final spate of poetry writing, which, while nothing like the activity of 1796-9, still furnished the albums of the time with short and by no means inconsiderable poems. Also at this time Coleridge was busy revising and editing the three-volume editions of 1828, 1829 and 1834. Coleridge's complete poetical works do not form a large corpus, even when fragments are included, and only a few of these have earned lasting attention but were it only for the existence of a few of those few, Coleridge's verdict of 'no poet' must have long been reversed by his readers.

Not all of Coleridge's journalistic pieces have much continuing interest but sometimes a more considered view of current events produced poetry of more lasting value. One of the earliest is the lyric included in *The Fall of Robespierre* and reprinted in the 1796 volume:[15]

> Tell me, on what holy ground
> May Domestic Peace be found?
> Halcyon daughter of the skies,
> Far on fearful wings she flies,
> From the pomp of Sceptred State,
> From the Rebel's noisy hate.
>
> In a cottag'd vale She dwells,
> Listening to the Sabbath bells!

Still around her steps are seen
Spotless Honour's meeker mien,
Love, the sire of pleasing fears,
Sorrow smiling through her tears,
And conscious of the past employ
Memory, bosom-spring of joy.

This poem is interesting because in spite of its apparent escapist attitude, it really contains a political statement: that Great Britain should not involve herself in the French war in order to maintain the British constitution and establishment, but rather should look for peace by supporting the British way of life. The second stanza probably adds more weight to Coleridge's later assertions that he never was a Jacobin than any of his more overtly political prose.

The non-political poems of this early period offer a clearer insight into the way in which Coleridge's poetic technique was to develop in maturity. The short poem 'To an Infant' anticipates Coleridge's later observations of his own children in the following lines:[16]

Ah! cease thy tears and sobs, my little Life!
I did but snatch away the unclasp'd knife:
Some safer toy will soon arrest thine eye,
And to quick laughter change this peevish cry!

Here, after the formality of the first line, Coleridge presents in simple language a picture of a child's tempers which convinces the reader that it was actually experienced. That Coleridge was aware of the difficulty of preserving the immediacy of the real especially when the subject had been taken over by formal patterns of verse, remote from reality, is made clear in 'To the Nightingale'. This early poem expresses the Romantic interest in the experience of the real world. Here in the simplest language Coleridge expresses the simplest fact of natural observation, 'But I *do* hear thee' and builds upon this a poem which skilfully combines the impact of the actual bird upon the listener and the thoughts of the poet processing his experience:[17]

Sister of love-lorn Poets, Philomel!
How many Bards in city garret pent,
While at their window they with downward eye
Mark the faint lamp-beam on the kennell'd mud,

And listen to the drowsy cry of Watchmen
(Those hoarse unfeather'd Nightingales of Time!),
How many wretched Bards address *thy* name,
And hers, the full-orb'd Queen that shines above.
But I *do* hear thee, and the high bough mark,
Within whose mild moon-mellow'd foliage hid
Thou warblest sad thy pity-pleading strains.
O! I have listen'd, till my working soul,
Waked by those strains to thousand phantasies,
Absorb'd hath ceas'd to listen!

The difference between the 'Bards'' reaction and that of the actual
experiencer of the real thing is pronounced, and it seems that
Coleridge learnt about this not from Wordsworth, whom he
scarcely knew, but from his schoolmaster:[18]

Lute, harp, and lyre, muse, muses, and inspirations, Pegasus,
Parnassus, and Hippocrene were all an abomination to him. In
fancy I can almost hear him now, exclaiming *'Harp? Harp?
Lyre? Pen and ink, boy, you mean! Muse, boy, Muse? Your
Nurse's daughter, you mean! Pieran spring? Oh aye! the
cloister-pump, I suppose!'*

This awareness of the unreality of poeticisms survives in the ironic
reference to 'the Poet's Philomel' (now clearly not a real nightingale
at all) in the original version of 'Dejection'. But as Coleridge
admits, lapses from grace were common and a fondness for certain
images shaped his thinking and characterised his poetry. The
Aeolian harp was one of these and gave its name to one of the most
successful poems in Coleridge's first collection. Coleridge uses the
harp to frame an idea of the 'undivided unity' which underlies so
great a variety of forms and which is a recurrent idea in Coleridge's
poetry as well as in his prose. The title was not added until 1817,
illustrating how the image held its importance for Coleridge over
those central years of his life which might by their turbulence have
broken the thread of his thinking. In fact, the Aeolian lute is found
in the poem which epitomises the troubles of his middle years,
'Dejection'. By now the poet is feeling that the lute 'better far were
mute' but it is not mute. Throughout this period when the poet's
sensitivity (for this is part of what the lute represents) brought him

nothing but pain, the poet himself could not deny the importance of his receptiveness to external images.

For J. D. Campbell, who records that Coleridge thought 'The Aeolian Harp' 'the most perfect poem I ever wrote', 'this poem marks an era in the development of Coleridge's powers of expression, both as regards melody and individuality'.[19] The musical beauty of the lines:[20]

> the long sequacious notes
> Over the delicious surges sink and rise,
> Such a soft floating witchery of sound
> As twilight Elfins make, when they at eve
> Voyage on gentle gales from Fairy-Land,

anticipates that skill in manipulating sound effects which is of paramount importance in Coleridge's greatest poems.

'Religious Musings', subtitled 'a desultory poem written on Christmas Eve', is not so much desultory as formless and unwieldy; its value is not aesthetic but as part of the history of Coleridge's ideas on politics and religion. There are moments, however, when the otherwise ill-digested content is amalgamated into poetry which transcends its source ideas:[21]

> There is one Mind, one omnipresent Mind,
> Omnific. His most holy name is Love.
> Truth of subliming import! with the which
> Who feeds and saturates his constant soul,
> He from his small particular orbit flies
> With blest outstarting! From himself he flies,
> Stands in the sun, and with no partial gaze
> Views all creation; and he loves it all,
> And blesses it, and calls it very good!
> This is indeed to dwell with the Most High!

As early as 1796 Coleridge is expressing his idea of the relationship between the creator and the created possible through the power he was later to define as imagination. In these few lines Coleridge foreshadows his mature belief in the oneness of creation, and the possibility which that created world offers to the imaginative perceiver of an insight into, a union with the Creator. Later, in the *Biographia*, he was to refine this idea by adding a secondary imagination which clarifies the role of the artist:[22]

The primary IMAGINATION I hold to be the living Power and prime Agent of all human Perception, and as a repetition in the finite mind of the eternal act of creation in the infinite I AM. The secondary Imagination I consider as an echo of the former,

'Religious Musings' purported to have been written on Christmas Eve 1795 (in fact, it was composed over a longer period); 'Ode to the Departing Year' was commissioned for the end of 1796 and is very much in the same mould. The footnotes are longer and more enlightening than the poem itself, which could not stand without them. The force in the note to stanza 8:

We have been preserved by our insular situation, from suffering the actual horrors of war ourselves, and we have shewn our gratitude to Providence for this immunity by our eagerness to spread those horrors over nations less happily situated. In the midst of plenty and safety we have raised or joined the yell for famine and blood.

quite overshadows the four lines to which it refers:[23]

> Abandon'd of Heaven! mad Avarice thy guide,
> At cowardly distance, yet kindling with pride –
> Mid thy herds and thy corn-fields secure thou hast stood
> And join'd the wild yelling of Famine and Blood!

Not until April 1798, when 'France, an Ode' appeared as a recantation of his earlier sympathy for the French cause, did Coleridge perfect a poem of this kind. The poem has greater strength than others which share its political, philosophical, religious themes: contrasting his former and his present attitudes to France enables Coleridge to see the cause of freedom more coherently because retrospectively:[24]

> When France in wrath her giant-limbs upreared,
>     And with that oath, which smote air, earth, and sea,
>         Stamped her strong foot and said she would be free,
> Bear witness for me, how I hoped and feared!
> With what a joy my lofty gratulation
>     Unawed I sang, amid a slavish band:
> And when to whelm the disenchanted nation,
>     Like friends embattled by a wizard's wand,

The Monarchs marched in evil day,
　And Britain joined the dire array;
　Though dear her shores and circling ocean,
　Though many friendships, many youthful loves
　　Had swoln the patriot emotion
And flung a magic light o'er all her hills and groves;
Yet still my voice, unaltered, sang defeat
　To all that braved the tyrant-quelling lance,
And shame too long delayed and vain retreat!

Written in the same month as 'France' and on the same theme, 'Fears in Solitude' is more personal, a 'conversation poem' shaped by the poet's situation. Here Coleridge expresses a deep love for the country to whose physical attributes the poem is so closely related:[25]

　　　　O divine
And beauteous island! thou hast been my sole
And most magnificent temple, in the which
I walk with awe, and sing my stately songs,
Loving the God that made me!

The fears of the title seem more important because the war and its devastations relate to an actual scene which the poetry makes as real and as loved to the reader as it is to the poet:

And now, beloved Stowey! I behold
Thy church-tower, and, methinks, the four huge elms
Clustering, which mark the mansion of my friend;
And close behind them, hidden from my view,
Is my own lowly cottage where my babe
And my babe's mother dwell in peace!

The relation of the horrors of war to the known and felt is central to the poem; only by feeling what war really is will the people of England have a proper understanding of what they are doing in France:[26]

　　　　Boys and girls,
And women, that would groan to see a child
Pull off an insect's leg, all read of war,
The best amusement for our morning meal! ...
And all our dainty terms for fratricide;

Terms which we trundle smoothly o'er our tongues
Like mere abstractions, empty sounds to which
We join no feeling and attach no form!
As if the soldier died without a wound;
As if the fibres of this godlike frame
Were gored without a pang; as if the wretch,
Who fell in battle, doing bloody deeds,
Passed off to Heaven, translated and not killed;
As though he had no wife to pine for him,
No God to judge him! Therefore, evil days
Are coming on us, O my countrymen!
And what if all-avenging Providence,
Strong and retributive, should make us know
The meaning our words, force us to feel
The desolation and the agony
Of our fierce doings?

Besides its concern for the misery and suffering of war, this passage
shows another concern, here closely related: that we should know
what words mean. To the end of his life, Coleridge insisted that
good action depended upon a proper understanding and use of
words uniting what might appear to be only literary critical with
the political:[27]

> The high importance of Words, and the incalculable moral
> and practical advantages attached to the habit of using them
> definitely and appropriately, the ill consequence of the contrary
> not confined to Individuals, but extending even to National
> Character and Conduct.

The passage from the poem hints at the point where the two
distinct attitudes to language of Wordsworth and Coleridge touch,
the relationship of a proper communication in words and the value
of the real communicated as plainly as possible. In Coleridge's case,
the passage makes clear the background from which the idea
emerged. It is related to the *Watchman* motto, 'That all may know
the truth and the truth may set them free.' Coleridge's experience
in journalism, the desire to make the news from France as vivid to
the reader (and equally in the case of lectures to the audience) as
local gossip, made him feel the importance of as direct a use of
language as possible. This, together with the schoolday training in

71

the use of plain terms, which was probably reinforced by Wordsworth's similar ideas, had an important effect on Coleridge's poetry.

The third poem in the 1798 pamphlet shows this attitude to
language bearing fruit in a non-political context. 'Frost at Midnight' concentrates on the poet, alone except for his baby son and
isolated in the quiet warm house from the world's cares; but even
here Coleridge reaches out from the personal:[28]

> But *thou*, my babe! shalt wander like a breeze
> By lakes and sandy shores, beneath the crags
> Of ancient mountain, and beneath the clouds,
> Which image in their bulk both lakes and shores
> And mountain crags: so shalt thou see and hear
> The lovely shapes and sounds intelligible
> Of that eternal language, which thy God
> Utters, who from eternity doth teach
> Himself in all, and all things in himself.

Again the idea of language is prominent in a concept of Creation
which looks forward to the 1817 *Lay Sermon*:[29]

> A Symbol (ὃ ἔστιν ἄει ταυτηγορικον) is characterized by a
> translucence of the Special in the Individual or of the General
> in the Especial or of the Universal in the General. Above all
> by the translucence of the Eternal through and in the
> Temporal. It always partakes of the Reality which it renders
> intelligible; and while it enunciates the whole, abides itself as a
> living part in that Unity, of which it is the representative.
> The other [allegories] are but empty echoes which the fancy
> arbitrarily associates with apparitions of matter.

When Coleridge later wrote that he was a metaphysician and not
a poet, he seemed to suggest that he was unable to embody his
thinking in true poetry. 'Frost at Midnight', one example among
many, illustrates how Coleridge underestimated his success. The
lines quoted contain truly Coleridgean metaphysics, and yet the
poem itself delights aesthetically as well as philosophically. The
silent poet, the baby and his home are vividly evoked, the poet's
thinking is perfectly embodied as fireside musing, and the relationship between the inner world of thought and the outer world
of persons, objects and events is depicted in just the way which
frosty weather, turning us in on ourselves, suggests.

'This Lime-tree Bower' is a more social poem because although the poet is solitary his thoughts reach out to his friends and their experience. Like 'Frost at Midnight' this poem shows how Coleridge could embody his thought in the finest poetry. Of all his celebrations of the beneficence of nature, this is perhaps the most persuasive because in it Coleridge, while using his own position, imprisoned by a burnt foot beneath the lime tree, also evokes his friend's situation on a familiar walk. This gives the poem a structure and enables Coleridge to make a richer study of nature, using both settings. The inclusion of 'Gentle-hearted Charles, to whom No sound is dissonant which tells of life' gives the poem a broader sympathy and under this influence Coleridge suggests we should:[30]

> lift the soul, and contemplate
> With lively joy the joys we cannot share.

The natural description in this poem is particularly beautiful, illustrating Coleridge's point that 'no plot so narrow' but affords scope for the sense:

> Pale beneath the blaze
> Hung the transparent foliage; and I watch'd
> Some broad and sunny leaf, and lov'd to see
> The shadow of the leaf and stem above
> Dappling its sunshine! And that walnut-tree
> Was richly ting'd, and a deep radiance lay
> Full on the ancient ivy, which usurps
> Those fronting elms, and now, with blackest mass
> Makes their dark branches gleam a lighter hue
> Through the late twilight:

The accuracy of the observation, the neat differentiation between degrees of shade and qualities of light, are such that reading the poem becomes an experience of nature reinforcing Coleridge's point about the effect of keeping 'the heart Awake to Love and Beauty'.

Before this was published in 1800, the conversational quality of these poems was brought to public notice in the *Lyrical Ballads*, where 'The Nightingale' was offered as an example. In part, this is an expansion of the earlier poem of the same title but now the poet is in company and the bird's song is not melancholy in fact as well as convention, but in reality is joyful:[31]

> 'Tis the merry Nightingale
> That crowds, and hurries, and precipitates
> With fast thick warble his delicious notes,

Now Coleridge really communicates as well as states the immediacy of his experience of the bird's song, and this complements his belief in the benign influence of nature, here, as in 'Frost at Midnight', expressed in relation to the baby Hartley:[32]

> Well! –
> It is a father's tale: But if that Heaven
> Should give me life, his childhood shall grow up
> Familiar with these songs, that with the night
> He may associate joy. – Once more, farewell,
> Sweet Nightingale! once more, my friends! farewell.

Here the conversational style makes the reader feel that this is not a mere poetic reflection of a philosophy of nature, but a genuinely felt reaction to a real bird singing. This represents one of the major themes of *Lyrical Ballads* and is expressed by Wordsworth in, for instance, 'The Tables Turned', where bird song again provides the first impulse:[33]

> Let Nature be your teacher.
>
> She has a world of ready wealth,
> Our minds and hearts to bless –
> Spontaneous wisdom breathed by health,
> Truth breathed by chearfulness.

Apart from two excerpts from the unpublished *Osorio*, Coleridge's only other contribution to *Lyrical Ballads* was 'The rime of the Ancyent Marinere', as it was called in the first edition. Wordsworth's remaining poems included 'Tintern Abbey', which expands on Nature's ability to 'inform The mind that is within us', and various narratives of life in rural England. 'The Ancient Mariner' seems to be set apart from the rest of the book by its language, its ballad-like narrative, and its South Seas setting. J. Livingston Lowes's exposition in his famous critical work of 1927, *The Road to Xanadu*, furthermore makes clear that this poem offers no abandonment of books for a first-hand apprehension of nature. But the final message from the Mariner to the wedding-guest relates the same moral:[34]

> He prayeth well, who loveth well
> Both man and bird and beast.
>
> He prayeth best, who loveth best
> All things both great and small;
> For the dear God who loveth us
> He made and loveth all.

To a certain extent Coleridge himself is responsible for our refusal to accept this message, which is strengthened in *Lyrical Ballads* by similar ideas of nature in other poems. In *Table Talk* he is recorded as answering Mrs Barbauld's criticism:[35]

> as to the want of a moral, I told her that in my own judgment the poem had too much; and that the only, or chief fault, if I might say so, was the obtrusion of the moral sentiment so openly on the reader as a principle or cause of action in a work of such pure imagination. It ought to have had no more moral than the 'Arabian Nights' tale of the merchant's sitting down to eat dates by the side of a well, and throwing the shells aside, and lo! a genie starts up, and says he *must* kill the aforesaid merchant *because* one of the date shells had, it seems, put out the eye of the genie's son.

As Humphrey House[36] has said, there is a moral implicit in the *Arabian Nights'* story and this should modify our feelings about the 'Ancient Mariner'. Indeed, Coleridge says that the poem's fault is 'the obtrusion of the moral sentiment so openly' – which is different from saying that there should have been no moral content. It is, in fact, difficult to imagine any narrative totally devoid of moral content, certainly not one by Coleridge. The comment shows Coleridge being mischievously perverse with Mrs Barbauld as a rebuke, possibly, for her inability to read an implicit moral, but this has done his poem a disservice. If we assume a parallel between the action of the Mariner and its awful outcome and the action of the merchant and its punishment, there is a third parallel in a notebook entry describing an attempt to shoot a hawk on the voyage to Malta:[37]

I heard firing, now here, now there/& nobody shot it/but

probably it perished from fatigue, & the attempt to rest upon
the wave! – Poor Hawk! O Strange Lust of Murder in Man! –
It is not cruelty/it is mere non-feeling from non-thinking.

Here the common factor is made explicit, 'non-feeling from non-
thinking'. This can be related to the lines from 'Fears in Solitude'
quoted above, with a special relevance to 'The Ancient Mariner' of
the 'all-avenging Providence' who will 'force us to feel The
desolation and the agony'. The work of 'pure imagination' parallels
the contemporary poem on topical reality.

There is much more to the poem than this, but there has been
so much written about the poem that to a certain extent the
narrative which wields such power over the reader has been
overwhelmed by critical apparatus. Perhaps a verse from *Lyrical
Ballads* is apt here:[38]

> Enough of science and of art;
> Close up these barren leaves.
> Come forth, and bring with you a heart
> That watches and receives.

This is not to deny the consummate artistry with which Coleridge
amalgamates the widest ranging sources to create a poem whose
effect is of direct communication. Here, for example, is an insight
into the 'desolation and the agony':[39]

> I closed my lids, and kept them close,
> And the balls like pulses beat;
> For the sky and the sea, and the sea and the sky
> Lay like a load on my weary eye,
> And the dead were at my feet.
>
> The cold sweat melted from their limbs,
> Nor rot nor reek did they:
> The look with which they looked on me
> Had never passed away.
>
> An orphan's curse would drag to hell
> A spirit from on high;
> But oh! more horrible than that
> Is the curse in a dead man's eye!
> Seven days, seven nights, I saw that curse,
> And yet I could not die.

To call this conversational language is to ignore the art which has pared away every unneeded word and made simple words convey simple facts with terrible nakedness, 'the balls like pulses beat', 'and yet I could not die'. In the use of these universally available words, Coleridge is calling on universal feelings of suffering, both physical and mental, relating the Mariner's experience to the experience of the reader, reinforcing his moral without making it explicit; counteracting the 'non-feeling from non-thinking' which in Coleridge's day was having such terrible effects on the civilised world.

The other two great poems of this period, 'Kubla Khan' and 'Christabel', were supposedly unfinished and therefore unpublished. A second part to 'Christabel' was written after the poet moved to Keswick in 1800, but Coleridge never seems to have attempted to add to 'Kubla Khan' which was published almost twenty years after it was written with the disclaimer that it was work done long ago. The well-known story of the man from Porlock who interrupted the transcription of the poem which came complete to Coleridge in a dream is now generally accepted to be apocryphal. But this note can still be a valuable guide to reading the poem, subtitled 'A Vision in a Dream', and Coleridge, who was always interested in dreams, has communicated an imagined, if not a real dream, in which many differing images are suspended without sequence in our consciousness. The incantatory magic of the poem achieves that 'willing suspension of the disbelief' which is as characteristic of dreams as it is of art. The poem's meaning has proved as elusive as that of any dream, and it would not be possible in this chapter to examine the many interpretations to be found elsewhere. If, as critics seem to agree, the last stanza expresses the poet's longing to revive lost powers, then it is ironically expressive of Coleridge's inability to rely on his own genius that he did not recognise the success with which he captures the mood of failure. For he does revive 'the symphony and song' of the Abyssinian maid, and he does recreate 'that sunny dome, those caves of ice' which despite the rich sources that tell us that these phenomena had an existence before Coleridge, can never have been so real as in this poem.

In the Preface to 'Christabel', Coleridge again carefully set the poem in his past, but he predicts its completion within the next year, because 'in my very first conception of the tale, I had the whole present to my mind, with the wholeness, no less than the liveliness of a vision'.[40] No more of the poem ever did appear, but it is interesting that Coleridge, ignoring its resemblance to a ballad, again compares his poem with a dream. The 'liveliness and wholeness of a vision' which has little to do with sequence of events or consistency of character is invoked. This may explain why it is so difficult to analyse the causes of the action or the nature of the characters of Geraldine, Christabel and Sir Leoline; they have surface but no substance.

The poem was begun at the same time as the 'Ancient Mariner' and in the same year Coleridge reviewed Lewis's Gothic novel *The Monk*, commenting:[41]

> The romance-writer possesses an unlimited power over situations; but he must scrupulously make his characters act in congruity with them. Let him work *physical* wonders only, and we will be content to *dream* with him for a while; but the first *moral* miracle which he attempts, he disgusts and awakens us ... The extent of the powers that may exist, we can never ascertain; and therefore we feel no great difficulty in yielding a temporary belief to any, the strangest situation of *things*. But that situation once conceived, how beings like ourselves would feel and act in it, our own feelings sufficiently instruct us; and we instantly reject the clumsy fiction that does not harmonise with them.

This represents a working interest in the form, showing how, in both the 'Ancient Mariner' and 'Christabel', Coleridge was concerned to explore the possibilities of the preternatural in a psychologically convincing framework. The entry of Geraldine and Christabel into the silent sleeping castle, for instance, is depicted with a careful regard for plausible characterisation, culminating in the picture of Geraldine as she undresses and prepares to lie down with Christabel:[42]

> Deep from within she seems half-way
> To lift some weight with sick assay,
> And eyes the maid and seeks delay;
> Then suddenly, as one defied,
> Collects herself in scorn and pride,
> And lay down by the Maiden's side!

It is this realism of character which involves the reader in the story, making its incompleteness so tantalising. Whether A. H. Nethercot[43] is right in his assertion that Geraldine belongs to the vampire tradition, or whether the psychological critics[44] are more accurate in thinking that Geraldine represents a usurping love precipitating Christabel's rejection by her father, still part of her fascination lies in the fact that she is not only 'preternatural' but shares recognisable characteristics with the reader.

In the poem 'Love', which replaced 'Christabel' in the second edition of *Lyrical Ballads,* Coleridge encapsules the incomplete narrative within a hearer's reaction. The device is used in the 'Ancient Mariner' to emphasise the story, but here the narrative is subordinate to the reactions of the listener, 'my own dear Genevieve'. E. H. Coleridge first ascribed the poem to the period just after Coleridge's meeting with Asra, and G. Whalley confirms the identity of Genevieve and Asra in his book on the Asra poems.[45] Coleridge's involvement with the poem's characters transfers attention from the story and its first person narrator to the poet, whose tale of a knight of old is of much less interest. Although it does not show the same mastery of narrator, narrative and listener as the 'Ancient Mariner', 'Love' is an interesting poem and skillfully done. It indicates, moreover, the direction in which Coleridge's poems were to develop from this time forward. Without the confidence to continue in the supernatural mode, and dissatisfied with his attempts to embody his thoughts in conversational poems, he increasingly turns inwards. The later poems lack the balance which 'Frost at Midnight', 'Lime-tree Bower' and 'The Nightingale' received from the external features referred to in their titles. Even Coleridge's final triumph in this style in its title 'Dejection' suggests the difference. The original verse letter written on 4 April 1802 was much longer and more personal than the version published six months later in the *Morning Post.* In its original private form[46] Coleridge probes his inmost thoughts about his personal situation and so provides a quarrying ground for excavations of hidden significance in his life and work.[47] The revelations are unsparing and reflect Coleridge's capacity for honest self-scrutiny:[48]

> 'My little Children are a Joy, a Love,
> A good Gift from above!
> But what is Bliss, that still calls up a Woe

> And makes it doubly keen
> Compelling me to *feel*, as well as KNOW,
> What a most blessed Lot mine might have been.
> Those little Angel Children (woe is me!)
> There have been hours, when feeling how they bind
> And pluck out the Wing-feathers of my Mind,
> Turning my Error to Necessity,
> I have half-wish'd, they never had been born!
> *That* seldom! but sad Thoughts they always bring,
> And like the Poet's Philomel, I sing
> My Love-song, with my breast against a Thorn.

The poem as published represents a truly Coleridgean achievement, the making out of his own situation a poem of permanent and general value. In the finished poem there is still a profoundly personal utterance:[49]

> But now afflictions bow me down to earth:
> Nor care I that they rob me of my mirth;
>     But oh! each visitation
> Suspends what nature gave me at my birth,
>     My shaping spirit of Imagination.

Here Coleridge examines the relation of the poet to the external world critically because that relationship is no longer a happy one:[50]

> It were a vain endeavour,
>     Though I should gaze for ever
> On that green light that lingers in the west:
> I may not hope from outward forms to win
> The passion and the life, whose fountains are within.

Coleridge is no longer able to experience with 'Joy' the nature whose beneficent influence his earlier work had commemorated. However, he shapes this statment of personal failure in such a way that the value and reality of the natural is preserved:[51]

> Those stars, that glide behind them or between,
> Now sparkling, now bedimmed, but always seen:
> Yon crescent Moon, as fixed as if it grew
> In its own cloudless, starless lake of blue;
> I see them all so excellent fair,
> I see, not feel, how beautiful they are!

It is the counterpoising of the external against Coleridge's scrutiny of his own inability to feel its influence which gives the poem, as published, its aesthetic poise and philosophical meaning, which has a value to the reader independent of its psychological insights into its writer.

'Hymn before Sunrise', written just before the 'Dejection' ode, is an instance of Coleridge's unequal poetic grasp at this time. Coleridge said that the poem was originally inspired by his emotions on seeing the sunrise from Scafell[52] but, as subsequent research has shown, it was heavily dependent on literary sources. The general verdict on the poem is that it represents shameless plagiarism cunningly concealed; maybe Coleridge was trying to remedy the loss of his 'shaping Spirit of Imagination' by using a framework of ideas already available in the poetry of others. 'The Picture', written later in 1802, owes its central idea, of a lover who vows to forget about love but breaks his vow at the first test, to a German poem. The description of the woodland scene mirrors the lover's self-preoccupation in its lack of particularity – 'this river, in this silent shade' and 'brook and bridge, and grey stone cottages, Half hid by rocks and fruit-trees' reflect an inability to realise the individual character of each seen object. When the poem closes with the lover's thoughts of his loved one, the identity of Coleridge with his lover is clear. His Asra too was:[53]

> full of love to all, save only me,
>   And not ungentle e'en to me!

'The Pains of Sleep', composed at Edinburgh in the autumn of 1803, discusses the same nightmares which notebook entries from this period record. Later Coleridge came to relate these night-time horrors to opium but when the poem was written the bewilderment was genuine:[54]

> wherefore, wherefore fall on me?
> To be beloved is all I need,
> And whom I love, I love indeed.

The poem's chief interest is psychological. The difficulties which Coleridge experienced at this period in producing a complete poem combining a history of external interest with his own emotions and ideas is typified by the fragment 'The Blossoming of the Solitary Date Tree'. In 1828 Coleridge published under this title what is really only a collection of working papers. It is subtitled 'A Lament' and is prefaced by an excerpt from a collection of Hebrew writers and a reference to Linnaeus, both of which illustrate the poem's theme, that without the company of a loved one, no matter how favourable other conditions, there can be no fulfilment and no peace. The verse fragment gives a poignant survey of Coleridge's positive attributes:[55]

> Imagination; honourable aims;
> Free commune with the choir that cannot die;
> Science and song; delight in little things,
> The buoyant child surviving in the man;
> Fields, forests, ancient mountains, ocean, sky,
> With all their voices – O dare I accuse
> My earthly lot as guilty of my spleen,
> Or call my destiny niggard! O no! no!
> It is her largeness, and her overflow,
> Which being incomplete, disquieteth me so!

The fragment ends:

> Why was I made for Love and Love denied to me?

This, the personal section of the poem, is all that there is; the opening which would have given the poem a more general philosophical background remains only in prose summary. What is true of this fragment is often true of other poems of this period. As N. Fruman said:[56]

> Though the poems are considerably diminished when considered solely in themselves, they take on a distinctly tragic quality in the context of his later life.

Towards the end of his life, Coleridge was able to produce poems which, making no claims to greatness, still have a certain grace and charm. Several of these appeared in the literary anthologies then fashionable, and one of Coleridge's most sustained later compositions appeared with an illustration in 1829. 'The Garden of Boccaccio' is really a conversation poem. The poet describes himself in 'one of those most weary hours' 'bereft alike of grief or glee', when a friend silently slides in front of him the illustration from Boccaccio, which awakens the poet from his dreary mood. He retraces his youth and visualises:[57]

> a matron now, of sober mien,
> Yet radiant still, and with no earthly sheen,
> Whom as a faery child my childhood woo'd
> Even in my dawn of thought – Philosophy;
> Though then unconscious of herself, pardie,
> She boreſno other name than Poesy;
> And, like a gift from heaven, in lifeful glee,
> That had but newly left a mother's knee,
> Prattled and play'd with bird and flower, and stone,
> As if with elfin playfellows well known,
> And life reveal'd to innocence alone.

Then, and only then, is the poet able to turn to the picture and

> descry
> Thy fair creation with a mastering eye,
> And all awake,

Here Coleridge is offering an example of the point he made in 'Dejection': 'O Lady! we receive but what we give'. The rest of the poem celebrates Boccaccio's Florence, the seat of the revival of Classical learning:[58]

> Rich, ornate, populous, – all treasures thine,
> The golden corn, the olive, and the vine.
> Fair cities, gallant mansions, castles old,
> And forests, where beside his leafy hold
> The sullen boar hath heard the distant horn,
> And whets his tusks against the gnarléd thorn;

Whereas in earlier conversation poems nature gives a frame of reference, this late poem uses art, the musings too are more narrowly personal, but essentially the form is little changed, and a coherence in Coleridge's poetic oeuvre seems to emerge.

In 1834, Coleridge's poem 'Youth and Age' appeared complete. It had previously been published as two separate halves, the first thirty-eight lines in 1828 and the last ten in 1832. Although the last lines are subdued:[59]

> Dewdrops are the gems of morning,
> But the tears of mournful eve!
> Where no hope is, life's a warning

> That only serves to make us grieve,
>   When we are old:

the first part is more jocular in tone as Coleridge refuses to believe
that he is no longer young:

> O Youth! for years so many and sweet,
> 'Tis known, that Thou and I were one,
> I'll think it but a fond conceit –
> It cannot be that Thou art gone!
> Thy vesper-bell hath not yet toll'd: –
> And thou wert aye a masker bold!
> What strange disguise hast thou put on,
> To make believe, that thou art gone?

The poem is not obsessively personal but explores a genuinely
meaningful comparison: its musical skill shows that the technique of
poetry has not deserted Coleridge. Although the idea of Coleridge's
youthful years being 'many and sweet' does not accord with one
side of his life, the poem truthfully perceives in the physically ailing
'sage of Highgate' the same interests and processes of thought which
made his youth so exciting.

Commonly we separate this later Coleridge from his youthful
self, the enthusiastic Pantisocrat and friend of Southey, the country
dweller and friend of Wordsworth, but the late poems show a unity
in Coleridge's thought and a coherence in the development of his
mind and art. In 'The Garden of Boccaccio', Coleridge implies that
what began as poetry developed as philosophy, but it is important
to remember that he is not suggesting two different 'spirits of
power' but merely a young one maturing. Coleridge's poetic work
has too often been fragmented by critics, who have isolated a few
poems and ignored the rest, and although recently more poems have
been singled out for critical attention, the process continues. That
some few of Coleridge's poems achieve the mastery of genius is
undeniable, that many fall well below that level is equally true, but
all Coleridge's poetry was the product of his own unique mind. The
poems in a collected volume may be very unequal in achievement,
but considered as part of his complete works, they illustrate, no less
than any of his other writings, the 'unity in multeity' which is at
the core of all Coleridge's thinking.

# 4

# Literary Criticism

Of all Coleridge's prose work, his critical studies, the *Biographia Literaria* and the *Shakespeare Criticism*, are most familiar to students. Although neither is particularly easy reading, both are related to an external subject which helps the reader find his way through the book. In the *Shakespeare Criticism* there is one main subject, the genius of Shakespeare, but the *Biographia* has a twofold object of study: the poetry and theory of Wordsworth and, as the title suggests, the poet's own life and opinions. Yet it is not only for the elucidation of the works of others that Coleridge is read; his unique contribution to the history of literary criticism consists in his efforts to understand the processes which underly the production of works of art. It is in this second aspect that difficulties occur, partly because Coleridge never really explained the problem to his and our satisfaction and was always hoping to expand his study in his great work, *Logosophia*, and also because, as the *Biographia* makes clear, an understanding of Coleridge's approach to philosophy (if not of the philosophical arguments themselves) is essential to a study of his critical theory. To a certain extent to follow Coleridge's critical theory necessitates following closely and sympathetically the development of his ideas as they were influenced by his own circumstances and his reading. As Coleridge was an energetic thinker and an indefatigable student, this involves considerable labour, and the *Biographia*, which could almost be regarded as the handbook for this study, is, accordingly, a monumental work.

Coleridge's critical career was a long one, but his output was mainly occasional or fragmentary and not intended for publication. In 1796 his first volume of poems was accompanied by a preface demonstrating an interest in poetic theory. At the same time he was reviewing novels and other contemporary works for the *Critical*

85

*Review*. Even earlier, if we include the dedicatory letter to Martin which accompanied *The Fall of Robespierre* (1794) and accept the authenticity of the review of *The Mysteries of Udolpho* which appeared in August 1794,[1] Coleridge the critic was perceptible to a discerning reader. Although Coleridge published nothing until the lectures of 1808, his critical powers developed significantly in the intervening years. The letters reveal a protracted debate with Wordsworth about poetic diction and Coleridge's scribblings in books not necessarily his own show a mind always engaged critically in reading. The notebooks where many of the central ideas of his later works are found, reveal a constantly evolving attitude to poetic creation, but Coleridge did not formulate his thinking for the public until, as J. R. de J. Jackson suggests,[2] there was a pressing financial need.

The lectures of 1808 at the Royal Institution were successful enough for Coleridge to give a second course at the Surrey Institution between November 1811 and January 1812. This is the series which provides the core of Coleridge's Shakespeare criticism, the 1808 series having left little record. By 1813 Coleridge was in Bristol and in October began a third series of lectures mostly on Shakespeare, but with two lectures on education added. At the same time another series was begun at Clifton nearby, but was unfinished since attendance was poor. The Bristol lectures were completed so successfully that at the last lecture on 23 November a new course was announced to begin on 8 December. This was to include:[3]

> Two [lectures] on those plays of Shakespeare which were not referred to in the former course and illustrative of the poetic and romantic character of our great dramatist, namely, *The Tempest, Midsummer Night's Dream, Merchant of Venice, As You Like It, Twelfth Night*, etc.; and four on the *Paradise Lost* and the character of Milton as a man and a poet; with an examination of Dr. Johnson's Preface to Shakespeare and his life of Milton.

No record of these lectures survives although they were probably given, as were the first four of a series of six proposed for April 1814.

Also in 1814, in *Felix Farley's Bristol Journal*, Coleridge published his 'Essays on the principles of genial criticism concerning the Fine Arts, more especially those of statuary and painting, deduced from the Laws and Impulses which guide the true artist in the production of his works'. These were intended, as Coleridge wrote in a letter to Stuart, 'to serve poor Allston, who is now exhibiting his pictures at Bristol'[4] but as the title suggests the subject soon moved from the particular, the works of the American painter whom Coleridge had first met in Rome, to general critical principles. A proposal to continue the series for the *Courier* came to nothing but the interest in critical principles emerged again in the preface which Coleridge began writing in 1815 for his proposed collection of poems, *Sibylline Leaves*. The criticism eventually expanded into a work in its own right, *Biographia Literaria*, which appeared in 1817. The 1818 series of lectures given in London, alternated with a series on philosophy, constituted Coleridge's last public appearance. In 1825, however, to fulfil an obligation to the Royal Society of Literature, from whom he received an annuity, Coleridge read an essay 'On the Prometheus of Aeschylus'; this is properly considered a work not of literary criticism but of comparative mythology, but it is interesting that literature was the starting point from which Coleridge wound ever deeper into what he aptly called 'the holy jungle of transcendental metaphysics'.[5]

This brief biographical survey illustrates the way in which Coleridge's critical thinking developed. He began with his own works and the works which he admired, and finished with a highly complex philosophy of art and criticism. His greatest achievements are in works where the interest in a specific work or passage is coloured by the overall philosophical perspective or, to put it another way, where his critical system is not divorced from reference to precise observation of actual works. It is a combination of the two strands that give the *Biographia* and the *Shakespeare Criticism* their importance.

The first impulse toward critical principles came from the process of creating his own poetry. A letter of 1796 to J. Thelwall illustrates how Coleridge's mind darted from his own work to the work of others producing flashes of critical insight indifferently from either:[6]

And now, my dear fellow! for a little sparring about Poetry. My first *Sonnet is obscure*; but you ought to distinguish between obscurity residing in the uncommonness of the thought, and that which proceeds from thoughts unconnected & language not adapted to the expression of them. When you

87

> *do* find out the meaning of my poetry, can you (in general, I mean) alter the language so as to make it more perspicuous - the thought remaining the same?

and:

> I feel strongly, and I think strongly; but I seldom feel without thinking, or think without feeling. Hence tho' my poetry has in general a *hue* of tenderness, or Passion over it, yet it seldom exhibits unmixed & simple tenderness or Passion. My philosophical opinions are blended with, or deduced from, my feelings: & this, I think, peculiarizes my style of Writing. And like every thing else, it is sometimes a beauty, and sometimes a fault. But do not let us introduce an act of Uniformity against Poets - I have room enough in *my* brain to admire, aye & almost equally, the *head* and fancy of Akenside, and the *heart* and fancy of Bowles, the solemn lordliness of Milton, & the divine Chit chat of Cowper: and whatever a man's excellence is, that will be likewise his fault.

In the same year as this letter was written Coleridge had published his *Poems on Various Subjects*. The prefaces to this and to the 1798 edition reveal Coleridge's first critical gropings. The same interest in the why and wherefore which characterises his later work is here, but as yet no critical principle is elucidated. Worried by a possible change of 'querulous egotism' he analyses the process of poetry:[7]

> The communicativeness of our nature leads us to describe our own sorrows; in the endeavour to describe them intellectual activity is exerted; and by a benevolent law of our nature from intellectual activity a pleasure results, which is gradually associated and mingles as a corrective with the painful subject of the description. 'True!' it may be answered, 'but how are the PUBLIC interested in your sorrows or your description?' We are for ever attributing a personal unity to imaginary aggregates. What is the PUBLIC but a term for a number of scattered individuals of whom as many will be interested in these sorrows as have experienced the same or similar?

As an analysis of the poet's point of view this works quite well, but as an account of the value of poetry to its readers it is woefully inadequate. Yet even in this early piece Coleridge is fumbling towards ideas which are to be significant in his future thought. His castigation of popular evasions, for instance:

> With what anxiety every fashionable author avoids the word *I*! – now he transforms himself into a third person, – 'the present writer' – now multiplies himself and swells into '*we*' – and all this is the watchfulness of guilt. Conscious that this said *I* is perpetually intruding on his mind and that it monopolizes his heart, he is prudishly solicitous that it may not escape from his lips.

anticipates his later philosophical awareness of self as the cornerstone of all knowledge, as he says in the *Biographia*:[8]

> The postulate of philosophy and at the same time the test of philosophic capacity, is no other than the heaven-descended KNOW THYSELF! (*E coelo descendit, Γνῶθι σεαυτόν*) . And this at once practically and speculatively. For as philosophy is neither a science of the reason or understanding only, nor merely a science of morals, but the science of BEING altogether, its primary ground can be neither merely speculative or merely practical, but both in one. All knowledge rests on the coincidence of an object with a subject. . . . For we can *know* that only which is true: and the truth is universally placed in the coincidence of the thought with the thing, of the representation with the object represented.

The difference between the two passages in formulation and content is wide, but it is possible to see the early passage as an enquiry into why the self was so ineradicable leading to the later philosophical concept of the importance of self-awareness.

Also in the 1797 edition of the poems Coleridge printed an 'Introduction to the Sonnets'. Among some fairly conventional writing on the form of the sonnet, which illustrates the debt to Bowles, appears this observation:[9]

> those Sonnets appear to me the most exquisite, in which moral Sentiments, Affections, or Feelings, are deduced from, and associated with, the Scenery of Nature. Such compositions generate a kind of thought highly favourable to delicacy of character. They create a sweet and indissoluble union between the intellectual and the material world.

As Coleridge admits in this Introduction, he was never very successful with sonnets but the above is a good description of his conversation poems and illustrates how Coleridge's mind was moving to that form. All the early prefaces show this close interrelation between the poems Coleridge was writing (or perhaps contemplating writing) and his critical thinking and make clear in a way which is not so obvious later that Coleridge's criticism is the work of a practising poet.

While these poetry volumes were appearing Coleridge was contributing anonymously to the *Critical Review*. Scholars disagree[10] as to exactly how many reviews Coleridge wrote, but even if he wrote all those ascribed to him, only a few add anything to our knowledge of his critical development. A review of *On the Prosodies of the Greek and Latin Languages* illustrates Coleridge's early interest in metre and perhaps indicates some of the preliminary thinking which shaped the metre of *Christabel*. More important is the review of Lewis's *The Monk* which appeared in February 1797. This was not the only Gothic novel which Coleridge was sent to review, and again Coleridge's interest is that of a writer as well as a reader. Although the review takes a stern view of the trappings of the Romance form, a letter to Bowles shows the high-spirited, half-mocking, half-serious interest which Coleridge had in this contemporary fashion:[11]

> I am almost weary of the Terrible, having been an hireling in the Critical Review for these last six or eight months – I have been lately reviewing the Monk, the Italian, Hubert de Sevrac & &c & &c – in all of which dungeons, and old castles, & solitary Houses by the Sea Side, & Caverns, & Woods, & extraordinary characters, & all tribe of Horror & Mystery, have crowded on me – even to surfeiting. –

In fact the review begins by castigating the public for its interest in the Gothic form:[12]

> We trust, however, that satiety will banish what good sense should have prevented; and that, wearied with fiends, incomprehensible characters, with shrieks, murders, and subterraneous dungeons, the public will learn, by the multitude of the manufacturers, with how little expense of thought or imagination this species of composition is manufactured.

Despite this Coleridge was very interested in the form, as he was in psychological abnormalities all his life. The description of Luther's throwing of the inkpot at the devil, for instance, was to occupy his attention in *The Friend*.[13] The conclusion to the argument takes us further towards understanding the psychological and philosophical base of Coleridge's mature criticism:[14]

> we feel no great difficulty in yielding a temporary belief to any, the strangest, situations of *things*. But that situation once conceived, how beings like ourselves would feel and act in it, our own feelings sufficiently instruct us;

This reference to his own feelings balances the philosophical reference to German ideas in Coleridge's criticism, making it unmistakably his own, even where there is a heavy dependence on the writings of others. This personal method was not infallible, as Coleridge's somewhat disproportionate admiration of Bowles's sonnets makes clear; but mainly Coleridge's feelings were, as he said in a letter to Thelwall, blended with his 'philosophical opinions'. Moreover, this appeal to common feelings gives Coleridge's criticism a universal reference. Later Coleridge further refined this appeal to the reader's reactions. He concludes the first essay 'On the Principles of Genial Criticism', with two postulates:[15]

> the only ones he deems necessary for his complete intelligibility:
> the first, that the reader would steadily look into his own
> mind to know whether the principles stated are ideally true;
> the second, to look at the works or parts of the works
> mentioned, as illustrating or exemplifying the principle, to
> judge whether or how far it has been realized.

As a test of critical principles this is a valuable formula and it illustrates how Coleridge's mind sought both external and internal verification for his ideas.

In 1800, the short preface to the original edition of the *Lyrical Ballads* was expanded to include the critical statements which make it such an important document in the history of the Romantic movement. In 1802 further expansion continued the public's initiation into a new way of thinking about poetry. Coleridge wrote none of these prefaces but, as Wordsworth was later to reveal, his influence was an important factor. Barron Field's manuscript biography of Wordsworth has a pencil note by Wordsworth himself:[16]

> I will mention that I never cared a straw about the theory & the Preface was written at the request of Mr. Coleridge out of sheer good nature.

This is probably a later exaggeration but Coleridge's contemporary letters show the two poets in close debate. By 1802 Coleridge was beginning to be aware of differences of opinion, for he wrote to William Sotheby:[17]

> I must set you right with regard to my perfect coincidence with his poetic Creed. It is most certain, that the Preface arose from the heads of our mutual Conversations &c - & the first passages were indeed partly taken from notes of mine/ for it was first intended, that the Preface should be written by me - and it is likewise true, that I warmly accord with W. in his abhorrence of these poetic Licences, as they are called, which are indeed mere tricks of Convenience & Laziness. ... In my opinion every phrase, every metaphor, every personification, should have it's justifying cause in some *passion* either of the Poet's mind, or of the Characters described by the poet - But *metre itself* implies a *passion*, i.e. a state of excitement, both in the Poet's mind, & is expected in that of the Reader - and tho' I stated this to Wordsworth, & he has in some sort stated it in his preface, yet he has not done justice to it, nor has he in my opinion sufficiently answered it. In my opinion, Poetry justifies, as *Poetry* independent of any other Passion, some new combinations of Language, & *commands* the omission of many others allowable in other compositions/ Now Wordsworth, me saltem judice, has in his system not sufficiently admitted the former, & in his practice has too frequently sinned against the latter. - Indeed, we have had lately some little controversy on this subject.

Some days later Coleridge wrote to Southey on the same subject:[18]

> I rather suspect that some where or other there is a radical Difference in our theoretical opinions respecting Poetry -/ this I shall endeavour to go to the Bottom of - and acting the arbitrator between the old School & the New School hope to

lay down some plain, & perspicuous, tho' not superficial,
Canons of Criticism respecting Poetry.

This clearly looks forward to the *Biographia*, which, significantly,
was written only after the quarrel in 1810 gave Coleridge a better
perspective on his friend's work. The *Lyrical Ballads* Preface was
undoubtedly the product of conversations between the two poets,
and from what we know of their habits of mind it seems probable
that the more philosophical element especially reflects Coleridge's
influence. However, the Preface was actually written by Wordsworth, and not until 1817 did Coleridge make public his view of
those early conversations.

The *Biographia* itself is in many ways a summary of Coleridge's
critical thinking up to that point in his life. One of the reasons why
Coleridge's criticism is so difficult to analyse is that his thinking was
organic, and in a constant state of growth, so that his critical prose
is merely a series of interim reports. Coleridge's lectures, too,
represent a selection from a continuous process of thought, for as he
said in a letter:[19]

> I would not lecture on any subject for which I had to *acquire*
> the main Knowledge, even though a month's or three months'
> previous time were allowed me; on no subject that had not
> employed my thoughts for a large portion of my life since
> earliest manhood, free of all outward and particular purpose

The impulse to publish an interim report was usually financial and
strengthened by support from outside. The *Biographia* was begun at
one of the lowest points in Coleridge's life, and the fact that he was
able to write it and prepare the volume of poems for which it was
originally intended as a preface is testimony to the understanding
and care of John Morgan. Coleridge, as he himself was well aware,
did not take kindly to pressure from without, but all too often he
needed a helping hand to enable him to produce his thoughts in
written form. The *Biographia* was dictated to Morgan, just as in an
earlier and equally unhappy period *The Friend* was dictated to Sara
Hutchinson. Although critical opinion now recognises an organised
unity in the *Biographia*,[20] the work still appears as a rather dis-
jointed whole at a first reading. This is partly because Coleridge had
to add material (Satyrane's letters; an edited version of his letters
from Germany in 1798-9, first published in *The Friend*; and a

critique of Maturin's *Bertram*[21] to fill out the second volume which the publisher decided, rather late, would be needed to accommodate what Coleridge had already written. Even if these additions are discounted, however, the work may appear to offer only a variety of topics unrelated to a central theme. For instance, most of Chapter Three is a defence of Southey from the castigations of the reviewers, Chapter Ten closes with a set of anecdotes from Coleridge's early life, Chapter Six is titled 'That Hartley's system, as far as it differs from that of Aristotle, is neither tenable in theory, nor founded in facts' and most of the second volume comprises a detailed criticism of Wordsworth's poetic theory and practice. However, despite appearances there are themes which unify the book.

Coleridge, clearly aware of the somewhat disparate nature of the contents of his book, suggested one thread for readers to follow:[22]

> I have used the narration chiefly for the purpose of giving a
> continuity to the work, in part for the sake of the
> miscellaneous reflections suggested to me by particular events,
> but still more as introductory to the statement of my
> principles in Politics, Religion, and Philosophy, and an
> application of the rules, deduced from philosophical principles,
> to poetry and criticism.

Not quite as much of the *Biographia* as this suggests is taken up with politics, religion and philosophy, but Coleridge's criticism is inextricably linked with his philosophical thinking, and it is not possible to understand fully any of Coleridge's most important critical theories without a knowledge of their philosophical base. Fortunately, it is not necessary for the purposes of criticism to understand the nature of Coleridge's contribution to philosophy as such, and those who are interested primarily in criticism can, I think, content themselves with seeing Coleridge's philosophy as Coleridge himself saw it. Similarly, for the purposes of understanding Coleridge's contribution to English literary criticism it is not necessary to understand in detail just how much and exactly what Coleridge borrowed from his German predecessors in the study of philosophical criticism. This is a vexed problem, but Coleridge's own remarks, if interpreted carefully, can help: referring to Fichte, he says:[23]

> In this instance, as in the dramatic lectures of Schlegel to
> which I have before alluded, from the same motive of

self-defence against the charge of plagiarism, many of the most
striking resemblances, indeed all the main and fundamental
ideas, were born and matured in my mind before I had ever
seen a single page of the German Philosopher; and I might
indeed affirm with truth, before the more important works of
Schelling had been written, or at least made public. Nor is this
coincidence at all to be wondered at. We had studied in the
same school; had been disciplined by the same preparatory
philosophy, namely, the writings of Kant; we had both equal
obligations to the polar logic and dynamic philosophy of
Giordano Bruno; and Schelling has lately, and, as of recent
acquisition, avowed that same affectionate reverence for the
labours of Behmen, and other mystics, which I had formed at
a much earlier period. ... To me it will be happiness and
honor enough, should I succeed in rendering the system itself
intelligible to my countrymen, and in the application of it to
the most awful of subjects for the most important of purposes.

Here, Coleridge is acknowledging that his ideas owe a debt to his
reading, but he is also saying that he has read critically. The
notebooks help us to understand the way in which his mind
worked. Certain questions interested Coleridge all his life and he
made use of whatever he saw or read to help him understand these
questions, but in the process the quality of his own thinking
transformed what he used. For instance, notes 4111-15 and 4265 in
Volume 2 of the *Notebooks* give source material which reappears
almost unchanged in the Lectures and in the *Biographia*, but on the
same subject and as early as 1801 antedating any known reading of
Schelling and, interestingly, prompted by a quotation from
Wordsworth - there is:[24]

> - and the deep power of Joy
> We see into the *Life* of Things -

i.e. - By deep feeling we make our *Ideas dim* - & this is what
we mean by our Life-ourselves. I think of the Wall - it is
before me, a distinct Image - here. I necessarily think of the
*Idea* & the Thinking I as two different & opposite Things.
Now <let me> think of *myself* - of the thinking Being - the
Idea becomes dim whatever it be - so dim that I know not
what it is - but the Feeling is deep & steady - and this I call *I*
- identifying the Percipient & the Perceived -

Coleridge makes it clear that a major impulse behind the *Biographia* is the author's reading by his subtitle 'Biographical Sketches of my Literary Life and Opinions'. Accordingly, the book opens with an account of the early influence of school on his attitude to poetic language; this follows his announced intention 'to effect, as far as possible, a settlement of the long continued controversy concerning the true nature of poetic diction'.[25] The issue is clearly related to the *Lyrical Ballads* preface, and much of what Coleridge has to say, especially in the second volume, is in response to Wordsworth's preference for 'the real language of men'. Coleridge takes this statement to pieces and exposes all its logical and actual weaknesses:[26]

> a rustic's language, purified from all provincialism and
> grossness, and so far reconstructed as to be made consistent
> with the rules of grammar (which are in essence no other than
> the laws of universal logic, applied to psychological materials)
> will not differ from the language of any other man of
> common-sense, however learned or refined he may be, except
> as far as the notions, which the rustic has to convey, are fewer
> and more indiscriminate.

But this is not the best of Coleridge's ideas on the subject, largely because he is so heavy-handed in his dissection of Wordsworth. Where Coleridge gives his own ideas, unrelated to the controversy, he makes a more positive contribution to the development of poetic technique. The important factor is 'the truth of passion'; this, says Coleridge, was Wordsworth's valuable contribution and it is expanded by Coleridge. As the letter to Thelwall quoted at the beginning of this chapter makes clear, the passion in poetry had long been an important concept, and this Coleridge now says should be the criterion for poetic language:[27]

> Our genuine admiration of a great poet is a continuous
> *under-current* of feeling; it is everywhere present, but seldom
> anywhere as a separate excitement. I was wont boldly to
> affirm, that it would be scarcely more difficult to push a stone
> out from the pyramids with the bare hand, than to alter a
> word, or the position of a word, in Milton or Shakespeare, (in
> their most important works at least,) without making the
> author say something else, or something worse, than he does
> say. . . .

The same 'under-current of feeling' underlies Coleridge's attitude to metre:[28]

> This I would trace to the balance in the mind effected by that spontaneous effort which strives to hold in check the workings of passion.

This in turn should have its effect on the choice of language:[29]

> First, that, as the *elements* of metre owe their existence to a state of increased excitement, so the metre itself should be accompanied by the natural language of excitement. Secondly, that as these elements are formed into metre *artificially*, by a *voluntary* act, with the design and for the purpose of blending *delight* with emotion, so the traces of present *volition* should throughout the metrical language be proportionately discernible. Now these two conditions must be reconciled and co-present. There must be not only a partnership, but a union; an interpenetration of passion and of will, of *spontaneous* impulse and *voluntary* purpose.

In the *Biographia* the discussion of the fusion of language and metre in accordance with the fused powers of feeling and control is clouded over by the argument with Wordsworth and a reader may well feel that the discussion has an element of personal exasperation when he reads Coleridge's:[30]

> I write in metre, because I am about to use a language different from that of prose.

Elsewhere Coleridge sums up his ideas just as succinctly and with more conviction:[31]

> The sole difference, *in style*, is that poetry demands a *severer keeping* – it admits nothing that Prose may not often admit; but it *oftener* rejects. In other words, it pre-supposes a more continuous state of Passion.

Another notebook entry enables us to see this principle at work:[32]

> It appears to me little less than a general rule, that wherever a phrase confessedly trivial & colloquial is introduced in poetry, it ought not to be disguised by position – but placed as it would be *in prose* – otherwise it makes poetry absolutely

97

ludicrous – and the reason is this: that the original ground of
the metathesis of words is *a passion* suggesting one idea before
others. ... it is that very passion which brought to the mind
the trivial instead of a thought-created sentence – Thus
Othello – Not a Jot! Not a Jot! – Where if he had said – No!
not a jot even! – this for a hint to myself – the remark is
Wise; but I have not happily exprest it. And I must not forget
in speaking of the certain Hub-bub, I am to undergo for
hypercriticism, to point out how little instructive any criticism
can be which does not enter into minutiae – & to contrast it
with the common reviews – take for instance any half dozen
from the Edinburgh –

This shows a concern for the practice of criticism which, as the
twenty-first chapter of the *Biographia* shows, is the basis for his
contempt of the reviews of the day, notably the *Edinburgh* and the
*Quarterly*. It is a recurring theme first announced in the third
chapter:[33]

till in the place of arbitrary dictation and petulant sneers, the
reviewers support their decisions by reference to fixed canons
of criticism, previously established and deduced from the
nature of man; reflecting minds will pronounce it arrogance in
them thus to announce themselves to men of letters, as guides
to their taste and judgement.

The *Biographia* makes and justifies a claim to be criticism founded
on such principles. It is to these that Coleridge refers in his criticism
of the poetry of Wordsworth, and significantly, the chapter on
reviews precedes Coleridge's analysis of Wordsworth's characteristic
defects and excellencies, as though Coleridge wished to dissociate his
criticism from that of the reviewers of the day who also listed 'faults
and beauties'.

The defects listed and illustrated by Coleridge relate almost
exclusively to the poems of rustic life. He speaks of incongruity of
language, matter-of-factness, a disproportion between knowledge
and intensity of feeling, resulting in 'an eddying, instead of
progression, of thought', 'mental bombast' where 'thoughts and
images are too great for the subject' and misuse of the dramatic
form:[34]

Either the thoughts and diction are different from that of the poet, and then there arises an incongruity of style; or they are the same and indistinguishable, and then it presents a species of ventriloquism, where two are represented as talking, while in truth one man only speaks.

This relates to Coleridge's hopes for Wordsworth, that he would finish the *Recluse*, of which we have only 'The Prelude' and 'The Excursion':[35]

What Mr. Wordsworth *will* produce it is not for me to prophecy: but I could pronounce with the liveliest conviction what he is capable of producing. It is the FIRST GENUINE PHILOSOPHICAL POEM.

And I think the list of defects illustrates Coleridge's feeling that in pursuing poetry of rustic characters Wordsworth was denying his true ability in a philosophic vein. S. M. Parrish in an article entitled 'The Wordsworth-Coleridge Controversy'[36] stresses this charge of ventriloquism, claiming that this and not the nature of poetic diction is central to the debate. This is true, I think, to the extent that the charge reveals where Coleridge thought Wordsworth's true ability lay, as he said later:[37]

I think Wordsworth possessed more of the genius of a great philosophic poet than any man I ever knew, or, as I believe has existed in England since Milton; but it seems to me that he ought never to have abandoned the contemplative position, which is peculiarly - perhaps I might say exclusively - fitted for him. His proper title is *Spectator ab Extra*.

Coleridge's high claims for Wordsworth are related to his high claims for the poet. In bitterness he had declared himself 'no poet' as early as 1802 but he still saw the poet as an ideal embodiment of 'unity in multeity'. The description of the poet represents Coleridge's prose at its best:[38]

The poet, described in *ideal* perfection, brings the whole soul of man into activity, with the subordination of its faculties to each other, according to their relative worth and dignity. He diffuses a tone and spirit of unity, that blends, and (as it were) *fuses*, each into each, by that synthetic and magical power, to which we have exclusively appropriated the name of imagination. This power, first put in action by the will and understanding, and retained under their irremissive, though gentle and unnoticed, controul (*laxis effertur habenis*) reveals itself in the balance or reconciliation of opposite or discordant qualities: of sameness, with difference; of the general, with the concrete; the idea, with the image; the individual, with the representative; the sense of novelty and freshness, with old and familiar objects; a more than usual state of emotion, with more than usual order; judgement ever awake and steady self-possession, with enthusiasm and feeling profound or vehement; and while it blends and harmonizes the natural and the artificial, still subordinates art to nature; the manner to the matter; and our admiration of the poet to our sympathy with the poetry.

This brings us to Coleridge's analysis of imagination, the importance of which is an undercurrent in the book. It is a key factor in his praise of Wordsworth:[39]

I challenge for this poet the gift of IMAGINATION in the highest and strictest sense of the word. In the play of *Fancy*, Wordsworth, to my feelings, is not always graceful, and sometimes *recondite*. ... But in imaginative power, he stands nearest of all modern writers to Shakespeare and Milton; yet in a kind perfectly unborrowed and his own.

It is appropriate that Coleridge makes use of the desynonymized terms, imagination and fancy, in discussing Wordsworth because, as he says:[40]

This excellence, which in all Mr. Wordsworth's writings is more or less predominant, and which constitutes the character of his mind, I no sooner felt, than I sought to understand. Repeated meditations led me to suspect, (and a more intimate analysis of the human faculties, their appropriate marks, functions, and effects matured my conjecture into full conviction,) that fancy and imagination were two distinct and widely different faculties, instead of being, according to the general belief, either two names with one meaning, or, at furthest, the lower and higher degree of one and the same power.

The desynonymizing process involved a long enquiry into the theory of Association which culminated in an abrupt dead-end, Coleridge interrupting himself with a letter supposedly from a friend and deciding that the enquiry was becoming disproportionate to the whole. The philosophical content of these chapters (5-13) will be discussed later. The enquiry starts with a more or less historically structured account of the Laws of Association, beginning with Aristotle, including Hobbes, Hartley, Descartes, Spinoza, and Leibnitz and showing how knowledge of the human powers of knowing was modified by these writers. Bruno, Behmen, Kant and Schelling appear in Chapter Nine to present a more sympathetic approach to the problem of the human mind. Then Coleridge, feeling for his readers' struggles in a work which was supposed to be 'Biographical Sketches' gives a 'Chapter of digressions and anecdotes'. Chapter Eleven, very short, contains 'an affectionate exhortation to those who in early life feel themselves disposed to become authors' – an exhortation based no doubt on Coleridge's present difficulties in subduing his hard-thought philosophy into a saleable form and on his recollections of youthful attempts to earn a living from writing. The twelfth chapter opens with a precept which should always be borne in mind by readers of Coleridge: 'until you understand a writer's ignorance, presume yourself ignorant of his understanding',[41] and concludes with the ten theses derived from Schelling. This cleared the way for Coleridge's treatment of imagination in Chapter Thirteen. He was working towards this by means of analysing the Kantian 'tertium aliquid', which is 'no other than an inter-penetration of the counteracting powers partaking of both',[42] when the letter (written, of course, by Coleridge himself) interrupts, protesting:[43]

> every reader, who, like myself, is neither prepared nor perhaps calculated for the study of so abstruse a subject so abstrusely treated, will, as I have before hinted, be almost entitled to accuse you of a sort of imposition on him. For who, he might truly observe, could from your title-page, viz. *'My Literary Life and Opinions'* published too as introductory to a volume of miscellaneous poems, have anticipated, or even conjectured, a long treatise on ideal Realism which holds the same relation in abstruseness to Plotinus, as Plotinus does to Plato.

The first volume of the *Biographia* then concludes with the definitions of imagination and fancy which have vexed critics ever since. There are those who think that Coleridge gives a distinction without a difference, and among the rest, interpretations of what the various terms mean in practice vary considerably. Certainly, the distinction has less value if it is not considered critically in relation to a philosophical system. Fancy presents few problems, 'a mode of Memory emancipated from the order of time and space';[44] it is that faculty which enables a poet to ornament his thought with images from differing aspects of life. Coleridge's example from Otway is unfortunate as it is inaccurately quoted ('lobsters' should be 'laurels'):

> Lutes, lobsters, seas of milk and ships of amber[45]

but others can be found, as, for instance, those given by I. A. Richards from Dryden.[46] Coleridge himself provides many fine examples, as these from the 'Ancient Mariner':[47]

> And ice, mast-high, came floating by,
> As green as emerald.

and:

> Her beams bemocked the sultry main,
> Like April hoar-frost spread;

The analysis of imagination causes more serious problems because of its division into primary and secondary. Of the latter he says:[48]

> It dissolves, diffuses, dissipates, in order to recreate; or where this process is rendered impossible, yet still at all events it struggles to idealize and to unify. It is essentially *vital*, even as all objects (*as* objects) are essentially fixed and dead

This is related to the description of the ideal poet and, provided we accept Coleridge's ideal unity as a valid concept, presents few difficulties. Problems arise because it is described as 'an echo' of:

> The primary IMAGINATION ... the living Power and prime Agent of all human Perception, and as a repetition in the finite mind of the eternal act of creation in the infinite I AM.

Although there are many interpretations of this, there are broadly two schools. The first, following Shawcross in his notes to his edition of the *Biographia*, consider it:[49]

the organ of common perception, the faculty by which we
have experience of an actual world of phenomena

Recently this has been considered inadequate. J. R. de J. Jackson in
*Method and Imagination in Coleridge's Criticism* gives an exposition of
the place of imagination in Coleridge's philosophical scheme of
human perception. For him primary imagination is akin to reason,
which, as Coleridge's philosophical studies make clear, held a special
place as intermediary between the consciousness of God and the
consciousness of man; this interpretation, I think, fits more closely
the idea that the secondary imagination is an echo: in Shawcross's
explanation it is, rather, a refinement. This gives the theory of
imagination a context in his thinking which Coleridge's treatment
leads us to expect. The distinction between imagination, a reflection
of the creative power of the Creator, and fancy, a literary device,
becomes clear. For Coleridge at least, the newly defined imagination
provided a useful critical tool:[50]

the sense of musical delight, with the power of producing it, is
a gift of the imagination

This refers to the ability to create harmony and a sense of unity
through rhythm and sound, an ability not only related to ordinary
perception but also, especially if we take into account Coleridge's
interest in Platonism, a known way of reflecting the divine creation
which Coleridge may well have had in mind during his discussion
of imagination, as his quotation from Sir John Davies's *Orchestra* at
the close of Chapter Fourteen shows.

The comment on musical delight comes in Coleridge's criticism
of *Venus and Adonis* and *The Rape of Lucrece;* more even than as a
critic of Wordsworth, Coleridge survives as a critic of Shakespeare.
This is because his thinking about the imagination enabled
Coleridge to display to subsequent readers and audiences the unity
of Shakespeare's creation. In Coleridge's day, when plays were
cut and rewritten for performance, criticism concentrated on
'beauties' while regretting that from want of judgement much of
Shakespeare's work was sadly blemished. Coleridge's criticism of
Shakespeare, however, is not a systematic exposition, like that of
Wordsworth in the *Biographia*, a series of separate utterances
surviving from lectures.

When, in 1806, after his return from Malta, Coleridge first
considered lecturing, Dorothy Wordsworth expressed her doubts:[51]

I fear his health would suffer from late hours and being led too much into company; and in the second place, I would fain see him address the whole powers of his soul to some great work in prose or verse, of which the effect would be permament, and not personal and transitory. I do not mean to say that much permanent good may not be produced by communicating knowledge by means of lectures, but a man is perpetually tempted to lower himself to his hearers to bring them into sympathy with him, and no one would be more likely to yield to such temptation than Coleridge;

Contrary to Dorothy Wordsworth's expectations, and although only a part of the lectures have survived, posterity has derived much permanent good from these lectures, and this partly because Coleridge has been able, with the stimulus of an actual audience, to make his ideas more accessible. The lectures were, however, very uneven in performance. Sometimes Coleridge was too ill to attend and lectures were postponed, sometimes the delivery was perfunctory and the matter heavy, but sometimes the audience was witness to a triumph of critical virtuosity. As J. P. Collier said in his explanation of the defects of his transcription of the lectures of 1811–12:[52]

I was not unfrequently so engrossed, and absorbed by the almost inspired look and manner of the speaker, that I was, for a time, incapable of performing the mechanical duty of writing.

Even so, H. C. Robinson felt that Coleridge's deficiency as a lecturer lay in his inability to meet his hearers' expectations. He wrote to his brother in December 1811:[53]

In a word, then, Coleridge's lectures do high honour to him as a man of genius, but are discreditable to him (perhaps I might use without injustice a stronger word) as a man who has a duty to discharge; . . . His pretended lectures are immethodical rhapsodies, moral, metaphysical, and literary, abounding in brilliant thoughts, fine flashes of rhetoric, ingenious paradoxes, occasionally profound and salutary truths, but they are not a scientific or instructive course of readings on any one subject a man can wish to fix his attention on. He is to lecture on Shakespeare, Milton, and the modern poets.

We have in fact had one lecture on the minor poems of
Shakespeare and have been *three nights* alone employed on
*Romeo and Juliet*, which we are promised the conclusion of.
The course is to consist of fifteen lectures, and eight are
over ! ! !

On the other hand, Kathleen Coburn suggests in a note to a
*Notebook* entry relating to the 1818 lectures that there is:[54]

an indication that much fun is missing from the reports of his
lectures. Perhaps the more amusing, the less reported from the
distractions of enjoyment and laughter and possibly from the
reporter's view that such levity did not merit serious
treatment.

Certainly, we cannot hope to recapture the experience of listening
to Coleridge lecture. In some ways this relieves us of the
exasperations shown by H. C. Robinson at the Milton lecture of
1808 when: 'the word poetry was not used till the lecture was
two-thirds over, nor Milton's name till ten minutes before the
close.'[55] On the other hand it means that transcripts by other
hands than Coleridge's are only a reflection of the original
experience.

T. M. Raysor's introduction to the first volume of his edition of
the *Shakespeare Criticism* illustrates clearly the background from
which it arose. Some critics concentrate more on those aspects in
which Coleridge was anticipated by others, but it is still true to say
that with Coleridge, English criticism began to base its reading of
Shakespeare on a respect for his craftmanship and thought.
Coleridge himself took the view that this was his central purpose.
In a fragment which probably relates to the 1818 series of lectures
he wrote:[56]

In all the successive courses delivered by me since my first
attempt at the Royal Institution, it has been and it still
remains my object to prove that in all points from the most
important to the most minute, the judgement of Shakespeare is
commensurate with his genius – nay, that his genius reveals
itself in his judgement, as in its most exalted form.

Having said this, the problem of Coleridge's debt to his German
predecessors again becomes prominent. Often Coleridge used ideas

formulated by Schlegel to make his points succinctly. When we come across:[57]

> No work of true genius dare want its appropriate form;
> neither indeed is there any danger of this. As it must not, so
> neither can it, be lawless! For it is even this that constitutes it
> genius – the power of acting creatively under laws of its own
> origination.

our immediate reaction is how Coleridgean an achievement this terse summary is, how neatly it brings into critical focus the philosophical enquiries into imagination and poetic genius. However, our exclamations are silenced by T. M. Raysor's footnote: 'These three sentences are a paraphrase of a similar passage in Schlegel (*Werke* vi. 157)'.

The combination of the two – the immediate reaction and the scholarly footnote – creates a sense of disappointment which is, I think, critically dangerous. It is, after all, possible that Coleridge paraphrased the sentences because the idea was in tune with his own thinking. Such was the view of Coleridge's daughter, Sara,[58] and of Kathleen Coburn in her edition of the notebooks, and this is the view I shall adopt here. It is important to recognize that many of Coleridge's phrases and critical ideas are directly traceable to Schlegel, Schelling and Kant but it is equally important to remember that Coleridge fully understood and agreed with these expressions because they were in keeping with his own investigations. Indeed, as R. H. Fogle suggests, in relation to Coleridge's ideas about dramatic illusion, the very 'multiplicity of his possible sources is so great as to neutralize the effect of any one in particular'.[59]

The recognition of the supreme skill of Shakespeare is closely related to the study of poetic language and the definition of imagination:[60]

> Shakespeare knew the human mind, and its most minute and
> intimate workings, and he never introduces a word, or a
> thought, in vain or out of place: if we do not understand him,
> it is our own fault or the fault of copyists and typographers;
> but study, and the possession of some small stock of the
> knowledge by which he worked, will enable us often to detect
> and explain his meaning. He never wrote at random, or hit

upon points of character and conduct by chance; and the smallest fragment of his mind not unfrequently gives a clue to a most perfect, regular, and consistent whole.

This in turn brought forward other problems.

One of these was the question of dramatic illusion. In notes on *The Tempest* the subject is discussed fully:[61]

> the drama is an *imitation* of reality, not a *copy* – and that imitation is contradistinguished from copy by this: that a certain quantum of difference is essential to the former, and an indispensable condition and cause of the pleasure we derive from it; while in a copy it is a defect, contravening its name and purpose.

The dramatist's task is to create an illusion and the way in which this is done is explained by analogy with dreaming:

> in sleep we pass at once by a sudden collapse into this suspension of will and comparative power: whereas in an interesting play, read or represented, we are brought up to this point, as far as it is requisite or desirable, gradually, by the art of the poet and the actors; and with the consent and positive aidance of our own will. We *choose* to be deceived.

Coleridge goes on to give instances of the dramatist's skill in maintaining this 'willing suspension of the disbelief':

> many obvious improbabilities will be endured as belonging to the groundwork of the story rather than to the drama, in the first scenes, which would disturb or disentrance us from all illusion in the acme of our excitement, as, for instance, Lear's division of his realm and banishment of Cordelia. But besides this dramatic probability, all the other excellencies of the drama, as unity of interest, with distinctness and subordination of the characters, appropriateness of style, nay, and the charm of language and sentiment for their own sakes, yet still as far as they tend to increase the inward excitement, are all means to this chief end, that of producing and supporting this willing illusion.

Here Coleridge replaces the classical unities of place, time and action with a new unity of interest. However, and no doubt influenced by his own activity in the theatre, Coleridge recognises the importance of particular effects and sees a tension between the two factors, local excellence and the whole illusion. He adds to the above paragraph:

> tho' the excellencies above mentioned are means to this end, they do not therefore cease to be themselves *ends,* and as such carry their own justification with them as long as they do not contravene or interrupt the illusion. It is not even always or of necessity an objection to them, that they prevent it from rising to as great a height as it might otherwise have attained; it is enough, if they are compatible with as high a degree as is requisite.

It is frequently objected that Coleridge's criticism has little to do with the theatre, which plays a relatively small part in his elucidation of the plays. This is because he was trying to recreate a Shakespeare whose essential characteristics he felt were mangled in contemporary performances. As the report of his lecture in Bristol in 1813 says:[62]

> he never saw any of Shakespeare's plays performed, but with a degree of pain, disgust, and indignation. He had seen Mrs. Siddons as Lady, and Kemble as Macbeth:- these might be the Macbeths of the Kembles, but they were not the Macbeths of Shakespeare. He was not therefore grieved at the enormous size and monopoly of the theatres, which naturally produced many bad and but few good actors; and which drove Shakespeare from the stage, to find his proper place in the heart and in the closet, where he sits with Milton, enthroned on a double-headed Parnassus;

Subsequent readers have inferred from this that Coleridge thought that Shakespeare should be read independently of any feeling for the theatre, but a glance at the earlier London lectures of 1811-12 shows that the root of the objection was the manner of contemporary theatrical presentation. Coleridge was well aware that Shakespeare was writing for the particular dramatic conditions of his day, when 'the circumstance of acting were altogether different from ours' and he goes on:[63]

> It was natural that Shakespeare should avail himself of all that imagination afforded. If he had lived in the present day and

had seen one of his plays represented, he would the first moment have felt the shifting of scenes. Now, there is so much to please the senses in the performance and so much to offend them in the play, that he would have constructed them no doubt on a different model .... All may be delighted that Shakespeare did not anticipate, and write his plays with any conception of that strong excitement of the senses, that inward endeavour to make everything appear reality which is deemed excellent as to the effort of the present day.

Certainly Coleridge felt that it was possible to transfer his ideas into practical acting, as a letter to Charles Mathews, the comedian, makes clear. After criticising in detail Mathews's performance in two popular plays, Colman's *Who Wants a Guinea?* and Macklin's *Love a la Mode*, which he had seen at the Bristol theatre, Coleridge turns his attention to general criticism:[64]

I once had the presumption to address this advice to an Actor on the London Stage. '*Think*, in order that you may be able to *observe*! *Observe*, in order that you may have materials to *think* upon! - And 3rdly, keep awake ever the habit of instantly *embodying* & *realizing* the results of the two: but always *think*.'

A great Actor, comic or tragic, is not to be a mere *Copy*, a *fac simile*, but an *imitation*, of Nature. A good actor is Pygmalion's Statue, a work of exquisite *art*, *animated* & gifted with *motion*; but still *art*, still a species of *Poetry*.

Not the least advantage, which an Actor gains by having secured a high reputation, is this: that those who sincerely admire him, may dare tell him the Truth at times, & thus, if we have sensible friends, secure his progressive Improvement: in other words, *keep him thinking*. For without *thinking* nothing *consummate* can be effected -

That this advice was taken in good part may be inferred from the friendship which Coleridge afterwards built up with Mathews's family. Another instance in which Coleridge's criticism was not felt to be irrelevant to the stage is that of the great actor-manager Macready, who heard Coleridge lecture.[65]

This analysis of the general principles of Shakespeare criticism is illuminated by close and careful readings of some of the plays themselves. For instance, although he speaks highly of *Romeo and Juliet*, he admits that:[66]

the poet is not ... entirely blended with the dramatist – at least, not in the degree to be afterwards noticed in 'Lear', 'Hamlet', 'Othello', or 'Macbeth'. Capulet and Montague not unfrequently talk a language only belonging to the poet, and not so characteristic of, and peculiar to, the passions of persons in the situations in which they are placed –

Coleridge's criticism of *Hamlet* is famous not so much on its own account but because of Coleridge's observation, 'I have a smack of Hamlet myself, if I may say so',[67] but despite a similarity between Coleridge's view of Hamlet and his view of his own personality, the characterisation of Hamlet still embodies Coleridge's critical principles. Shakespeare:[68]

intended to pourtray a person, in whose view the external world, and all its incidents and objects, were comparatively dim, and of no interest in themselves, and which began to interest only, when they were reflected in the mirror of his mind.

but this is balanced by the initial external fact of the ghost:

Hamlet's own disordered fancy has not conjured up the spirit of his father; it has been seen by others: he is prepared by them to witness its re-appearance, and when he does see it, Hamlet is not brought forward as having long brooded on the subject. The moment before the Ghost enters, Hamlet speaks of other matters: ... the preternatural appearance has all the effect of abruptness, and the reader is totally divested of the notion, that the figure is a vision of a highly wrought imagination. Here Shakespeare adapts himself so admirably to the situation – in other words, so puts himself into it – that, though poetry, his language is the very language of nature. No terms, associated with such feelings, can occur to us so proper as those which he has employed, especially on the highest, the most august, and the most awful subjects that can interest a human being in this sentient world.

*Miscellaneous Criticism*, edited by T. M. Raysor, contains what remains of the 1818 lectures on subjects other than Shakespeare and Volume 3 of the *Collected Notebooks* supplements these fragments with preparatory notes. The prospectus for the course indicates a wide range of topics, including troubadour poetry and Cervantes as well as Shakespeare's contemporaries, and the notes that survive suggest that Coleridge allowed himself full rein in covering these subjects. In addition to the lectures, *Miscellaneous Criticism* also gives an insight into what might almost be thought of as a Coleridgean form, marginalia. Raysor goes so far as to say:[69]

> The fragment was the literary *genre* which was natural to Coleridge, and only in the fragments of marginalia was he entirely himself. He could carry over the results and use them in his oral lectures only in part.

This seems to underestimate Coleridge's desire to make his thought move, however erratically, towards a whole but Charles Lamb had it right when he wrote:[70]

> Reader ... lend thy books; but let it be to such a one as S.T.C. – he will return them (generally anticipating the time appointed) with usury; enriched with annotations, tripling their value. I have had experience. Many are these precious MSS. of his – (in *matter* oftentimes, and almost in *quantity* not unfrequently, vying with the originals) – in no very clerkly hand – legible in my Daniel; ... I counsel thee, shut not thy heart, nor thy library, against S.T.C.

In marginal comments, more clearly because more unselfconsciously, Coleridge reveals the principles on which he expounded in public utterances. For instance, his interest in metre and poetic language shows in his notes on Lamb's edition of Samuel Daniel's poetical works:[71]

> the accents and scansion of Daniel's Lines more assist the reading of the sense, than in any work, I know. If the Line runs ill to you, you may be sure, you have not read it in it's exact sense. The whole represents a grave easy man talking seriously to his friends. Sometimes too he breaks up, for a moment, the feeling of versification; but never by a *contradiction to* it, but by heightening the feeling of conversation ex.gr. by putting 3 important words in the most important Line of an aphorism; as if at each of the 3 words the Speaker gave a wise nod aided by the motion of a forefinger, 'To *greatness,* who *Love* and *opinion* hath.'

And again, on his copy of Donne's poems:

> To read Dryden, Pope, &c., you need only count syllables; but to read Donne you must measure *time*, and discover the time of each word by the sense of passion.

and:[72]

> In poems where the writer *thinks*, and expects the reader to do so, the sense must be understood in order to ascertain the metre.

The fourteenth in the 1818 series on style was Coleridge's last public statement on this subject:[73]

> Style is, of course, nothing else but the art of conveying the meaning appropriately and with perspicuity, whatever the meaning may be, and one criterion of style is that it shall not be translateable without injury to the meaning. Johnson's style has pleased many from the very fault of being perpetually translateable; he creates an impression of cleverness by never saying any thing in a common way.

It is a remark of which Coleridge's early teacher would have approved[74] and it illustrates how the same principles underly Coleridge's literary criticism when they apply to purely literary matters, no matter how his philosophical thinking, so closely related, evolved.

It is not possible in a short chapter to give a representative sample of Coleridge's insights into the poetry of others, and I have concentrated instead on Coleridge's critical principles because these, I believe, have conditioned the way in which poetry is read now, and the way in which Shakespeare is performed and understood. These principles underly the occasional insights and give them their vitality. Even the famous quip about Kean, 'to see him act is like reading Shakespeare by flashes of lightning',[75] is made more interesting when it is set against Coleridge's philosophical sense of the unity of the plays.

Many of Coleridge's more abstruse insights have been abandoned, or at least questioned; there is no agreement about the value of the distinction between imagination and fancy, no universal acceptance of his interpretation of *Hamlet*, but these two discussions have added immeasurably to our comprehension of the way in which poetry is produced, not least because they are the product of a great poet.

Moreover, Coleridge has made a great contribution to the practice of criticism by his method. Allied as his statements are to a world view of all-embracing seriousness, yet they are none the less closely related to the texts under study. Some aspects of the results of the Coleridgean method of criticism I hope have been illustrated in this chapter; more will be clear to anyone who reads the criticism itself. What will not perhaps be so apparent, but which is no less important, is that the way in which he reads will be subtly, and possibly at several removes, influenced by the way in which Coleridge read.

# 5

# Political Journalism

In 1789, when the Bastille was stormed, Coleridge at seventeen was still a schoolboy; when Napoleon was finally dispatched to St Helena, Coleridge was forty-three and writing his *Literary Life*. In those twenty-six years Europe had seen one of its foremost countries, racked by violent changes in government, turn the full weight of its violence outwards involving most of the known world in bitter fighting. Against the background of the dual phenomenon of the French Revolution and the Napoleonic Wars, Coleridge wrote on contemporary events. Although attempts to land troops in England were largely unsuccessful so that there was never fighting in the country, the war and its consequences touched closely on almost every aspect of life, not only for its duration but also for the decade following.

One of the longest lasting effects of the Revolution in England was upon attitudes in the government towards freedom of expression and civil rights. Electoral reform, a seriously considered prospect in 1789, did not come until 1832 – not only because the nation had other preoccupations but because in the minds of the Establishment reform had come to seem akin to revolution. Attitudes to reform predictably changed in the intervening years. Coleridge as a young man declared in his prospectus to the *Watchman*[1] that one of its aims was a wider suffrage and in a public lecture said bravely:[2]

> The right of election therefore, as it at present exists in
> England, must be considered not as an exception to Despotism,
> but as making it more operose and expensive from the
> increased necessity of corruption. The people at large exercise
> no sovereignty either personally, or by representation.

114

But when, in 1831, a measure of reform was introduced Coleridge was bitterly opposed to it, as H. N. Coleridge recorded in *Table Talk:*[3]

> The miserable tendency of all is to destroy our nationality, which consists, in a principal degree, in our representative government, and to convert it into a degrading delegation of the populace. There is no unity for a people but in a representation of national interests; a delegation from the passions or wishes of the individuals themselves is a rope of sand

Whereas in the early passage he criticises the system as being despotic, in the second he considers the same system to be the best safeguard of a representative government. Two factors account for this change, which was by no means unique to Coleridge.[4] The first is age; in 1795 Coleridge was a young man fired by ideals and untrammelled by those domestic ties which overcast ideals with practicalities. Second, the events of the French Revolution made most Englishmen consider the effects of popular power as potentially dangerous. Southey, for instance, co-founder of Pantisocracy, could write in 1832:[5]

> No man defends the aristocracy more earnestly than I do, because no man can be more thoroughly convinced of the utility and necessity of such an order of the state.

Attitudes to Coleridge, and also to Southey and Wordsworth, tend to be modified according to which of these factors, the personal or the actual, is considered more predominant. In their lifetimes all three suffered for their changed attitudes to democratic reform, notably at the hands of Hazlitt, who was quite convinced that prospects of preferment were responsible for a change of heart. Coleridge frequently defended himself from charges that he had changed his position, and a few examples from his many utterances on this, perhaps the central issue of his day, may serve to give coherence to his development.

Coleridge's involvement with the principles of the French Revolution was fairly brief and is marked by his activities in Bristol, lecturing, pamphleteering and producing the *Watchman.* Even in this period, Coleridge's enthusiasm was distinguished by a refusal to abandon his Christian faith so that he was able to confound one critic on his *Watchman* tour:[6]

> Mr Fellowes (to whom I was introduced by a letter from Mr. Strutt) gave one of my Prospectuses to an Aristocrat – He glanced his eye on the motto 'That All may know the Truth, and that the Truth may make us free' – A *Seditious* beginning! quoth he – . Sir! said Mr Fellowes – the motto is quoted from another Author – Poo! quoth the Aristocrat – what Odds is it whether he wrote it himself or quoted it from any *other seditious Dog?* Please (replied Mr F.) to look into the 32nd [Verse of the 8th] Chapter of John, and you will find, Sir! that that *seditious Dog was* – JESUS CHRIST!

At this most revolutionary period of his life Coleridge's religious sympathy was with Dissent and specifically with the Unitarian movement. But his family background in the established church had not altogether ceased to influence him and by 1798 he was writing to his brother:[7]

> I wish to be a good man & a Christian – but I am no Whig, no Reformist, no Republican – and because of the multitude of these fiery & undisciplined spirits that lie in wait against the public Quiet under these titles, because of them I chiefly accuse the present ministers – to whose folly I attribute, in great measure, their increased & increasing numbers.

Although Coleridge's desire to impress his older, orthodox brother must be taken into account, other statements support this one. The execution of Emmet, an Irish patriot and rebel, in 1803 caused Coleridge to review his youthful opinions:[8]

> Like him, I was very young, very enthusiastic, distinguished by Talents & acquirements & a sort of turbid Eloquence; like him, I was a zealous Partisan of Christianity, a Despiser & Abhorrer of French Philosophy & French Morals; like him, I would have given my body to be burnt inch by inch, rather than that a French Army should have insulted my native Shores/ & alas! alas! like him I was unconsciously yet actively aiding & abetting the Plans, that I abhorred, & the men, who were more, far more unlike me, in every respect, in education, habits, principles &

feelings, than the most anathematized Aristocrat among my opponents.

This is supported by an article in the *Morning Post* for 8 January 1800 criticising the English attitude of 'open war' with France, who under Buonaparte as First Consul had made overtures of peace:[9]

> The ministers, however, have passed 'sentence for open war'. We protest solemnly against that sentence, *because we are Anti-Gallicans, and Anti-Jacobins;* because, if the war be unsuccessful, it will raise Jacobinism from its present state of suspended animation into new and frantic life.

Early in his career Coleridge had abandoned the sympathy for the Revolution which characterises his Bristol lectures and publications; even at the height of his enthusiasm he was aware of pitfalls and in his lecture of early 1795 boldly stated:[10]

> The example of France is indeed a 'Warning to Britain'. A nation wading to their Rights through Blood, and marking the track of Freedom by Devastation! . . . French Freedom is the Beacon, that while it guides us to Equality should shew us the Dangers, that throng the road.

This illustrates the twin strands of Coleridge's political thinking: an awareness of the needs of the people and a recognition of the dangers of popular rule. The balance of his opinion shifted from the former to the latter as he grew older, but both elements are clearly evident thoughout. The older Coleridge could still show sympathy for the victims of pre-Revolutionary abuse, as is shown by a notebook entry probably written in June 1810:[11]

> If you find the empire in many respects more prosperous than a good man would almost wish, if you find an insufficiency of retributive Sufferings for their guilt & cowardice, if the Great Towns (the principal Scene of Crimes) are dull and languid, but the roads alive & stirring, the fields spreading over wastes & commons, & separate Farms studding the face of France, like Primroses on a Bank – to what can you attribute these blessings but to the measures of the First Constituent Assembly.

As late as July 1820 persisting identification with his youthful revolutionary self is found in a manuscript note on a copy of *Conciones ad Populum*, first published in 1795:[12]

> Except the two or three passages involving the doctrine of
> Phil. Necessity & Unitarianism I see little or nothing in these
> outbursts of my youthful zeal to *retract*, & with the exception
> of some flame-coloured Epithets applied to Persons, as Mr Pitt
> & others, or rather Personifications (for such they really were
> to *me*) as little to regret.

Coleridge reprinted the lecture in the 1818 *Friend*, where he hoped
it would give the lie to accusations of early Jacobinism.

Much in the *Conciones* anticipates Coleridge's later political
thought, and Coleridge might with justice claim that his underlying
political theory suffered little change throughout his life, though the
application to events did change, producing a marked contrast
between his statements at different times. Political theory will be
treated in a separate chapter, here I want to concentrate on
Coleridge's writings about the events of his day.

Coleridge's first political contribution to a newspaper was a
poem. He had already had several other poems printed in the
*Cambridge Intelligencer* and the *Morning Chronicle* when, in
December 1794, the latter published 'To a Young Ass', making
several thrusts on behalf of Liberty. At the same time a series of
*Sonnets on Eminent Characters*, in which Coleridge made his pro-
Revolutionary sympathies clear with poems on Lafayette, Kosciusko
and Pitt, appeared. In 1795 several poems were published in the
*Watchman* but the next major contribution was 'Ode to the
Departing Year', which was written for the *Cambridge Intelligencer*
at the end of 1796. The next year, when Wordsworth's influence
was greatest, produced little for the papers, but towards its close Sir
James Mackintosh recommended Coleridge to the notice of Daniel
Stuart, editor and proprietor of the *Morning Post*. Stuart offered
Coleridge a small salary for occasional verses. The verses, as Stuart
later recorded, were very occasional[13] but 'Fire, Famine and
Slaughter', a thinly disguised attack on Pitt, created a minor
sensation on 8 January 1798 and 'The Devil's Thoughts', a satirical
depiction of the English establishment as Devil's agents, composed
jointly with Southey, sold the paper out on 6 September 1799 and
for several days after. 'France, an Ode' appeared in April 1798 and
'Recantation, illustrated in the Story of the Mad Ox' in July of the
same year. By the end of 1799 Coleridge was a contributor on a
full-time basis but poetic contributions continued sporadically until

Stuart gave up the *Morning Post* in 1803. After 1800 few of the contributions were of significance as comments on the news, but Coleridge's activity as a journalist is put into better perspective if it is recognised that over fifty poems of varying length and merit first appeared in daily papers. Indeed, the *Morning Chronicle*, in publishing 'To Fortune' on 7 November 1793, probably gave Coleridge his first public appearance in print. Sir James Mackintosh's recognition was not of a complete nobody for besides the poems Coleridge was known for the Bristol lectures, but it offered Coleridge the opportunity to publish his views on contemporary events, providing him with the groundwork of his political theory.

Apart from the poetry, there are three distinct periods of journalistic activity, 1795-6, 1799-1802 and 1809-11. The first marks Coleridge's earliest prominence before the public in the city of Bristol. In January 1795 Coleridge, Southey and a third would-be Pantisocrat, George Burnett, were all living together in lodgings in College Street. The lecture series begun by Coleridge in late January or early February was one of several ideas for financing the Pantisocratic venture. Soon after, Southey joined in the series. Only a confused account of lectures survives and the introduction in the Collected Works is the best source for following the various pieces of evidence. The lectures for which Coleridge charged one shilling caused a stir in Bristol, arousing the disapproval of the Establishment, but as a contemporary review recorded:[14]

> Undaunted by the storms of popular prejudice, unswayed by magisterial influence, he spoke in public what none had the courage in this City to do before, – he told Men that they have Rights.

In fact, in a later letter Coleridge suggests that he was not only undaunted but encouraged by his position among the few whose Revolutionary principles made them the object of official disapproval:[15]

> tho' I detested Revolutions in my calmer moments, . . . – yet with an ebullient Fancy, a flowing Utterance, a light & dancing Heart, & a disposition to catch fire by the very rapidity of my own motion, & to speak vehemently from mere verbal associations, choosing sentences & sentiments for the very reason, that would have made me recoil with dying away

of the Heart & an unutterable Horror from the actions expressed in such sentences & sentiments - namely because they were wild, & original, & vehement & fantastic! - I aided the Jacobins, by witty sarcasms & subtle reasonings & declamations full of genuine feeling against all Rulers & against all established Forms!

Coleridge was obliged to publish the first lecture, 'A Moral and Political Lecture', because it was suspected of treason, and a projected fourth lecture had to be abandoned probably because of difficulty in finding a room for such seditious meetings. The political lectures were followed by a historical series given by Southey and a series on revealed religion by Coleridge, but as the prospectus for the latter made clear, the connection with current events was not completely forgotten. The sixth lecture is announced as:[16]

The grand political views of Christianity - that far beyond all other Religions, and even sects of Philosophy, it is the Friend of Civil Freedom - the probable State of Society & Government if all men were Christians.

The close connection between politics and religion is one of the constants of Coleridge's thinking and has a profound influence on his political theory. By mid-June Coleridge was back to more pressing contemporary issues. He delivered a lecture on the slave trade, which was revised and reprinted in the *Watchman,* and Cottle records lectures on the hair-powder tax, and the Corn Law, of which no trace survives. By the end of 1795, after his marriage and a short retirement in Clevedon, Coleridge was again addressing the people of Bristol. In October the king had been attacked on his way to open Parliament, and a government already so nervous of any expression of dissent that the Habeas Corpus Act had been suspended the previous February was considering two bills put forward by Pitt and Grenville forbidding meetings of fifty or more without the consent of the magistrates, who were also empowered to disperse meetings. The bills redefined treason to include incitement, and printing and lecturing were also liable to restraint if considered to be against the king. In November there were two meetings in Bristol at which Coleridge spoke and a petition against the bills was sent to Parliament. On the 26th Coleridge gave a lecture on the subject, which was published as 'The Plot Discovered', probably in early December. Coleridge also issued 'An Answer to a "Letter to Edward Long Fox, M.D."' defending himself and several leading Bristol liberals, from the strictures of the writer.

The *Watchman*, like the lectures, was a response to an immediate political issue: a fear that England's government was undermining England's traditional freedoms. Whereas later, when popular feeling ran high against the government, Coleridge was fearful that revolution and bloodshed would result, now he was concerned only that England should share the freedom which France enjoyed. The two bills which became law in December threatened that freedom, but various political pressure groups hoped to mobilise public opinion and overthrow the government. As the Prospectus states, Coleridge planned in the *Watchman*:[17]

> to co-operate (1) with the WHIG CLUB in procuring a repeal of Lord Grenville's and Mr Pitt's bills, now passed into laws, and (2) with the PATRIOTIC SOCIETIES, for obtaining a Right of Suffrage general and frequent.

The people of Bristol promised support for the venture and to augment that Coleridge set off, in January 1796 on the *Watchman* tour of Midland towns immortalised in the *Biographia*. This was interrupted by Coleridge's recall to Bristol because Sara, who was pregnant, was ill, and Coleridge began the work for the periodical in an atmosphere of urgent domestic need. This, as he wrote in a letter to Poole, gave him an insight into the needs of others:[18]

> Mrs Coleridge's increasing danger at home added to the gloomy prospect of so many mouths to open & shut, like puppets, as I move the string – in the eating & drinking way – but why complain to you? Misery is an article with which every market is so glutted, that it can answer to no one's purpose to export it. – Alas! alas! – Oh! Ah! Ah! Oh! – &c. I have received many abusive letters – post-paid, thanks to the friendly Malignants – but I am perfectly callous to disapprobation, except where it tends to lessen profit. – There indeed I am all one Tremble of Sensibility, Marriage having taught me the wonderful uses of that vulgar commodity, yclept *Bread*. – The Watchman succeeds so as to yield a *bread-and-cheesish* profit.

The profit, however, proved to be illusory and by 13 May the tenth issue appeared with an address to the readers:[19]

> This is the last Number of the WATCHMAN. –
> Henceforward I shall cease to cry the State of the political Atmosphere. While I express my gratitude to those friends, who exerted themselves so liberally in the establishment of this Miscellany, I may reasonably be expected to assign some reason for relinquishing it thus abruptly. The reason is short and satisfactory – the Work does not pay its expences.

Coleridge sums up the reasons for the paper's failure in the *Biographia* as 'lack of worldly knowledge'.[20] The political climate changed during the paper's existence because of peace moves and potential readers of the *Watchman* became more insistent that the magazine should meet their expectations, which, as Coleridge pointed out, were quite diverse. Some, for instance, wanted more poetry; others less. Equally, Coleridge did not get the contributions he hoped for, his London agent, Parsons, did not pay for the copies he sold and finally, Coleridge's views on the international situation were beginning to change as France became more obviously the aggressor in the war. Close inspection of parliamentary reports and repeated stories of bloodshed from France probably furthered Coleridge's general disillusion, as he wrote to Flower, editor of the *Cambridge Intelligencer,* another provincial paper on the Whig side:[21]

> I am tired of reading butcheries and altho' I should be unworthy the name of Man, if I did not feel my Head & Heart awefully interested in the final Event, yet, I confess, my Curiosity is worn out with regard to the particulars of the Process.

Three years passed before Coleridge again turned his attention to the affairs of the day.

By the end of 1799, the illusion of domestic stability had vanished and Coleridge was entering his long middle period of change and misery. Wordsworth had made good his intention to move north and by Christmas was living at Dove Cottage with Dorothy. Coleridge was torn between Wordsworth and Poole and was unable to find a replacement for the house at Nether Stowey, which had become too small. After a trip to the Lake District with Wordsworth, he finally took up an offer from Daniel Stuart to write regularly for the *Morning Post* and he and his family moved into the lodgings off the Strand which Stuart had arranged. On the last day of the year he wrote to Poole: 'I work from I-rise to I-set (that is from 9 AM. to 12 at night), almost without intermission.'[22] Before long he was writing to Southey:[23]

> I have not a moment's time - & my head aches - I was up
> till 5 o clock this morning - My Brain so overworked, that I
> could doze troublously & with cold limbs, so affected was my
> circulation / I shall do no more for Stewart.

Also at this time Coleridge was working on the *Wallenstein* translations for Longman, and it is not surprising perhaps that by March, his contributions to the *Morning Post* were becoming somewhat less frequent. Coleridge isolated the central problem in a letter to Stuart at the beginning of March:[24]

> I will do what I can - only not for any regular *Stipend*.
> - That harrasses me - I know, that hitherto I have received
> from you much more than I have earned - & this must not
> be - I have no objection to be payed for what *I do*, but a great
> objection to be paid for what I *ought* to do -.

Daniel Stuart, who used to call at Coleridge's lodgings to discuss the day's leading article and even on occasion, when Coleridge was ill, to write the articles from dictation, was well aware of the difficulty:[25]

> he could never write a thing that was immediately required of
> him. The thought of compulsion disarmed him.

Stuart was a shrewd editor and raised the *Morning Post* sales from 350 a day to 4,500 and sold the paper he bought for £600 in 1795 for £25,000 eight years later. Coleridge claimed greater responsibility for this rapid improvement than Stuart would allow, and certainly the editor must take final responsibility, not least for securing the services of a Coleridge and persevering in getting articles from him against the odds. Clearly, Coleridge was not an ideal newspaper correspondent and after a spate of activity in early 1800, the articles gradually became more infrequent despite a series sent from Greta Hall in the autumn of 1802. However, most of the articles were closely argued and represent careful and intelligent study of the current affairs involved. The time limits imposed by a daily paper created difficulties for Coleridge, who felt he could not discuss each subject so throughly as he wished. On the other hand, the need to compress his thoughts, the deadline always close at hand, meant that these articles are written in a style which is much less involved than is common in Coleridge's prose.

In 1809 Coleridge's work again appeared in a paper controlled by Stuart. By now it was the *Courier*, an evening paper edited by T. G. Street and only part owned by Stuart, who still maintained his influence. Stuart helped Coleridge with the setting up of the *Friend* in 1808, advising him on business matters, procuring and even paying for some of the paper. In November 1809 Stuart reprinted an article in the *Courier* from the *Friend* and, according to E. L. Griggs,[26] it was to repay the debt for paper that Coleridge sent the eight 'Letters on the Spaniards' which appeared from December 1809 to 20 January 1810. Thus, when Coleridge left Montagu's house because of his words about Wordsworth and found himself relying on his own support entirely, it was not unnatural that he should turn again to Stuart; in April 1811, when the winter months had restored some equilibrium to his mind and affairs, he wrote to Stuart tentatively suggesting that he should work for the *Courier:*[27]

> it struck me, that by devoting myself for the next half year to the Courier, as a regular Duty, I might prove useful to the Paper: as, if it were desirable, I could be at the office every morning by ½ past 9, to read over all the Morning Papers &c, & point out whatever seemed noticeable to Mr Street, - that I might occasionally write the leading Paragraph when he might wish to go into the City or to the Public offices - and besides this, I would carry on a series of articles, a column and a half or two columns each, independent of small paragraphs, poems etc, as would fill whatever room there was in the Courier whenever there was room. In short, I would regularly furnish six Colums to Mr Street, which [he] might suffer to accumulate in busy times -.

Coleridge talks of the plan as being 'pleasing to Street' but there can be no doubt that he also considered that the rather easy-going timetable would suit him too. To modern eyes it seems a very lackadaisical way to run an important daily paper, but on 5 May 1811 Coleridge was able to report to Stuart that Street had agreed and that he was intending to start the next day at 8.30 a.m. Coleridge clearly fulfilled his obligation because there are some forty-five articles reprinted by Sara Coleridge from the period May to September 1811, and the letters to Stuart from this time reveal Coleridge's commitment to the paper and its interests. By October, though, the letters are full of plans for articles which never appeared and were probably never written. The reasons for this seem to be threefold: first, an article by Coleridge on the re-appointment of the Duke of York as commander-in-chief of the army was suppressed by government interference, which made Coleridge feel that the paper was becoming a party organ; second, Coleridge was beginning to make plans for a second series of lectures which began in November, and third, there seem to have been problems about remuneration.

In the *Biographia* Coleridge added to his claim that he had made the *Morning Post* what it was:[28]

in these labours I employed, and, in the belief of partial friends wasted, the prime and manhood of my intellect.

Stuart felt that this was overstated but suppressed his feelings during Coleridge's life and continued to supply him with funds for his annual holiday by the sea. When *Table Talk* and Gillman's *Life* both repeated this claim, Stuart spoke out in a series of letters to the *Gentleman's Magazine,* and while generously acknowledging Coleridge's occasional and profitable insights, he fairly states:[29]

A few weeks in 1800, and a few weeks in 1802, that was all the time he ever wasted on the Morning Post; as for the Courier, it accepted of his proffered services, as a favour done to him, when, everything having failed, he could do nothing else.

Daniel Stuart was an old man when he wrote these letters and there is an understandable sense of grievance at the way in which his generosity was being turned against him, but the articles do not have the bitterness of Cottle's *Reminiscences* and offer valuable insights into the ways of editors and correspondents at this period. Stuart rightly stresses his financial help but does not emphasise, as he might have done, the encouragement he gave Coleridge to develop his political thinking, to test his theories against events, to control his vast and speculative thoughts into a commentary on the daily news. To posterity Coleridge is first of all a poet, then a critic and possibly a philosopher; in his own day he must have been known equally as a commentator on contemporary issues. A contributor to the press, a founder of periodicals, a lecturer exploiting what media there were; this side of Coleridge has not appealed uniformly to posterity, which has taken its cue from the *Biographia*, but it represents more fully that side of Coleridge which was in touch with the actual affairs of his day. Indeed, at one time it seemed possible that events might overtake him. Napoleon, who was very resentful of press criticism, took a tyrant's line with Coleridge and tried to have him arrested when he was in Italy because of articles which had forecast the imminent and inevitable downfall of the French Emperor. Friends and connections helped Coleridge to escape from Rome but the experience no doubt left its mark on his political thinking.

After 1811 Coleridge wrote only two letters for the papers, both in defence of Southey, whose early revolutionary play *Wat Tyler* had been reprinted without permission. Southey, by now a respected and conservative Poet Laureate, had been bitterly attacked by a Mr William Smith. Coleridge's letters appeared in the *Courier* in 1817, where Stuart's influence still stood Coleridge in good stead, possibly because Southey too had been an early contributor to the *Morning Post*.

In April 1818 Coleridge published his last work directly concerned with contemporary affairs, *Two Addresses on Sir Robert Peel's Bill*. Passing into the statute books in 1819, this bill reduced the hours worked by children from fifteen to twelve and prevented the employment of children under nine years of age. Coleridge's attention, especially in the first address, is focused on the fear that the bill would encourage further curtailment of the liberty of trading manufacturers. The callousness of some objections was another target:[30]

[Picture] a child employed on tasks the most opposite to all
its natural instincts were it only from their improgressive and
unwearying uniformity – in a heated stifling impure
atmosphere, fevered by noise and glare, both limbs and spirits
outwearied, – and that, at the tenth hour he has still three,
four or five hours more to look forward to. Will he, will the
poor little *sufferer*, be brought to believe, that these hours are
mere trifles – or the privilege of going home, not worth his
thanks? Generalities are apt to deceive us. Individualize the
sufferings which it is the object of this bill to remedy: follow

up the detail in some one case with a human sympathy and the deception vanishes.

This is the same approach as is found in the early anti-war poetry, where Coleridge bitterly rebukes:[31]

> all our dainty terms for fratricide;
> Terms which we trundle smoothly o'er our tongues
> Like mere abstractions, empty sounds to which
> We join no feeling and attach no form!

It also shows that Coleridge's changed attitudes to electoral reform meant no lessening of sympathy for those who suffered in the service of the system.

The Introductory Address to his *Conciones ad Populum* (1795) is a good example of Coleridge's attempts to relate the day's events to some more permanent principle. There is an evident debt to Godwin and to Hartley. As Peter Mann points out in his introduction to the *Lectures*, Godwin's influence on Coleridge was always modified by his Christian belief, but in areas where the two did not clash – especially in benevolism, a belief that if men's circumstances were improved, man himself would improve morally and socially – Godwin's influence is pervasive, coupled with that of David Hartley, whose theory of association Coleridge had not yet rejected. Of the poor, Coleridge writes:[32]

> They too, who live *from Hand to Mouth*, will most frequently become improvident. Possessing no *stock* of happiness they eagerly seize the gratifications of the moment, and snatch the froth from the wave as it passes by them. Nor is the desolate state of their families a restraining motive, unsoftened as they are by education, and benumbed into selfishness by the torpedo touch of extreme Want. Domestic affections depend on association. We love an object if, as often as we see or recollect it, an agreeable sensation arises in our minds. But alas! how should *he* glow with the charities of Father and Husband, who gaining scarcely more, than his own necessities demand, must have been accustomed to regard his wife and children, not as the Soothers of finished labour, but as Rivals for the insufficient meal!

Coleridge always differed from Godwin in his attitude to the influence of domestic affection on a wider sympathy and here states categorically:[33]

> The paternal and filial duties discipline the Heart and prepare it for the love of all Mankind. The intensity of private attachments encourages, not prevents, universal Benevolence.

This difference from Godwin helped to shape one of the central concerns of Coleridge's political thought, the importance of a personal and immediate involvement in social problems. The theoretical introduction provides the basis for the examination of the more immediate aspects of the situation in the second lecture, 'On the Present War'. It is very useful reading to anyone interested in the life of the times and makes good use of standard rhetorical devices:[34]

> We will now take a rapid survey of the consequences of this unjust because unnecessary War. I mean not to describe the distressful stagnation of Trade and Commerce: I direct not your attention to the wretches that sadden every street in this City, the pale and meagre Troop, who in the bitterness of reluctant Pride, are forced to beg the Morsel, for which they would be willing to 'work their fingers to the bone' in honest Industry: I will not frighten you by relating the distresses of that brave Army, which has been melted away on the Continent, nor picture to your imaginations the loathsome pestilence that has mocked our Victories in the West-Indies: I bid you not hear the screams of the deluded Citizens of Toulon – I will not press on your recollection the awful Truth, that in the course of this calamitous contest more than a Million of men have perished – a MILLION of men, of each one of whom the mangled corse terrifies the dreams of her that loved him, and makes some mother, some sister, some widow start from slumber with a shriek! These arguments have been urged even to satiety – a British Senator has sneeringly styled them mere common-place against wars. I could weep for the criminal Patience of Humanity! These arguments are *hacknied*; yet *Wars* continue!

A whole history of government mismanagement is alluded to here. The West Indian campaign, undertaken largely to appease the influential sugar plantation owners (the same men who so retarded the abolition of the slave trade), the surrender of Toulon to Lord Hood, who was blockading the port, a campaign in Flanders where the Duke of York led English troops fighting alongside the Allies, and a projected expedition to Brittany to mobilise Royalists in France all made claims on England's slender manpower. Toulon was lost because a force was not sent until it was too late; the Flanders campaign was unsuccessful because the force there was too small. The West Indian campaign in the years 1793-6 lost the army 80,000 men, mainly from disease, half of them dying, the others returning home unfit for service. The government would not allow the use of negro troops who could withstand the conditions, did not issue tropical kit and finally surrendered many of its expensive captures in the later Peace of Amiens. This was the final touch to a campaign which represented the early mismanagement of the war at its worst.

The suspension of the Habeas Corpus Act also occupies Coleridge's attention and here his sense of underlying principles gives an important added depth to his argument:[35]

> Not one definite reason assigned, not one fact proved, we have
> been impelled by dark and terrifying Generalities to sacrifice
> the personal Security of ourselves and perhaps of our posterity.
> The august and lofty Tree, which while it rose above the
> palace of the Monarch, sheltered the distant dwelling of the
> Cottager, stripped of its boughs, now stands the melancholy
> memorial of counquered Freedom. - We can only water its
> roots with our tears, or look forward with anxious eye to the
> distant Springtide, when it shall branch forth anew! - We are
> no longer Freemen, and if we be more secure here than in
> Morocco or at Constantinople, we owe this superiority to the
> mildness of our Masters, not to the protection of our Laws.

Coleridge goes on to allude to Hardy, one of those involved in the State Trials of 1794 and imprisoned in May of that year, whose wife had died after a mob attack on her house. Hardy was subsequently acquitted but what worried Coleridge was that the arbitrarily falling axe of the executioner seemed to be related not to a concept of justice but to the dictate of a frightened government. Coleridge's fears for more and more violent repression were unfulfilled. As the war progressed, the violence of the opposing army united the British people behind their government in its prosecution of the war. Not until there was, in the post-war depression, more popular demonstration of discontent did the government again need the support of Gag Acts.

A sign of this changing climate of opinion is apparent in the *Watchman*. 'A Remonstrance to the French Legislators' appeared in the eighth issue for 27 April 1796, rebuking their refusal to treat for peace after the British overtures made earlier in the month. Perhaps the most important passage in this crucial article is where Coleridge refers to France's condition of treaty that she retain the Netherlands. He begins by putting the case from the French point of view:[36]

> the inhabitants of the Netherlands themselves wish this union: and it would be unworthy a generous Republic to yield them up to their former Despotism. We should not use those arguments, of which our adversaries may equally avail themselves. To the same motives expressed in the same words the horrors of La Vendée are to be attributed. That no nation has the right of interfering with the affairs of another Country, is a general law: and general laws must not be dispensed with in compliment to the supposed justice of a particular case.

The thread of the argument is not easy to follow. What Coleridge is saying is that, while the French government claims the will of the people as a justification for the annexation of the Netherlands, it cruelly repressed the uprising in the Vendée, where the French themselves expressed their will as a desire for a return to the monarchy. In this, foreign countries, in accordance with the general law referred to in the final sentence, did not interfere. Nor, therefore, ought France to undermine the government of Holland by an appeal direct to the people. In effect, Coleridge is taking sides with the government, even an unpopular government, as representing the embodiment of general law. This is a point of view which he was to develop more fully later in life and it led to his changed attitude to electoral reform.

The final paragraph contains a typical mixture of shrewdly accurate prophecy (Buonaparte is clearly foreshadowed) and unrealistically applied idealism. He asks the French legislators:[37]

If however you persevere in your intentions, will your soldiers

fight with the same enthusiasm for the Ambition as they have
done for the Liberty of their Country? Will they not by
degrees amid the stern discipline of arms and the horrors of
War, forget the proud duties of *Citizens,* and become callous
to the softer claims of domestic life? . . . May not the rising
generation, who have only *heard* of the evils of Despotism but
have felt the horrors of a revolutionary Republic, imbibe
sentiments favourable to Royalty? Will not the multitude of
discontented men make *such* regulations necessary for the
preservation of your Freedom, as in themselves destroy
Freedom? Have not some of your supposed Patriots already
deemed it expedient to limit the liberty of the Press?

The *Watchman,* although most of its articles relate to France or to
the domestic situation as affected by the war, was not wholly
confined to such subjects. It also included a small number of poems,
by Coleridge and other contributors, and among the articles there
is a review of a collection of essays by a Count Rumford, whose
plans, including one for preventing smoky chimneys, greatly
impressed Coleridge. There are also articles culled from other
periodicals – for instance, one on the Ireland Shakespeare forgeries.
The most important of the articles unrelated to the Revolution and
its effects is 'On the Slave Trade', adapted from the lecture given the
previous year. The revisions throw more emphasis on to the two
main points of the article: the moral indefensibleness of the slave
trade and what the English people could do to abolish the trade
without the passing of a law, over which Pitt's government was
procrastinating. The prime aim of both article and lecture is to
emphasise the connection between the unthinking sweetening of tea
and the terrible tortures of the West Indian slave trade. The same
desire to connect cause and effect, where circumstance and habit
have divorced the two in the public's sensibility, is a central concern
of Coleridge's thinking. The opening, essentially unaltered from the
lecture, shows Coleridge groping towards a theory of perception and
related action. Characteristically, he begins with a questioning of the
sources of ideas:[38]

Whence arise our Miseries? Whence arise our Vices? From
*imaginary* Wants. No man is wicked without temptation,
no man is wretched without a cause. But if each among us
confined his wishes to the actual necessaries and real comforts

of Life, we should preclude all the causes of Complaint and all the motives to Iniquity. What Nature demands, she will supply, asking for it that portion only of Toil, which would otherwise have been necessary as *Exercise*. But Providence, which has distinguished Man from the lower orders of Being by the progressiveness of his nature, forbids him to be contented. It has given us the restless faculty of *Imagination*. . . . I have the firmest Faith, that the final cause of all evils in the moral and natural world is to awaken intellectual activity. Man, a vicious and discontented *Animal*, by his vices and his discontent is urged to develop the powers of the Creator, and by new combinations of those powers to imitate his creativeness. And from such enlargement of the mind Benevolence will necessarily follow. . . . In my calmer moments I have the firmest Faith that all things work together for Good. But alas! it seems a long and dark Process . . . I have dwelt anxiously on this subject, with a particular view, to the Slave-trade, which, I knew, has insinuated in the minds of many, uneasy doubts respecting the existence of a beneficent Deity. And indeed the evils arising from the formation of *imaginary* Wants, have in no instance been so dreadfully exemplified, as in this inhuman traffic. We receive from the West-India Islands Sugars, Rum, Cotton, Logwood, Cocoa, Coffee, Pimento, Ginger, Indigo, Mahogany, and Conserves. Not one of these articles are necessary; indeed with the exception of Cotton and Mahogany we cannot truly call them even useful: and not one of them is at present attainable by the poor and labouring part of Society.

I have quoted this at length as it illustrates all the ramifications of Coleridge's thought. The passage displays an amalgamation of ideas from favourite philosophers (the optimism is a corollary to Hartleian necessarianism) and the germ of later essentially Coleridgean ideas. The development of the imagination and its relation to religious truth was to be central to Coleridge's political theory and his mature philosophy. To find it in a political setting is surprising, maybe, but for Coleridge political concerns were always moral and, hence, philosophical concerns. Thus, he seems even more concerned with the moral condition of the English than he is with the physical sufferings of the negro:[39]

There is observable among the Many a false and bastard

sensibility that prompts them to remove those evils and those evils alone, which by hideous spectacle or clamorous outcry are present to their senses, and disturb their selfish enjoyments. Other miseries, though equally certain and far more horrible, they not only do not endeavour to remedy - they support, they fatten on them. . . . To this grievous failing we must attribute the frequency of wars, and the continuance of the Slave-trade. The merchant finds no argument against it in his ledger: the citizen at the crouded feast is not nauseated by the stench and filth of the slave-vessel - the fine lady's nerves are not shattered by the shrieks! She sips a beverage sweetened with human blood, even while she is weeping over the refined sorrows of Werter or of Clementina. Sensibility is not Benevolence. Nay, by making us tremblingly alive to trifling misfortunes, it frequently prevents it, and induces effeminate and cowardly selfishness.

This is the basis of the details and figures with which Coleridge tries to impress the English people with the enormity of the negro's suffering. Relating this to the Christian precept, 'do unto others as ye would have that others do unto you', he asks:[40]

Would *you* choose, that a slave merchant should incite an intoxicated Chieftain to make war on your Country, and murder your Wife and Children before your face, or drag them with yourself to the Market? Would you choose to be sold?

Finally, Coleridge proposes that the discontinuance of the use of sugar and rum by a significant number of the population would bring to an end the slave trade without government intervention. Coleridge had an easy enough task in this essay, since the enormity of the trade itself impressed many people by means of such books as the *Impolicy of the African Slave Trade* by Thomas Clarkson, which Coleridge quoted extensively, and by means of Wilberforce's repeated introduction of bills in Parliament. The bulk of support for abolition came from Dissenters and especially Quakers, who in all probability formed the greater part of the *Watchman*'s readership. Possibly as he was preaching to the converted, Coleridge felt that he could approach the subject more philosphically.

In 1808, when abolition had become law, Coleridge reviewed the

*History of the Abolition of the Slave Trade* written by Thomas Clarkson, now a friend of some years' standing, in the *Edinburgh Review*. The article gives a readable account of the book and of Clarkson's tireless efforts to assemble facts to reinforce the case for abolition. Coleridge expresses a:[41]

> doubt, which of the two will be the greater final gain to the moral world, – the removal of the evil, or the proof thereby given what mighty effects single good men may realize by self-devotion and perseverance.

Later he analyses the effect of the slave trade on the traders. Here is a fine example of Coleridge's combined focus, not only on the event but on its significance in the world of principle and permanent truth:[42]

> The sufferings of the Africans were calculated, no doubt, to make a more rapid and violent impression on the imaginations and bodily sympathies of men; but the dreadful depravity that of necessity was produced by it on the immediate agents of the injustice; the almost universal corruption of manners which at the present day startles the reflecting traveller on passing from the Northern States of America into those in which slavery obtains; and the further influence of such corruption on the morals of the countries that are in the habits of constant commercial intercourse, and who speak the same language; these though not susceptible of colours equally glaring, do yet form a more extensive evil, – an evil more certain, and of a more measurable kind. These are evils in the form of guilt; ... which, therefore on a well-disciplined spirit, will make an impression deeper than could have been left by the mere agony of body, or even anguish of mind; in proportion as vice is more hateful than pain, eternity more awful than time.

If it seems that Coleridge's interest in underlying principle has chilled his sympathy, it should be remembered that legislation had made the suffering a thing of the past, or ought to have done. On the other hand, Coleridge's perception of the moral issue involved in the political action can make his commentary on contemporary issues more incisive. 'The Essay on Fasts' which appeared in the second *Watchman* brought Coleridge a good deal of criticism, largely on account of his flippantly used motto from Isaiah,

'Wherefore my Bowels shall sound like an Harp'. But by exposing the fallacy behind these fast days which were devised by the church but used to further the government's cause, Coleridge performed a valuable service. Coleridge's point is made in three parts. First, that the fasting of the poor is 'ridiculous' as they eat so little normally, and if they do not fast the propitiatory nature of the fast is undermined, especially as the rich minority hold themselves aloof from the country's present troubles:[43]

> Secondly, Altho' the higher classes of society were inclined to make atonement for the vices of their ragged relations in the family of human nature, and fast in their behalf – yet as it were foolish to expect total abstinence the poor would prove ungrateful, and forsooth because *they* can afford to eat nothing but bread and cheese on Christmas days, will pretend not to be able to conceive, how an hearty dinner on salt fish, egg sauce, and parsnips, can be *fasting* on any day.

Finally, Coleridge invokes Scripture to support his claim that the practice is 'superstitious or hypocritical'.

It was because he considered him to be motivated by prudence rather than principle that Coleridge was opposed to Pitt, whose watchword was 'Security'. In the 1795-6 period, Pitt, being of the war party, was naturally opposed by Whigs and Radicals and all those who were against the war, but Coleridge's opposition survived this period.

By 1800, Coleridge was not so staunch in his dislike of the war and like many of his contemporaries he hoped that the creation of Buonaparte as First Consul in the autumn of 1799 would lead to European peace. In December of that year, Buonaparte sent peace proposals to the English government, which repudiated him as an upstart. The government were undoubtedly right, on military grounds, to refuse to treat with a soldier who was in fact seeking a truce in order to renew his attack with greater vigour. The country as a whole, however, was not so sure that peace would not equally allow them to improve living standards in times of poor harvests, high taxation and widespread poverty. On 17 February 1800 Pitt made a speech in the House of Commons defending the continuance of the war. Coleridge was in the House for the *Morning Post* and stayed up all night to prepare his report, of which Canning is reputed to have said, 'It does more credit to his head than to his memory'.[44] This was only a month before his character of Pitt appeared in the same paper, and there is a clear link between the two. Coleridge's reaction to Pitt's speech was immediately critical. He wrote to Southey, 'He is a *stupid, insipid* Charlatan, that *Pitt*' and to Poole:[45]

> My report of Pitt's Speech made a great noise here – What a degraded Animal Man is to see anything to admire in that wretched Rant – ! –

The report of the speech certainly owes a good deal to Coleridge's view of the man, as a comparison between Coleridge's version and that in the 1806 edition of Pitt's speeches shows. For instance, where the official version has:[46]

> I do not say that we must wage war until the principle of Jacobinism is extinguished in the mind of every individual; were that the object of the contest, I am afraid it would not terminate but with the present generation. I am afraid that a mind once tainted with that infection never recovers its healthful state.

Coleridge produced the following:[47]

> The mind once tainted with Jacobinism can never be wholly free from the taint; I know no means of purification; when it does not break out on the surface, it still lurks in the vitals; no antidote can approach the subtlety of the venom, no length of quarantine secure us against the obstinacy of the pestilence.

Here Coleridge is rather creating than reporting, and much the same is true of the whole report. The *Times* report too, though it gives the immediacy of the debate more accurately, is not faithful, except in the most general way. Nor really can it have been expected that speeches would be reported with minute accuracy in the days before shorthand was prevalent.

Oddly, the speech as printed in the collected edition gives a clearer sense of the cool, efficient Pitt who so provoked Coleridge to anger than does his own report. The following may be excellent policy, but it lacks any sense of the human suffering entailed in war:[48]

> Peace is most desirable to this country: *but* ... *if* the prosecution of the war afford the prospect of attaining

complete security; and *if* it may be prosecuted with increasing commerce, with increasing means, and with increasing prosperity, except what may result from the visitations of the seasons; then I say, that it is prudent in us not to negociate at the present moment.

Coleridge's attack on Pitt – for it is an attack rather than a 'Character' – is grounded on Pitt's ability to divorce words from reality, an ability which is exemplified in the speech, where no reference is made to lives lost or ruined by war, or to the starvation and real want which Pitt dismisses as 'the visitations of the seasons'. This, says Coleridge, was due in the first place to his father's training of the boy in oratory and was fostered by Pitt's natural coldness, which kept him aloof from the vital experience of the young. This made the young Prime Minister:[49]

A plant sown and reared in a hot-house, for whom the very air that surrounded him, had been regulated by the thermometer of previous purpose; to whom the light of nature had penetrated only through glasses and covers; who had had the sun without the breeze; whom no storm had shaken; on whom no rain had pattered; on whom the dews of heaven had not fallen! – A being, who had had no feelings connected with man or nature, no spontaneous impulses, no unbiassed and desultory studies, no genuine science, nothing that constitutes individuality in intellect, nothing that teaches brotherhood in affection!

Such a background disabled Pitt, Coleridge claims, from apprehending the true nature of the French Revolution. Instead, he had to rely on Burke's phrases without Burke's knowledge or principles.

Coleridge illustrates this by recounting Pitt's reply to critics who refer to the food shortage:[50]

This (it is replied) is owing to our PROSPERITY – all *prosperous* nations are in great distress for food! – still PROSPERITY, still GENERAL PHRASES, unenforced by one *single image*, one *single fact* of real national amelioration, of any one comfort enjoyed, where it was not before enjoyed; of any one class of society becoming healthier, wiser, or happier. These are *things*, these are realities; and these Mr Pitt has

137

neither the imagination to body forth, nor the sensibility to feel for.

Hence, Coleridge's criticism of Pitt's speeches is a criticism of the whole man:

> One character pervades his whole being. Words on words, finely arranged, and so dexterously consequent, that the whole bears the semblance of argument, and still keeps awake a sense of surprise; but when all is done, nothing rememberable has been said;

From the first Coleridge had used Pitt's oratory to illustrate his fundamental weaknesses. In the 1795 lecture 'On the Present War', he asked:[51]

> what question proposed to him by his great political
> Adversary has he ever directly answered? His speeches which
> seemed so swoln with meaing, alas! what did they mean?

As a critique of a politician, Coleridge's article is unusual in that it lacks the vituperative references to personal shortcomings common at the time (though there is a veiled mention of Pitt's fondness for port) but, on the other hand, makes capital out of his lack of such common touches. Like Pitt's speech, though, it is more impressive as a piece of writing than as political analysis. Coleridge's knowledge of contemporary politics was limited to what he heard in the House and read in the papers. He had little knowledge of how the system, both foreign and domestic, worked or how it could be made to work. His reaction to Pitt fits perfectly with his general attitude to the use of language in public life – that it should, contrary to common usage, reflect reality and make it more widely known. This is central to Coleridge's political theory, but it does not offer any understanding of how to act to ameliorate the situation. The ways and means were of scant interest to Coleridge, and this constitutes a serious limitation of his ability as a political commentator. For instance, Coleridge castigates Pitt for the failure of his Poor Bill (glossing over the fact that the introduction of such a bill runs counter to his theory of Pitt's unawareness of the condition of the people) but he gives no indication of the difficulty of passing what was a very advanced social reform through a very conservative legislature. In a different way, the reference to Burke points up Coleridge's weakness in political commentary. Pitt, whatever his lack of theory, followed Burke on the subject of the French Revolution, and events, as Coleridge was later to acknowledge, proved Burke right. At the same period, Coleridge put his weight behind the other party, the supporters of Fox, who, in turn, supported the revolutionaries without any conception of what the Revolution would lead to.

What Coleridge expected from men in public life was a commitment of the whole man which united mental power and a feeling for the experience of men and women in general. It is the same union of head and heart which underlies his poetry, his criticism and indeed his whole philosophy. A peroration to his sixth 'Letter to the Spaniards' which appeared in the *Courier* in December 1809 defended the use of heated language against Buonaparte:[52]

> There is a class of men, Sir, who make a point of rejecting or
> disregarding all arguments that are enforced with warmth of
> feeling and illustrated by the lights of imagination. (The latter
> is indeed the effect of the former; for the boldest figures of
> speech are the natural language of profound feeling and a heart
> affected in good earnest.)... A complete tranquillity, a cold
> self-possession, in the contemplation and defence of man's
> highest interests and most awful concerns, is the commencement
> of that depraved indifference, that deadness of the moral and
> religious sense, which (a morbid accumulation being the usual
> consequence of an unnatural obstruction) so easily passes into
> the brutal and stupid revolution-phrenzy, and then having
> raved out its hour of madness, sinks to sleep in the
> strait-waistcoat of military despotism.

There is much here that relates to the characterisation of Pitt, and in this, I think, Coleridge was astute to recognise how the repressive effect of aloofness would cause outbreaks of violence, necessitating more organised repression. Although this fear was to be realised in the period of post-war depression, Coleridge's immediate concern was that the people would be prepared by this indifference for a state where an invading Buonaparte would easily overcome them. To a modern reader secure in the knowledge that the French did not invade, this may seem rather obscure here but it is apparent in a later article. Responding to a plea in the House that Buonaparte should not be subject to 'vile and general abuse', Coleridge warns:[53]

> Nothing can so effectually prepare us for the yoke of tyranny as this idea of speaking with respect and moderation of the tyrant, and we declare to God that if this change be produced in the public mind, it will in our opinion be a greater victory to Bonaparte than any he has ever gained.

This shows how firmly held was Coleridge's belief in the importance of a rightly thinking public. It goes back to the *Watchman* days and looks forward to the *Lay Sermons* and it is at the root of his sense of the value of a free press and a more widespread education.

Not all Coleridge's contributions were on the subject of the war, though it was the pressure of war-time which brought many of the other issues to prominence. In the speech quoted above Pitt referred the corn shortage to bad weather conditions and at intervals during the war grain harvests were depleted by bad weather; the shortage was exacerbated by war-time restrictions on trade and the inadequate policies of those in charge. In 1795, an attempt was made to ameliorate the condition of the poor at Speenhamland and as a result farmers were encouraged to pay low wages in the knowledge that the parish would take them up to subsistence level. This was to undermine the economic condition of the rural poor, which had already suffered as a result of the enclosure of common land. In 1800 a summer drought and a very wet autumn ruined the crops, and as the 1799 harvest had also been poor, there was widespread starvation and bread riots resulted. Plans were made to import grain, but the war made that difficult. The Baltic trade was threatened and Russia was then a French ally. When Pitt referred to prosperity, he was truthfully referring to commercial success, but this, too, created new needs among a new labouring class. The price of staple commodities was very high, the population was rising and wages were falling. This was a recurring problem. The articles which Coleridge and Poole prepared for the *Morning Post* in October 1800 were still relevant in September 1811 when extracts appeared in the *Courier*. These articles on the corn trade were an attempt to demonstrate that the scarcity of wheat was not only not caused by, but was indeed detrimental to the farmer. The political importance of this should not be overlooked; the aim of the articles was to prevent disturbance and riots among the poor. This Coleridge made explicit in the 1811 version:[54]

as it appears, that owing to mildew, the wheat crops in many of the arable districts have been less productive than last year, though, in some measure, compensated for by the uncommon excellence of the oat and barley crops, we anticipate that faction will avail itself of ignorance and prejudice, to spread gloom and excite vindictive passions among the labouring class, and throughout the lower orders of society.

The social changes, accelerated but not caused by the war, which aggravated the corn scarcities, also created other problems. Pitt's new commerical enterprise, besides creating a new labouring class, also brought changed pressure on the country's monetary system. In 1811 a prolonged shortage of gold coin caused Parliament to consider when it could expect the Bank of England to resume payment in cash for paper money. There were two opposing schools, those who thought that the Bank should at a named time resume cash payments and those who thought that it should be left open. Coleridge was one of the latter party, but his interest was really in the principles involved. He gives a definition of money as '*whatever* has a value among men according to what it *represents*, rather than to what it *is*'.[55] This may seem obvious to a modern reader but it was a useful formulation in a time when gold and silver were the common coinage. In true Coleridgean fashion, the definition involves:[56]

a brief history of the transit from barter to money, then of money in its first form to the complexity of the present circulating medium, and lastly, of the action and re-action of money and barter on each other, and inclusively or by consequence on all the social relations of civilised man.

This is followed by a lively account of the evils of barter quoted from a contemporary book of American travels. In a second article Coleridge, as is his habit, attacks the subject through the words, claiming that the argument is:[57]

a mere *logomachy*, the final decision of which is either unattainable, or at best belongs not to law-makers, but to makers of dictionaries.

The word 'depreciation' is meaningless, he asserts, because it means equally that goods are worth more and that money is worth less.

This is well enough as far as it goes, but it clearly stops short of a professionally trained commentary on a complex issue and it illustrates again the weakness of Coleridge's political journalism. His strength lay in combining a long view of the consequences and a close scrutiny of the verbiage of politics.

There is a common concern underlying Coleridge's articles both on grain prices and on bullion, which he himself states:[58]

> if the dry and difficult question of Bullion and Paper Currency can be hammered out into a weapon of offence, with far greater ease and to far worse purposes will a false alarm concerning the immediate subsistence of the people be seized and employed by our present malcontents, the true successors of the old French faction, who wear the old mantle with a double portion of that spirit of malignant prophecy by which ominous prediction hopes to realize what it predicts.

This represents the true change in Coleridge's political thinking. Whereas in 1795, for instance, his sympathy was with protest without thought for the consequences, now he is apprehensive that the consequence will bring rebellion and social upheaval. It is a change of emphasis rather than a change of side, for as his 'Cotton Bill Addresses' show, he was still capable of active sympathy with the sufferings of the labourer. That sympathy was only allowed to develop where there was no danger to law and order. 'Security' had not become his watchword, maybe, but it was his first concern for the state. To modern eyes it may seem a sad loss of vision, but to Coleridge's generation it was a normal reaction to the dreadful suffering which the French Revolution caused not only the ruling class but society as a whole. Moreover, the events of the Revolution made thinking men critical of the ability of the lower classes to organise society even for their own benefit.

Many of Coleridge's later contributions to the *Courier* are concerned with Ireland. The question was immediately one of Catholic Emancipation; this, like electoral reform, had suffered long delay as a result of the war. It eventually became law in 1829 but as early as 1801, after an Act of Union between Ireland and England, Pitt had been obliged to resign because of King George's obdurate refusal to consider emancipation. The question was kept alive because of continuing trouble in Ireland and a consequent fear that discontent would ally Ireland with France. Catholic Emancipation was considered primarily as a means of reducing the risk of rebellion rather than as a right. Coleridge was not intolerant of practitioners of varying religions but he had scant respect for almost all sects and his especial fear was that Catholic allegiance to the Pope would undermine allegiance to the English government. Events in Ireland fostered this fear and on 3 September 1811 Coleridge reported a meeting at which 'it was declared and repeated, that the Catholic Emancipation was but a means to an end, the end being a repeal of the Union'. To Coleridge this clearly signalled a desire for Catholic sovereignty. He characterises the petitioners as saying:[59]

> Let us first secure the means of a Catholic Parliament, with Catholic officers of state, then dissolve the union with Great Britain, and then – Caetera quis nescit?

Having said this Coleridge is, however, mindful of the obligations of England to the Irish:[60]

> If we have done wrong, it is iniquitous to urge the effects of that wrong as exempting us from the duty of compensating for it. ... We may have kept him in the dark till his eye hates the light: the memory of past scourgings may make the wound in the heart ache and bleed at the sight of us, when scarce a scar is visible in the body. In this case, we cannot indeed all at once trust hate with power, or blindness with guidance; but we can, and we are bound to exert all our invention in the discovery, all our power in the application, of the best means to reconcile the eye, to conciliate the heart, for the purpose and with the earnest intent of gradually conceding the whole claim, as soon as, and in proportion as, we shall have succeeded in disentangling our own ravel, in recalling the claimant himself to a capability of receiving and using his own claim. Measures not without hazard must yet be hazarded, where the demand is pressing, and the final right manifest and notorious.

This recalls Coleridge's early optimism about man, for he adds:

> The history of man has almost warranted the policy of a bold and flattering confidence.

In a second letter on the subject Coleridge emphasises the importance of the principles behind the policy of emancipation, and in a third letter begins the examination of the relation of Church and State which these principles affect, looking forward to his later book, *On the Constitution of Church and State:*[61]

> Church and State – civil and religious rights – to hold these essential powers of civilized society in a due relation to each other, so as to prevent them from becoming its burthens instead of its supports; this is perhaps the most difficult problem in the whole science of politics.

These articles of 1811 show a broader sympathy with the movement of the people than is elsewhere apparent in Coleridge's later journalism. This is in contrast to his 'Letters to Judge Fletcher' signed 'An Irish Protestant' which appeared in the *Courier* from September to December 1814. These letters, written in response to a change to the jury which was regarded as an encouragement to popular reform movements, illustrate all Coleridge's later fears of popular dissidence:[62]

> Not only associations for objects avowedly political, but all combinations of private individuals, confirmed by oath, stand excluded in the strictness of my general rule. However good and fair their first-fruits might seem, I should still expect them to prove more or less baneful to the real interests of civilisation and philosophy.

It is remarks like this which illustrate the traditional side of Coleridge's attitude to politics. The French Revolution held back the liberalizing movement for more than forty years, but the pre-war stability of a hierarchical, predominantly rural society was never to be recovered. When in the mid-Victorian period England did regain a measure of peace and plenty, this was to be coupled with a steady movement towards alleviating the condition of the worker and making him more able to participate in the government of his country. Although he maintained a lively sympathy with the first movement, Coleridge could not anticipate any step, however small, in the direction of achieving the second, without grave fear that disorder and rebellion would ensue. His attitude to the working man was of the paternalistic fashion common among eighteenth-century landlords. He had every sympathy with them as people, but no respects for their rights as a class.

# 6

# Political Theory

Coleridge's very first public political utterance, significantly entitled 'A Moral and Political Lecture', offers in its motto, quoted from Akenside, a useful introduction to Coleridge's political theory:[1]

> To calm and guide
> The swelling democratic tide;
> To watch the state's *uncertain* frame:
> To baffle Faction's *partial* aim;
> But chiefly with determin'd zeal
> To quell the servile Band that kneel
> To Freedom's jealous foes;
> And Lash that Monster, who is daily found
> Expert and bold our country's peace to wound,
> Yet dreads to handle arms, nor manly counsel knows.

This aim, perhaps barely recognised in 1795, underlies Coleridge's political thinking, almost to the end of his life. The words 'calm and guide' are the significant ones, not to swell nor to stem the progressing tide of democracy, but to contain and organize it was Coleridge's life-long desire in politics.

To some extent, all Coleridge's political theory had a journalistic element just as the journalism was never devoid of an appeal to principles and I hope that the division of the political works between two chapters will not prevent readers from seeing them as forming a whole. Any tendency to consider the later Coleridge as a thinker cut off from life's realities should be corrected by looking at the occasions for the works in this chapter. The *Lay Sermons*, for instance, were written in the winter of 1816-17 at the instigation of the publisher, Rest Fenner, as pamphlets on current economic and social problems. *On the Consitution of Church and State*, although

145

written well before the event, was published as a response to the Catholic Emancipation Act of 1829. Most of all, *The Friend*, which began life as a stamped newspaper, can make a claim to be considered as journalism. There is, however, a distinction between these works and those covered in the previous chapter, best seen in *The Friend*. Although Coleridge's work as editor, proprietor and chief contributor of this periodical adds an important dimension to our appraisal of his work as a journalist, *The Friend* was never intended to be anything else but an exposition of principles. The word echoes through the work, repeated in titles to sections and always prominent in the discussion of individual topics. A letter to George Coleridge in April 1809, soliciting subscriptions makes the point emphatically:[2]

> I have been asked if it will be at all *political*. My answer has
> been – if by political be meant the events of the day, or
> discussions on the events of the day, or personalities ministerial
> or anti-ministerial, or *party*-politics in any shape, or disguise,
> THE FRIEND will not be *political*... my Object is to draw
> the attention of my countrymen, as far as in me lies, from
> *expedients* & short-sighted tho' quick-sighted Expedience, to
> that grand Algebra of our moral nature, *Principle* & Principles –
> in public as in private life, in criticism, ethics, & religion.

The story of the birth of *The Friend* is the most complicated, even among Coleridge's works. The prospectus itself caused great worry as the original printer had to be abandoned and a new one found. All the bother over the means of production helped Coleridge to clarify his thoughts about this work. For instance, a letter to Stuart about the prospectus discusses not only Coleridge's purpose but also his projected audience:[3]

> I do not write in this work for the multitude of men; but for
> those, who either by Rank, or Fortune, or Official situation,
> or by Talents & Habits of Reflection, are to influence the
> multitude – I write to found true PRINCIPLES, to oppose
> false PRINCIPLES in Legislation, Philosophy, Morals,
> International Law.

The prospectus when it did appear promised the first number for January 1809 but by that time Coleridge had neither publisher nor printer; and there was still confusion over whether the periodical was to be a newspaper, stamped and sent by post, or a pamphlet unstamped and sent by coach to coaching towns. Stuart favoured the latter, but Coleridge the former and he prevailed. A plan for a press at Dove Cottage was abandoned and finally a printer in Penrith, John Brown, was found. As there was no direct post from Ambleside to Penrith, Coleridge stayed at Keswick to begin with and later relied on Southey to read proofs. Whenever Coleridge had to see Brown, he walked over the fells. Paper was always a problem and the eighth issue was printed in two batches as the paper ran out. Collecting subscribers, which might have been a major problem, proved to be the simplest part of the venture. Indeed, the subscribers ensured the eventual failure of the periodical merely by their facile unthinking willingness to subscribe to a paper which they probably had little desire to read and no desire to pay for. The plan was that payment should be due after the twentieth issue, and while this seems ludicrously unbusinesslike to modern minds, Daniel Stuart, a very successful newspaper proprietor, approved it:[4]

> You can say nothing in the Advertisement respecting the mode of payment. It is quite unusual to call for money before hand, & such a call would not be attended to . . .

As well as these problems Coleridge had to work without the support of his immediate circle. Wordsworth went so far as to write to Poole:[5]

> I am sorry to say that nothing appears to be more desirable than that his periodical should never commence. It is in fact *impossible* - utterly impossible - that he should carry it on; and, therefore, better never begin it;

Southey felt the same and it was not long before they were proved right. However, Stuart, who was better qualified than either of the poets, saw no reason to withdraw his support, even though Wordsworth twice wrote to him expressing his despair of Coleridge's success. In many ways the production of *The Friend* is an important point in Coleridge's career. He himself felt new hope as he wrote to Poole:[6]

> I will make a covenant with you. Begin to count my Life, as a Friend of your's from 1 January, 1809 . . . my Health & spirits are better [than] I have known them for years.

and he continues to talk with enthusiasm of *The Friend* as:

> the main Pipe, thro' which I shall play off the whole reservoir of my collected Knowledge and of what you are pleased to believe Genius.

There is no greater testimony to Coleridge's faith in this new project than the dogged way in which he surmounted the practical difficulties which beset the venture. It is difficult to see how he could have been unaware of Wordsworth's attitude and yet this too did not affect his energy. Dorothy Wordsworth records that in the end Coleridge was tired and could not go on,[7] but he did not give up until the disastrous results of the subscription collection made it plain that he was working for a loss. Coleridge was no impractical dreamer and when he recognised that his work was not commercially successful, he had no heart to continue. It was the same with the *Watchman*. It is, however, difficult to see how the periodical could have been successful. Its professed intention was to appeal to a small audience, but the demands it makes are unrealistic for the readers of any periodical. The following, for instance, is a difficult sentence to understand fully:[8]

> He gave us Reason and with Reason Ideas of its own
> formation and underived from material Nature,
> self-consciousness, Principles, and above all, the Law of
> Conscience, which is the power of a holy and omnipotent
> Being *commands* us to attribute Reality – among the numerous
> ideas mathematical or philosophical, which the Reason by the
> necessity of its own excellence, creates for itself – to those,
> (and those only) without which the Conscience would be
> baseless and contradictory; namely, to the ideas of Soul, the
> Free Will, Immortality, and God.

To the subscribers, the thought was further complicated because the first part of the sentence appeared in the fifth issue for 14 September 1809 and the remainder, from 'mathematical' onwards, appeared the following Thursday. Nor was this the only instance of extra difficulties created by the plan of founding a periodical on principles. As time went on, concessions were made and lighter material was introduced. The eleventh issue, for instance, contained, as well as a continuation of the tenth issue, 'Specimens of Rabbinical Wisdom', 'The Hymn before Sunrise' (reprinted from the *Morning*

*Post*) and a letter to R. L. defending *The Friend* against the accusation that it was too difficult and promising alleviation in future; but typically, Coleridge does not promise easy reading:[9]

> No real information can be conveyed, no important errors rectified, no widely injurious prejudices rooted up, without requiring some effort of thought on the part of the Reader.

It was Coleridge's intention to have extra copies of the periodical printed on unstamped paper and bound to be sold in volumes, and he must have had hopes of more readers when *The Friend* appeared in this form in 1812, but this was not really as success. The 1818 'rifacciamento' which organised the work in a more permanent form is used in the Collected Works edition of *The Friend* and it is the one discussed in detail later in the chapter. The immediacy of the original version has an historical interest but it lacks the form of the 1818 revision and is more difficult to follow.

The years between the first appearance and the 1818 edition fully justify a conception of a crisis at its birth. Relations with Sara Hutchinson, Coleridge's amanuensis for *The Friend* finally and permanently broke down and when she left for Wales in spring 1810, no more *Friend* was written. Shortly afterwards, Coleridge left Wordsworth's house for London, the quarrel which followed was precipitated by Montagu, but as we have seen, in saying that Wordsworth had no hope of Coleridge he was only speaking the truth, even if unauthorised to do so. There was one final visit to the Lakes to collect proofs and other material for the 1812 issue of *The Friend* and then Coleridge came no more to the society of mountains, lakes, and his early friends but turned finally to the Gillmans and London intellectuals. When the 1818 *Friend* appeared, Coleridge was established in London, the *Biographia* and the *Lay Sermons* had been published, *Remorse* had been a great, even a financial success in the theatre, lecture series had attracted public attention and people were beginning to visit 'the sage of Highgate'.

The world, too, had changed in the intervening years, as Coleridge is careful to remind readers of the later version.[10] The Napoleonic struggle which was beginning to seem hopeless in 1809 was over and done with by 1818, and war-time commercial expansion had given way to depression and unrest. This is the background to the two *Lay Sermons*, which appeared in 1816 and 1817. Coleridge was asked originally to provide a tract for Rest

Fenner, a publisher with a religious bias, for which he was to receive no remuneration. He warmed to the task and by September 1816 was writing to a young admirer:[11]

> There will soon appear half a dozen theologico-metaphysico-political Essays, of every unequal lengths, by me, under the name of 'a Lay Sermon with Comments & Essays connected with the Study of the Scriptures' – The title – The Bible, the Statesman's best manual &c. It is sent off to the Publishers; and will make a *thin* book.
>
> I mention it because in the 4th I have endeavoured to explain myself at large on that distinction between the Reason and the Understanding, which I deem of such vital Importance – & with this some leading points of my scheme of philosophy, as contrasted with the Mechanic, Locke, Hartley and Condilliac System. –
>
> It will be followed by two other Lay Sermons, one to the Middle Classes, the other to the Labouring Classes, on the present real and asserted distresses – my object – to unvizard our Incendiaries.

The work which was about to appear was *The Statesman's Manual* complete with appendices. The one to the middle classes followed in a few months but the third never appeared, possibly because Coleridge found it impossible to address his thoughts to the labouring classes in a language which they could follow and partly, no doubt, because he felt, as he said in *The Friend*:[12]

> It is the duty of the enlightened Philanthropist to plead *for* the poor and ignorant, not *to* them.

Moreover, suspecting that Rest Fenner was not so reliable and helpful a publisher as he had at first seemed, Coleridge turned his thoughts to more profitable work. Certainly, the labour expended on *The Statesman's Manual*, which seems to have been done to deadline, was so great that Coleridge was ill on its completion and retired to Muddiford with the Gillman family for six weeks, so beginning a habit of autumn seaside holidays which lasted most of the rest of his life.

*The Statesman's Manual* is concerned to help the 'Learned and Reflecting of all Ranks and Professions' to a better political understanding by referring them to the Bible, whereas the second *Lay*

*Sermon* (confusingly given that tile, but often known as 'Blessed are ye that sow' from its motto), which Coleridge thought '(comparatively, at least) popular both in matter and style',[13] discusses more closely the actual situation of 1817, when Habeas Corpus was suspended after riots and the threat of an English revolution seemed as real as it ever had in the early days of the French Revolution. *The Statesman's Manual* is one of the least attractive of Coleridge's prose works in itself and is overshadowed by its own appendices, especially Appendix C, where Coleridge enlarges that differentiation between Reason and Understanding which is crucial to his thought at this period. The attraction of the Bible to Coleridge as a manual in political affairs is that:[14]

> In the Bible every agent appears and acts as a self-subsisting individual: each has a life of its own, and yet all are one life.

Here is that 'unity and multeity' which was central to Coleridge's mature thought, but he makes a poor job of convincing a modern reader, at least, either of its applicability to the Bible or its usefulness in relating the Bible to everyday politics. The *Manual* is useful because it displays a groping towards a theory more fully developed in the 1818 *Friend* and *On Church and State*. 'Blessed are ye that sow', on the other hand, is useful because it illustrates Coleridge's ability to relate a theory of government to specific cases; since it is amply illustrated with references to contemporary events, it also gives the background in which the theory was evolved. Here Coleridge makes the connection between Christian belief and political theory seem more fundamental and more useful. In the closing paragraphs of a *Lay Sermon* he asserts:[15]

> If we are a christian nation, we must learn to act nationally as well as individually, as Christians. We must remove half-truths, the most dangerous of errors ... by the whole Truth ... Our manufacturers must consent to regulations; our gentry must concern themselves in the *education* as well as in the *instruction* of their natural clients and dependents, must regard their estates as secured indeed from all human interference by every principle of law, and policy, but yet as offices of trust, with duties to be performed, in the sight of God and their Country.

*On the Constitution of Church and State according to the Idea of each* reflects Coleridge's perplexed response to the Catholic question, which caused Coleridge great perplexity because he did want religious toleration but he could not countenance the division of loyalty which he felt the Catholic church demanded. Accordingly, he was at pains to isolate the state from any purely Christian attribute and wrote:[16]

> In relation to the national Church, Christianity or the Church of Christ, is a blessed accident

but only if we underestimate the weight of 'blessed' will we be misled into divorcing Coleridge's political theory from his religious belief, and the same sentence goes on to add:

> a providential boon, a grace of God, a mighty and faithful friend, the envoy indeed and liege subject of another State, but which can neither administer the laws nor promote the ends of this other State, which is not of this world, without advantage, direct and indirect, to the true interests of the States, the aggregate of which is what we mean by the world, that is, the civilised world.

*Church and State* was first conceived as one of six supplementary disquisitions to *Aids to Reflection*, and was referred to, in that work, four years before it eventually appeared. According to the advertisement to *Church and State*, Coleridge wrote the piece originally at the suggestion of his influential friend, J. H. Frere, who, in turn, hoped to bring it to the attention of Lord Liverpool, then Prime Minister. *On Church and State* is neither an immediate response to a particular political act nor a philosophical treatise remote from contemporary problems. It represents the sort of thinking about political events which Coleridge was hoping to encourage in the readers of *The Friend* and vindicates his hopes for that periodical in so far as *Church and State* was the most influential of Coleridge's prose works. Its most powerful advocate was J. S. Mill, who used the work to reinforce his point that Coleridge added an important dimension to political thinking because of his inclusion of Idealist philosophy. Since Mill's article in the *Westminster Review* in 1840 (reprinted in *Dissertations and Discussions*, 1859) it has become accepted that Coleridge was a 'Tory philosopher'. This view of Coleridge survives, for instance, in D. P. Calleo's book *Coleridge and the Idea of the Modern State* (1966), where he says:[17]

Coleridge's later political philosophy is not a melancholy record of declining energy, but an important moment in the creation of a dynamic conservative tradition in English political thought. For it is Coleridge even more than Burke who is the true philosopher of that tradition.

I believe Coleridge would have thought that this was claiming both more and less than he claimed for himself. He would have resented being appropriated by any one faction and equally been disappointed that the educational aim of his political writings, the creation of a more politically aware governing class, had been overlooked. He would, too, have recognised that nowhere has he attempted a systematic philosophy of government.

In some ways, the phrase 'Tory philosopher' is a contradiction in terms, at least with reference to Coleridgean philosophy, and I think it is important to recognise at the outset that the accompaniment to Coleridge's political writings of religious and philosophical matter is not another instance of his inability to discipline his thoughts but an expression of his feeling that in the final analysis political solutions are not enough. In the section of *The Friend* which deals with the 'Principles of Political Philosophy', Coleridge demonstrates that government cannot be according to reason but must be related to expediency. This seems a very un-Coleridgean assertion, except in its rejection of Rousseauism, but Coleridge concludes the essay with an examination into his motives for an enquiry into political principles; his:[18]

> third motive is, that by detecting the true source of the influence of these principles, we shall at the same time discover their natural place and object: and that in themselves they are not only Truths, but most important and sublime Truths; and that their falsehood and their danger consist altogether in their misapplication. Thus the dignity of Human Nature will be secured, and at the same time a lesson of humility taught to each individual, when we are made to see that the universal necessary Laws, and pure IDEAS of Reason, were given us, not for the purpose of flattering our Pride and enabling us to become national legislators, but that by an energy of continued self-conquest, we might establish a free and yet absolute government in our own spirits.

This is an odd way to begin an enquiry into political principles but for Coleridge and for students of Coleridge it is the right one because it places politics as a study outside his concern to unite all knowledge into one philosophical system. Coleridge was too astute a commentator on contemporary events to think that any philosophical system could provide the answers to exigencies of government – and his handling of the British siezure of the Danish fleet[19] shows clearly how, without sacrificing his belief in principle, he can demonstrate that no system can provide all the answers. Thus, although Coleridge wrote a great deal about political theory, he never really approached a formulation of a theory of his own, not because, as happened with other projects, the task was too great for him, but because he did not consider politics reducible to a satisfactory theory. He did think, as the conclusion to *A Lay Sermon* quoted above shows, that political action had to be grounded on sound principles, and to the elucidation of these principles, which owe as much to religion and philosophy as to what we would call political science, he devoted much of his political writing.

*The Statesman's Manual* is perhaps the least political of all Coleridge's political writings and the least successful. The attempt to show that the Bible is the best guide to political action is fraught with difficulties, not the least of which is that it leads Coleridge into discussions which have little to do with the matter in hand. Here, Coleridge does seem to be making the claim that reason will solve all political problems:[20]

The histories and political economy of the present and preceding century partake in the general contagion of its mechanic philosophy, and are the *product* of an unenlivened generalizing Understanding. In the Scriptures they are the living *educts* of the Imagination; of that reconciling and mediatory power, which incorporating the Reason in Images of the Sense, and organizing (as it were) the flux of the Senses by the permanence and self-circling energies of the Reason, gives birth to a system of symbols, harmonious in themselves, and consubstantial with the truths, of which they are the *conductors.*

This is an important and useful statement about the relation between reason and imagination and, as L. C. Knights points out in

'Idea and Symbol: Some Hints from Coleridge'[21] a valuable statement about symbol but it has little to do with political principle. Furthermore, his claims for the Bible seem more appropriate to a work of religious principles:[22]

> The elements of necessity and free-will are reconciled in the higher power of an omnipresent Providence, that predestinates the whole in the moral freedom of the integral parts. Of this the Bible never suffers us to lose sight. The root is never detached from the ground. It is God everywhere: and all creatures conform to his decree, the righteous by performance of the law, the disobedient by the sufferance of the penalty.

A further passage relates this to Coleridge's conception of the State:[23]

> Herein the Bible differs from all the books of Greek philosophy, and in a two-fold manner. It doth not affirm a Divine Nature only, but a God: and not a God only, but the living God. Hence in the Scripture alone is the *Jus divinum*, or direct Relation of the State and its Magistracy to the Supreme Being, taught as a vital and indispensable part of all moral and of all political wisdom, even as the Jewish alone was a true theocracy.

It is impossible to disentagle the religious from the political here, and we are reminded of the Elizabethan concept of world order, and of Coleridge's great respect for the political writers of that period. Coleridge expresses the same idea more philosophically later in *The Statesman's Manual*:[24]

> The Bible alone contains a Science of *Realities*: and therefore each of its Elements is at the same time a living GERM, in which the Present involves the Future, and in the Finite the Infinite exists potentially. The hidden mystery in every, the minutest form of existence, which contemplated under the relations of time presents itself to the understanding retrospectively, as an infinite ascent of Causes, and prospectively as an interminable progression of Effects – that which contemplated in Space is beheld intuitively as a law of action and re-action, continuous and extending beyond all bound – this same mystery freed from the phenomena of Time

and Space, and seen in the depth of *real* Being, reveals itself to the pure Reason as the actual immanence of ALL in EACH.

Towards the end of the essay, Coleridge emerges from the more philosophical aspects and applies himself to current issues. He reminds his readers that he appeals: 'To men in whom I may hope to find, if not philosophy, yet occasional impulses at least to philosophic thought'[25] and goes on to reaffirm one of his earliest beliefs, that in the education of the people. Coleridge repudiates:[26]

> the disposition to think, that as the Peace of Nations has been disturbed by the diffusion of a false light, it may be re-established by excluding the people from all knowledge and all prospect of amelioration. O! never, never! Reflection and stirrings of mind, with all their restlessness, and all the errors that result from their imperfection, from the *Too much*, because *Too little*, are come into the world. The Powers, that awaken and foster the spirit of curiosity, are to be found in every village: Books are in every hovel. The Infant's cries are hushed with *picture*-books: and the Cottager's child sheds his first bitter tears over pages, which render it impossible for the man to be treated or governed as a child. Here as in so many cases, the inconveniences that have arisen from a thing's having become too general, are best removed by making it universal.

Coleridge puts into practice his belief that reformers should 'plead *for* the poor and ignorant, not *to* them' by appealing to the learned classes to remove impediments which prevented the education of the poor:[27]

> Virtue would not be Virtue could it be *given* by one fellow creature to another. To *make use* of all the means and appliances in our power to the actual attainment of Rectitude, is the abstract of the Duty which we owe to ourselves: To *supply* those means as far as we can, comprizes our Duty to others. The question then is, what are these means? Can they be any other than the communication of Knowledge and the removal of those Evils and Impediments which prevent its reception? It may not be in our power to combine both, but it is in the power of every man to contribute to the former, who is sufficiently informed to feel that it is his Duty. If it be said, that we should endeavor not so much to remove Ignorance,

as to make the Ignorant religious: Religion herself, through her
sacred oracles, answers for me, that all effective Faith
presupposes Knowledge and individual Conviction.

Thus, he refutes the argument that 'incendiaries' will inflame a
literate poor with pamphlets inciting revolt. Coleridge did not want
to see the poor rise up against the state, nor did he want the state
to repress the poor; he believed in a balance of interests, where all
would contribute to the greater good of the whole. That the
education of the poor would bring with it political problems he did
not anticipate, and he belonged to an era before the inevitability of
a class struggle was recognised.

Appendix C to *The Statesman's Manual* seems on the surface to
have little to do with the political problems of the times. However
the differentiation between reason and understanding also appears in
a political context in the 1818 *Friend* and, on closer inspection, it
becomes apparent that it was the study of politics which brought
Coleridge to make this distinction which is so important in his later
thought. To rescue what Coleridge sees as a divine attribute of man
from the narrow mechanical philosophy of the French, he makes
the distinction between reason, which 'first manifests itself in man
by the *tendency* to the comprehension of all as one',[28] and the
understanding, 'which concerns itself exclusively with the quantities,
qualities, and relations of particulars in time and space'. In this
Appendix Coleridge is careful to show that reason must be accompanied by the other members of the 'tri-unity' of man, religion
and the will, and to the appeal to reason in isolation he attributes
the false political doctrine of Jacobinism:[29]

For Jacobinism is *monstrum hybridum*, made up in part of
despotism, and in part of abstract reason misapplied to objects
that belong entirely to experience and the understanding. Its
instincts and mode of action are in strict correspondence with
its origin. In all places, Jacobinism betrays its mixt parentage
and nature, by applying to the brute passions and physical
force of the multitude (that is, to man a mere animal,) in
order to build up government and the frame of society on
natural rights instead of social privileges, on the universals of
abstract reason instead of positive institutions, the lights of
specific experience, and the modifications of existing
circumstances. *RIGHT* in its most proper sense is the creature

of law and statute, and only in the technical language of the courts has it any substantial and independent sense. In morals, Right is a word without meaning except as a correlative of Duty.

These thoughts, related as they were to Coleridge's experience of the French Revolution, are fundamental to an understanding of his political writings.

The second *Lay Sermon*, prefaced by an introduction in which Coleridge again affirms the importance of principles, has the motto 'Blessed are ye that sow beside all waters' and also, from the eighth chapter of Jeremiah, 'We looked for peace, but no good came'. This is the central subject of the *Lay Sermon* and as it deals with an economic problem, so in this work Coleridge came as near as he ever could to economic theory. Generally speaking, Coleridge did not have a high opinion of the relatively new science of economics, and as the following anecdote makes clear, this was a matter not of opinion only, but of principle. Coleridge had been discussing the depopulation and consequent depression of the Scottish Highlands and adds:[30]

I was sometimes afterwards told by a very sensible person who had studied the mysteries of political economy, and was therefore entitled to be listened to, that more food was produced in consequence of this revolution, that the mutton must be eat somewhere, and what difference where? If three were fed at Manchester instead of two at Glencoe or the Trossacs, the balance of human enjoyment was in favor of the former. I have passed through many a manufacturing town since then, and have watched many a group of old and young, male and female, going to, or returning from, many a factory, but I could never yet persuade myself to be of his opinion. Men, I still think, ought to be weighed not counted. Their *worth* ought to be the final estimate of their value.

This is the basis from which Coleridge makes what he calls a 'humble contribution' to the debate on the causes of the present distress:[31]

They appear to me, however, resolvable into the OVERBALANCE OF THE COMMERCIAL SPIRIT IN

## CONSEQUENCE OF THE ABSENCE OR WEAKNESS OF THE COUNTER-WEIGHTS:

Counterbalances continued, according to Coleridge, in 'the ancient feeling of rank and ancestry, compared with our present self-complacent triumph over these supposed prejudices',[32] 'the austerer studies' of philosophy and theology and the 'influence of Religion'. Coleridge concentrates on this last and in a long disquisition, which he rightly feared would anger his friends the Quakers, he described what has come to be popularly known as the Protestant ethic of trade:[33]

> We are - and, till its good purposes, which are many, have been all achieved, and we can become something better, long may we continue such! - a busy, enterprizing, and commercial nation. The habits attached to this character must, if there exist no adequate counterpoise, inevitably lead us, under the specious names of utility, practical knowledge, and so forth, to look at all things thro' the medium of the market, and to estimate the Worth of all pursuits and attainments by their marketable value. In this does the Spirit of Trade consist.

The only effective counterbalance to this is provided not by the religion of the Quakers, which on the contrary encourages such worldly transactions, but the religion of sixteenth- and seventeenth-century England. Next, Coleridge turns his attention to 'this overbalance as displayed in the commercial world itself'. One example of this is the 'periodical Revolutions of Credit'. This was a newly recognised phenomenon and that Coleridge was aware of it shows his astuteness in following contemporary affairs. While Coleridge recognised the cyclical theory accurately enough, as a cause of the economic depression, he found its implied cruelty repugnant. The passage in which he makes the point illustrates how vivid a prose writer Coleridge could be, even when the material was unpromising:[34]

> We shall perhaps be told too, that the very Evils of this System; even the periodical *crash* itself, are to be regarded but as so much superfluous steam ejected by the Escape Pipes and Safety Valves of a self-regulating Machine: and lastly, that in a free and trading country *all things find their level*. ... Thus instead of the position, that all things *find*, it would be less

equivocal and far more descriptive of the fact to say, that Things are always *finding*, their level: which might be taken as the paraphrase or ironical definition of a storm, ... But Persons are not *Things* – but Man does not find his level. Neither in body nor in soul does the Man find his level! After a hard and calamitous season, during which the thousand Wheels of some vast manufactory had remained silent as a frozen water-fall, be it that plenty has returned and that Trade has once more become brisk and stirring: go, ask the overseer, and question the parish doctor, whether the workman's health and temperance with the staid and respectful Manners best taught by the inward dignity of conscious self-support have found *their* level again!

Here Coleridge demonstrates that his concern is ultimately not political but moral, and he amplifies this in the conclusion to the *Lay Sermon*, where he expands his motto:[35]

Let us become a better people, and the reform of all the public (real or supposed) grievances, which we use as pegs whereon to hang our own errors and defects, will follow of itself. In short, let every man measure his efforts by his power and his sphere of action, and do all he can do! Let him contribute money where he cannot act personally; *but let him act personally and in detail* wherever it is practicable. Let us palliate where we cannot cure, comfort where we cannot relieve; and for the rest rely upon the promise of the King of Kings by the mouth of his Prophet, 'BLESSED ARE YE THAT SOW BESIDE ALL WATERS'.

This moral concern is Coleridge's constant in all his political thought. More specifically, it is a concern that we should each of us act as feeling and thinking beings. This is made clear, for instance, in both the political poetry, especially 'Fears in Solitude', and the early journalism, especially the demolition of Pitt in the *Morning Post* for 19 March 1800. This in turn involves a recognition that economic and political activity involves 'people not things' and results in such practical action as the support for Sir Robert Peel's Cotton Factory Workers Bill.

While the *Lay Sermons* are relatively short works deliberately limited in intention, *The Friend* was a much more ambitious undertaking perhaps best summed up in Coleridge's own words:[36]

> THE FRIEND does not indeed exclude from his plan
> occasional interludes; and vacations of innocent entertainment
> and promiscuous information, but still in the main he proposes
> to himself the communication of such delight as rewards the
> march of Truth, rather than to collect the flowers which
> diversify its track, in order to present them apart from the
> homely yet foodful or medicinable herbs, among which they
> had grown. To refer men's opinions to their absolute
> principles, and thence their feelings to the appropriate objects,
> and in their due degrees: and finally, to apply the principles
> thus ascertained, to the formation of stedfast convictions
> concerning the most important questions of Politics, Morality,
> and Religion – these are to be the objects and the contents of
> his work.

Here is the same emphasis on the individual rather than the group and it is in the training of this individual that Coleridge offers his help and advice in *The Friend*, as the title suggests. *The Friend* is a long work and at first sight formless, going on merely until it stops. The earlier periodical version could hardly avoid this but in the 1818 version there is a quite clearly defined pattern. The work begins with sixteen introductory essays, broadly speaking, on the subject of communication of truth, especially as related to the liberty of the press. After this comes the first landing-place, which Coleridge describes on an analogy with a 'Magnificent stair-case'.[37]

The first landing-place contains an essay comparing Erasmus and Voltaire, Luther and Rousseau, an essay recounting Luther's encounter with the devil at the Wartburg, a further commentary on ghosts and apparitions, a résumé of the introductory essays and, finally, the distinction between reason and understanding. This may seem rather hard work for a landing-place but in fact the writing is discursive and easy to follow and this in itself refreshes the mind. The other landing-places are much less demanding. The story of Maria Eleanore Schöning, for instance, is a swiftly moving narrative. But before that is the central section, misleadingly entitled 'Section the First', but more helpfully subtitled 'On the Principles of Political Knowledge'. Then, after the second landing-place, the final section, after an introductory section in which Coleridge reprints a letter from 'Mathetes' and the reply to it by Wordsworth, elucidates the grounds of morals and religion. This includes the essay on method, which Coleridge salvaged from the introduction to the *Encyclopaedia Metropolitana*, where it had been considerably altered by the publishers. Finally, the third landing-place is taken up with sketches of the life of Sir Alexander Ball, under whom Coleridge served as public secretary while he was in Malta.

As this short survey indicates the work is far from formless. Even the landing-places have relevance to the main political theme: the story of Maria Schöning is a tragedy of the conflict of a good citizen and a bad state, and the life of Sir Alexander Ball is an exemplum of the good ruler. Not that this structure makes the *Friend* easy reading, for that Coleridge made no claim, but it does help to make the difficulty of the subject matter less daunting. The third section of *The Friend* – which is not, strictly speaking, political, although related to politics by the vital cord of morality – will be dealt with in the philosophy chapter. The first two sections contain the core of Coleridge's political principles and are therefore of greater interest, I think, than the more narrowly based political scheme discussed in *On Church and State*.

The section in which Coleridge deals with the question of censorship of the press and the communication of truth is closely related to his treatment of the same subject in the *Lay Sermons*, and was doubtless made more important to Coleridge by his own experience as a journalist. In Coleridge's day, the press was closely and clandestinely controlled by the government, who used all sorts of methods to gain control over the way the news appeared. Only seldom did this include suppression of articles, though this did happen to Coleridge's article on the re-appointment of the Duke of York. More frequently, control was exercised by positive inducements, especially regular financial aid, and A. Aspinall's book, *Politics and the Press c. 1780-1850*, gives an insight into these transactions. It is this corruption of the press which compelled Coleridge to speak frankly to Stuart in a letter of May 1816. He praised the paper for its stand during the Napoleonic War, 'you did more against the French Scheme of Continental Domination than the Duke of Wellington has done', but since then he regrets:[38]

> the Courier itself has gradually lost that sanctifying Spirit,
> which was the Life of it's Life, & without which even the best
> and soundest principles lose half their effect on the human

mind – I mean, the *faith* in the *faith* of the person or paper which brings them forward.

Stuart took this to heart and decided to leave Street, who was more impressed by 'Nods & Shakes of the Hand from Lord This or That;' to conduct the paper in his own way. Here Coleridge speaks out bravely against a commonplace abuse; and less tactfully he made the point publicly in the *Biographia*.[39] At this time, the Establishment of England, afraid for its own existence, wished to curb the production of newspapers and pamphlets which could raise popular feeling to revolutionary pitch. Against this background, Coleridge's defence of the freedom of the press becomes a positive political gesture. The essays proceed logically from an assertion of the importance of the truth to a discussion of the difficulties of conveying it adequately to a wide audience. To a propensity to deliver what he calls 'pious frauds', Coleridge attributes the religious crisis of the French Revolution:[40]

> to this doctrine chiefly, and to the practices derived from it,
> we must attribute the utter corruption of the Religion itself
> for so many ages, and even now over so large a portion of the
> civilized world. By a system of accommodating Truth to
> Falsehood, the Pastors of the Church gradually changed the life
> and light of the Gospel into the very superstitions which they
> were commissioned to disperse, and thus paganized Christianity
> in order to *christen* Paganism. At this very hour Europe groans
> and bleeds in consequence. ... Truth, Virtue, and Happiness,
> may be distinguished from each other, but cannot be divided.
> They subsist by a mutual coinherence, which gives a shadow
> of divinity even to our human nature.

This is the framework from which Coleridge operates, and it is as much religious and moral as it is political.

This does not mean, however, that Coleridge was unaware of the difficulties which beset the diffusion of the truth among the masses. Recognising that most people have neither the time nor the desire nor the training to pursue higher truth, he asks:[41]

> To whom then do we owe our ameliorated condition? To the
> successive Few in every age (more indeed in one generation
> than in another, but relatively to the mass of mankind always
> few) who by the intensity and permanence of their action

have compensated for the limited sphere, within which it is at any one time intelligible; and whose good deeds posterity reverence in their results,

This is the beginning of the idea of a 'clerisy' which was more fully developed in *On Church and State*.

From this assertion of the fundamental value of Truth, Coleridge proceeds to discuss the question of the liberty of the press. Here, he stands by the dictum of Milton, one of Coleridge's few:[42]

the Law of England has done well and concluded wisely in proceeding on the principle so clearly worded by Milton: that a book should be as freely admitted into the world as any other birth; and if it prove a monster, who denies but that it may justly be burnt or sunk in the sea?

Coleridge recognises the difficulties which the law of libel raises:[43]

The statute of libel is a vast aviary, which incages the awakening cock and the geese whose alarum preserved the capitol, no less than the babbling magpye and ominous screech-owl.

But he fears that if all restraint is removed:

every principle, feeling that binds the citizen to his country and the spirit to its Creator, will be undermined – not by reasoning, for from that there is no danger; but – by the mere habit of hearing them reviled and scoffed at with impunity.

From this, Coleridge passes to tolerance and toleration, and he boldly affirms that a recognition of the importance of truth carries with it a duty to recognise falsehood:[44]

There is one heart for the whole mighty mass of Humanity, and every pulse in each particular vessel strives to beat in concert with it. He who asserts that truth is of no importance except in the sense of sincerity, confounds sense with madness, and the word of God with a dream. If the power of reasoning be the gift of the Supreme Reason, that we be sedulous, yea, and *militant* in the endeavour to reason aright, is his implied Command.

Hence, Coleridge sees his duty as the communication of truth:[45]

I have not a deeper conviction on earth, than that the
principles both of Taste, Morals, and Religion, which are
taught in the commonest books of recent composition, are
false, injurious, and debasing. If these sentiments should be just,
the consequences must be so important, that every
well-educated man, who professes them in sincerity, deserves a
patient hearing.

The central section of The Friend properly begins with the distinction between reason and understanding. This complex issue, as
the context makes plain, results from Coleridge's perplexity about
Rousseau's claims for reason, which resulted in such a disastrous
political system. Coleridge is concerned to demonstrate that the
equal possession of reason, which he does not dispute, is not grounds
for assuming total equality:[46]

> though the reason itself is the same in all men, yet the means of
> exercising it, and the materials (i.e. the facts and ideas) on
> which it is exercised, being possessed in very different degrees
> by different persons, the practical Result is, of course, equally
> different - and the whole ground work of Rousseau's
> Philosophy ends in a mere Nothingism.

So it is that the political section of The Friend is dominated by an
examination of Rousseau's politics. First of all, Coleridge asserts the
importance of law, more especially of law voluntarily agreed to
rather than law enforced by the sword, for:[47]

> if there be any difference between a Government and a band
> of robbers, an act of consent must be supposed on the part of
> the people governed.

Coleridge applies the test of reason sternly and asks why, if reason
is equal in all, women and children are excluded or, conversely, if
there are grounds for the exclusion of women and children, why
not also for the exclusion of the poor and infirm? Then he
concludes:[48]

> That Reason should be our guide and governor is an
> undeniable Truth, and all our notion of right and wrong is
> built thereon: for the whole moral nature of man originated
> and subsists in his Reason. From Reason alone can we derive
> the principles which our Understandings are to apply, the Ideal
> to which by means of our Understandings we should

endeavour to approximate. This however gives no proof that Reason alone ought to govern and direct human beings, either as Individuals or as States. It ought not to do this, because it cannot. The Laws of Reason are unable to satisfy the first conditions of Human Society.

This is because:

the proof is wanting that the first and most general applications and exertions of the power of man can be definitely regulated by Reason unaided by the positive and conventional laws in the formation of which the Understanding must be our guide, and which become just because they happen to be expedient.

More precisely, this is because the object of founding a state was not 'the protection of their lives but of their property' and 'it is impossible to deduce the Right of Property from Pure Reason'. There was a time when Coleridge would have gone from this to deny the virtue of property, but the decline of the early pantisocratic ideals in the face of Southey's possible inheritance and preferment had taught him that this was contradictory to the nature of man. Coleridge goes on to attack, instead, the 'rights of man' school of political thinking, though conceding:[49]

the system had its golden side for the noblest minds: and I should act the part of a coward, if I disguised my convictions, that the errors of the Aristocratic party were full as gross, and far less excusable.

He lengthily rebukes the English aristocratic party for pushing those who with 'warm benevolence and the enthusiasm for liberty' sympathised with the early French revolutionaries into an extreme position. Much of this section comes from an article which Coleridge wrote for the *Morning Post*, probably in October 1802,[50] entitled 'Once a Jacobin always a Jacobin' and its relevance to Coleridge's own experience cannot be overlooked. However, as so often with Coleridge, the personal is transcended and a more general principle deduced:[51]

From my earliest manhood, it was an axiom in Politics with me, that in every country where property prevailed, property must be the grand basis of government; and that that government was the best, in which the power or political influence of the individual was in proportion to his property, provided that the free circulation of property was not impeded by any positive laws and customs, nor the tendency of wealth to accumulate in abiding masses unduly encouraged.

The important proviso added in 1809 demonstrated how Coleridge's conception of the state was that it should preserve a balance between conservatism and change.

Coleridge next turns his attention to high war-time levels of taxation, which he defends on the grounds that taxes do not take away the nation's wealth but redistribute it. This seems not to have been sound economically for the time[52] but it provides an interesting example of Coleridge's willingness to see the state intervene to re-allocate national resources to the benefit of a wider section of the population. This is in contrast to his refusal to see any advantage in an increased suffrage, which in turn leads him to ask:[53]

What are the ends of Government? They are of two kinds, negative and positive. The negative ends of Government are the protection of life, of personal freedom, of property, of reputation, and of religion, from foreign and from domestic attacks. The positive ends are, 1st. to make the means of subsistence more easy to each individual: 2d. that in addition to the necessaries of life he should derive from the union and division of labour a share of the comforts and conveniences which humanize and ennoble his nature; and at the same time the power of perfecting himself in his own branch of industry by having those things which he needs provided for him by others among his fellow-citizens; including the tools and raw or manufactured materials necessary for his own condition and that of his children ... 3dly. The Hope of bettering his own condition and that of his children . . . Lastly, the development of those faculties which are essential to his human nature by the knowledge of his moral and religious duties, and the increase of his intellectual powers in as great a degree as is compatible with the other ends of the social union, and does not involve a contradiction.

Coleridge finds his own government satisfactory on the first three counts but wanting on the fourth. For a possible remedy to this deficiency Coleridge refers the reader to the end of this section, a reprinting of the 1795 'Moral and Political Lecture', which emphasises the value of 'domestic affection', and while he affirms his 'faith in the doctrine of philosophical necessity ... That vice is the effect of error and the offspring of surrounding circumstances, the object of condolence not of anger',[54] he reacts against Godwin's repudiation of private benevolence. This represents an important development in Coleridge's political thought:[55]

> The searcher after truth must love and be loved; for general benevolence is a necessary motive to constancy of pursuit; and this general benevolence is begotten and rendered permanent by social and domestic affections. Let us beware of that proud philosophy, which affects to inculcate philanthropy while it denounces every home-born feeling by which it is produced and nurtured. The paternal and filial duties discipline the heart and prepare it for the love of all mankind. The intensity of private attachments encourages, not prevents, universal Benevolence.

It remained central, as Coleridge's treatment of international law shows:[56]

> Patriotism itself is a necessary link in the golden chain of our affections and virtues, and turns away with indignant scorn from the false Philosophy or mistaken Religion, which should persuade him that Cosmopolitism is nobler than Nationality, and the human race a sublimer object of love than a people;

The assertion:[57]

> The law of nations is the law of common honesty, modified by the circumstances in which States differ from individuals.

is illustrated by reference to the British seizure of the Danish fleet when that seemingly neutral fleet was a threat to Britain's safety. He parallels this with the anecdote of men attacked by a robber, in which one man steals the fowling piece of the other, a Quaker, to shoot the robber and protect his life. Coleridge adduces a principle of self-protection to explain the seeming advocacy of expediency and the argument he offers is cogent and convincing, fully illustrating how adherence to principle need not incapacitate man or country when it comes to safe political action.

It is not possible to do justice to the depth of Coleridge's thinking, much less to the comprehensive discussion of the wide range of political activities, in such a short summary, and there is much that could have been dealt with more fully. Earlier I compared *The Friend* with the *Biographia*, Coleridge's only other large scale prose work, but *The Friend* has never taken its place beside the *Biographia* as the prose masterpiece that, despite its difficulties, it is. Of course, Coleridge has long and rightly been recognised as a great literary critic and he enjoys no such reputation as a political commentator. Nevertheless, *The Friend* deserves more recognition for its work on the overlapping areas of politics and morality, and because it represents the best of the mature thought of a great mind on a subject of central interest.

*On Church and State* (1830) is remarkable among Coleridge's prose works for its adherence to a preconceived plan given in the title 'The Constitution of Church and State according to the idea of each'. Coleridge deals with the State first then the Church and gives especial attention, as befits a work intended as an Aid 'towards a Right Judgment on the late Catholic Bill' to the Church of Rome, which he designates the Church of Anti-Christ. To twentieth-century eyes this seems such a harsh judgment that it is worth emphasising the Coleridge's objection to Roman Catholicism is political rather than religious:[58]

> it is ... my full conviction that the rights and doctrines, the *agenda et credenda* of the Roman Catholics, could we separate them from the adulterating ingredients combined with, and the use made of them by the sacerdotal Mamelukes of the Romish monarchy for the support of the Papacy and Papal hierarchy, would neither have brought about, nor have sufficed to justify, the conclusive separation under Leo X.

In the work as a whole, Coleridge depicts a society which he thought would best reconcile 'the two antagonist powers or opposite interests of the State under which all other state interests are comprised, ... those of permanence and progression'.[59] This is Coleridge's solution to the most pressing problem of his time, how to preserve the establishment from the corrosive effects of reform or the devastation of revolution. That he seems to favour permanence rather than progression illustrates how the French Revolution had changed the hopes of Coleridge's generation into mistrust and fear.

Even as late as 1862, Disraeli could refer to a Reform Bill which gave only a limited suffrage as 'a leap into the dark'. Coleridge was, however, aware that unless there was scope for change within the system, repression would lead to revolt. Southey too, although more of a Tory than Coleridge, was aware of the need for concessions, particularly to the new urban working masses, and only Wordsworth of the three former Revolutionary sympathisers entrenched himself behind a wall of old-fashioned High Toryism.[60]

Coleridge describes the National Church in a passage which looks back to Elizabethan times as:[61]

> the third great venerable estate of the realm; the first being the estate of the land-owners or possessors of a fixed property, consisting of the two classes of the Barons and Franklins; and the second comprizing the merchants, the manufacturers, free artizans, and the distributive class. To comprehend, therefore, the true character of this third estate in which the reserved Nationality was vested, we must first ascertain the end or national purpose for which such reservation was made. Now as in the first estate the permanency of the nation was provided for; and in the second estate its progressiveness and personal freedom; while in the king the cohesion by interdependence, and the unity of the country, were established; there remains for the third estate only that interest which is the ground, the necessary antecedent condition of both the former.

This brings Coleridge back to principles, to reason and to the assertion:[62]

> In fine, religion, true or false, is and ever has been the centre of gravity in a realm, to which all other things must and will accommodate themselves.

Hence, Coleridge's national church is not specifically Christian but rather a repository of higher values. For Coleridge, of course, it must preferably be a Christian church but not in any narrow sense:[63]

> The Christian Church, I say, is no state, kingdom or realm of this world; nor is it an estate of any such realm, kingdom or state; but it is the appropriated opposite to them all collectively – the sustaining, correcting, befriending opposite of the World,

the compensating counterforce to the inherent and inevitable evils and defects of the state, and without reference to its better or worse construction as a particular state; while whatever is beneficent and humanizing in the aims, tendencies, and proper objects of the State, the Christian Church collects in itself as a *focus*, to radiate them back in a higher quality;

Coleridge goes beyond the theoretical to show how the nation should set aside a portion of its wealth to maintain the national church and, specifically, pastors and teachers in every parish. This latter group, Coleridge's 'clerisy', were to be responsible for radiating higher values, remedying the deficiency which he had remarked in *The Friend* of a 'knowledge of moral and religious duties'. The importance of individual recognition of moral truth, when pushed to logical conclusions and provided with all the paraphernalia to make it realisable, seems very out of tune with political and social reality. Nevertheless, Coleridge's work on this had considerable influence, not only on J. S. Mill but also on F. D. Maurice, the Christian Socialist, and on Thomas Arnold,[64] and so helped to bring about a climate of opinion which made the Tory government of the 1860s see the need to follow up the extended suffrage with other social reforms, including more readily available education.

I have dealt briefly with *On Church and State* because it has attracted more attention elsewhere, notably in D. P. Calleo's full-length study *Coleridge and the Idea of the Modern State*. The work is, I think, more valuable because it demonstrates how Coleridge considered the practical problems than because of any intrinsic value in the proposals he makes. Whereas Coleridge, as a poet and philosopher, is well qualified to discuss the underlying principles of political thinking, the same qualifications do not seem sufficient to create a viable system. Indeed, even J. S. Mill, who sets such value on the work, does so chiefly because it affirms the need for non-utilitarian values rather than because it promulgates a theory of how these can be incorporated into the state.

Coleridge was not really a political thinker, as he would have been ready to admit, and in many ways he was out of sympathy with political studies, especially 'the sublime philosophy of the sect of Economists. They worship a kind of non-entity under the different words, the State, the Whole, the Society, &c'.[65] At the

171

same time, as a man thinking and feeling with other men, he involved himself in the struggles and ideas of his time. From 1795 to 1830 he demonstrates his concern for the government of his country. If that concern was moral or educational rather than narrowly political, it nevertheless makes a valuable contribution to our understanding of one of the most active periods in the development of human society.

# 7
# On Religion

Coleridge, whose father had been vicar and schoolmaster of Ottery
St Mary, always considered himself a religious man and a Christian,
even when political sympathies allied him with atheists like Thelwall and Godwin. While it is true that the preponderance of his
writing on religion comes from his later years, there is a sense in
which all his writing is religious, in so far as it is nowhere totally
free from the all-pervading moral-religious-philosophical desire to
find 'unity in multeity'. This underlies the poetry and much of the
critical prose and, as was seen, in politics Coleridge often preferred
religiously supported moral solutions to political ones. In his letters
too, Coleridge from his early years focused his attention on religion,
often explaining a change of heart. These changes are no less
dramatic seemingly than those in other areas of Coleridge's thought.
The Coleridge who in 1794 wrote of his fears that in America Mrs
Fricker would be 'teaching the Infants *Christianity*, – I mean – that
mongrel whelp that goes under it's name'[1] and was reluctant to
have his own children baptised, in 1832 stood by his long-estranged
wife at the christening of their granddaughter Edith, a symbol of all
that is of the Establishment in English religion. Coleridge's attitude
to organised religion was always ambiguous, as the following
anecdote shows. The scene is a Welsh inn at Bala:[2]

Shortly after, in came a Clergyman well drest, and with him 4
other Gentlemen – I was asked for a public Character – I gave,
Dr Priestley – the Clergyman whispered his Neighbour who it
seems, is the Apothecary of the Parish – (Republicans!)
– Accordingly when the *Doctor* (as they call apothecaries) was to
have given a name, 'I gives a sentiment, Gemmen! May all
Republicans be *gull*oteen'd! [']Up starts the Democrat 'May all
Fools be gulloteen'd – and then you will be first! ['] – Fool,

173

Rogue, Traitor, Liar &c flew in each other's faces in hailstorms of Vociferation. This is nothing in Wales – they *make* it –: necessary vent-holes for the sulphureous Fumes of their Temper! I endeavoured to calm the Tempest by observing – 'that however different our Political Opinions might be, the appearance of a Clergyman in the Company assured me, that we were all *Christians* – though I found it rather difficult to reconcile the last sentiment with the spirit of Christianity.' 'Pho.' quoth the Clergyman! 'Christianity! Why an't at *Church* now – are we? The Gemmans Sentiment was a very good one, because it shows him to be *sincere* in his principles.'

Here the connection between religious and political thought which was so much a part of general thinking at the time of the French Revolution is clearly apparent. It is possible to see in the trend towards greater religious orthodoxy a parallel to the adoption of more conservative, if not more purely Tory, views in politics. However, Coleridge's religious thinking is also closely involved in his interior development. The move away from the optimism of Hartleian necessarianism to a deeply felt dependence on the atonement of Christ for salvation, which is reflected in many of Coleridge's mature works, is a development which underpins the failures of Coleridge's life – his marriage, his opium-addiction, his loss of friends. To these twin strands of religious thought Coleridge brought the experience of his literary criticism, which enabled him to turn to the interpretation of the Bible for help in his desire to reconcile his inner needs with the orthodox creeds of the English church. He did not publish his biblical scholarship, though it is reflected in, for instance, his comments on Luther's *Table Talk* in *Literary Remains*,[3] but his work in this field is not without importance because, together with his plea for greater freedom in interpreting the Bible made in *Confessions of an Inquiring Spirit*, it anticipates the Victorian interest in the field.

The ground of Coleridge's faith was, however, personal and hard won, so the Confessio Fidei, dated 3 November 1816, reflects in silent contradiction the framework of his early thought:[4]

I. I believe that I am a Free Agent, inasmuch as, and so far as I have a will, which renders me justly responsible for my actions, omissive as well as commissive. Likewise that I possess

Reason, or a law of Right and Wrong, which uniting with my sense of moral responsibility constitutes the voice of Conscience.

II.   Hence it becomes my absolute Duty to believe, and I do believe, that there is a God, that is a Being in whom Supreme Reason and a most holy Will are one with an infinite Power; and that all holy Will is coincident with the Will of God, and therefore secure in its ultimate Consequences by His Omnipotence; – having, if such similitude be not unlawful, such a relation to the goodness of the Almighty, as a perfect Time-piece will have to the Sun.

The inner integrity which this demonstrates gives his writings on religion their value, for, considered as an orthodox Christian commentator, Coleridge betrays, I think, one fundamental flaw. He had, in the last analysis, no sense of the reality and otherness of a divine power (notice his indefinite 'a God') so that his religious writing lacks that dimension of faith reflected in a child's simple belief in Bible stories and at a different level in the one phrase 'I know that my Redeemer liveth'. In fact, Coleridge's religious thought is concentrated on the believer, or would-be believer, and here, more than anywhere else, he is quarrying his own mind and experiences with ruthless honesty. This self-centred religious interest is reflected in the Confessio Fidei. It is because he believes he is a free agent (a belief which he attained only after abandoning his youthful necessarianism) that he believes in a God. God is needed to make the system complete, but it is a system whose focus is Coleridge himself.

This is not the product of a naturally self-centred mind, although self-knowledge was always at the core of Coleridge's philosophy, but I think the result of winning his freedom from the various influences which from the first set up impossible conflicts. The family belonged to the Anglican establishment, as the memorials bearing the Coleridge name in the parish church of Ottery St Mary still show. The natural piety of Coleridge, as a boy, we must assume was satisfied by this, but at school outside influences began to make their mark so that 'bewildered by theological controversy' found, no doubt, in his reading, he sought solutions from the minds of others:[5]

In my friendless wanderings on our *leave-days*, ... highly was I delighted, if any passenger, especially if he were drest in black,

175

would enter into conversation with me. For I soon found the means of directing it to my favourite subjects.

> Of Providence, fore-knowledge, will, and fate,
> Fix'd fate, free will, foreknowledge absolute,
> And found no end in wandering mazes lost.

From this time onwards Coleridge's mind was to take the impression of many conflicting views. The notes to the Collected Coleridge edition of the *1795 Lectures* demonstrate the extent of his reading. Contact with Southey left its mark too, and in Bristol Coleridge easily became part of the Unitarian circle, taking up a connection formed, largely for political reasons, in Cambridge. It seems that Coleridge gave occasional sermons and was on the brink of joining the Unitarian ministry, when the Wedgwoods' annuity allowed him to make his first really personal stand in religious matters. This is best seen in Coleridge's letter to the prominent Bristol Unitarian, the Reverend J. P. Estlin:[6]

> To the cause of Religion I solemnly devote all my best
> faculties – and if I wish to acquire knowledge as a philosopher
> and fame as a poet, I pray for grace that I may continue to
> feel what I now feel, that my greatest reason for wishing the
> one & the other, is that I may be enabled by my knowledge
> to defend Religion ably, and by my reputation to draw
> attention to the defence of it ... While I could not devote my
> time to the service of Religion without receiving money from a
> particular congregation, I subdued the struggles of reluctance &
> would have submitted to receive it – Now I am enabled – as I
> have received freely, freely to give.

Some of this is special pleading but the core of it represents the reality of the situation. Coleridge did not want to be tied by a salary to a particular religious view, and at the same time he did think that the furtherance of a religious philosophy was part of his life's work. So it turned out to be. Coleridge's own system of belief does not fit into any orthodox creed; on the other hand, it would be hard to find any sustained passage in his works which did not add an implicit religious dimension to its main content.

Coleridge's first published religious work was the poem 'Religious Musings', which depends heavily on Hartley and Berkeley and emphasises Jesus as a 'Man or Woes' in true Unitarian fashion, ignoring his divine attributes. This was followed by the series of 'Lectures on Revealed Religion Its Corruptions and Political Views' given specifically at the request of a group of Bristol Unitarians. There is no record of the delivery of the lectures and they have survived in a copy taken from Coleridge's original notes by E. H. Coleridge. The probability is that they were delivered from 19 May to 9 or 12 June 1795 at the Assembly Coffee-house on the Quay, Bristol. We know nothing of their reception and little of Coleridge's attitude to the lectures, which are heavily dependent on his reading. After this, for twenty years no explicitly religious works were published, though *The Friend* and the *Lay Sermons* have an important religious content. In these middle years, while Coleridge's belief in the value of religion was by no means diminished, he was uncertain what exactly he believed. The notebooks and letters of these middle years give some useful indications of Coleridge's changing attitudes which will be supplemented when we have an edition of the marginalia which dates the comments. Among a cluster of notebook entries in the early months of 1805 which deal with religious problems, Coleridge wrote the following:[7]

> 7 or 8 years ago ... my mind then wavering in its necessary passage from Unitarianism (which as I have often said is the Religion of a man, whose Reason would make him an Atheist but whose Heart and Common sense will not permit him to be so) thro' Spinosism into Plato and St. John/No Christ, No God! – This I now feel with all its needful evidence, of the Understanding: would to God, my spirit were made conform thereto – that No Trinity, no God – That Unitarianism in all its Forms is Idolatry ... O that this Conviction may work upon me and in me/and that my mind may be made up as to the character of Jesus, and of his historical Christianity, as clearly as it is of the Logos and intellectual and spiritual Christianity, – that I may be made to know either their especial and peculiar Union, or their absolute disunion in any peculiar sense.

Three letters written in October 1806 reflect further developments. The two letters to his young nephew are more personal, that to Thomas Clarkson more philosophical. To George Fricker Coleridge wrote:[8]

I was for many years a Socinian; and at times almost a Naturalist, but sorrow, and ill health, and disappointment in the only deep wish I had ever cherished, forced me to look into myself; I read the New Testament again, and I became fully convinced, that Socinianism was not only not the doctrine of the New Testament, but that it scarcely deserved the name of a religion in any sense.

This concession was not enough for the more orthodox Fricker, and Coleridge in his next letter is pushed into probing further. Coleridge describes his earlier statement:[9]

as comprising such doctrines, as a clear Head & honest Heart assisted by divine Grace might in part discover by self-examination and the light of natural conscience, & which *efficiently* and *practically* believed would prepare the way for the *peculiar Doctrine* of Christianity, namely, Salvation by the Cross of Christ. I meant these doctrines as the Skeleton, to which the death & Mediation of Christ with the supervention of the Holy Ghost were to add the Flesh, and Blood, Muscles, nerves, & vitality. – God of his goodness grant, that I may arrive at a more living Faith in these last, than I now feel. What I now feel is only a very strong *presentiment* of their Truth and Importance aided by a thorough conviction of the hollowness of all other Systems. Alas! my moral being is too untranquil.

The letter to Thomas Clarkson examines much the same material, but more extensively and in a more abstract way. Here, Coleridge affirms a belief in the 'thrice sacred doctrine of the Tri-unity' and then moves on to consider the soul. This reveals Coleridge's persistent interest in the fundamental nature of man's thought processes, which are now seen in a religious light:[10]

with a certain degree of satisfaction to my own mind I can define the human Soul to be that class of Being, as far as we are permitted to know, the first and lowest of that Class, which is endued with a reflex consciousness of it's own continuousness, and the great end and purpose of all it's energies & sufferings is the growth of that reflex consciousness: that class of Being too, in which the Individual is capable of

being itself contemplated as a Species of itself, namely, by it's
conscious continuousness moving on in an unbroken Line,
while at the same time the whole Species is capable of being
regarded as one Individual.... A spacious field here opens itself
for moral reflection, both for Faith, and for Consolation, when
we consider the growth of consciousness (and of what kind
our's is, our *conscience* sufficiently reveals to us: for of what use
or meaning could *Conscience* be to a Being, who in any state
of it's Existence should become to itself utterly lost, and
entirely new?) as the end of our earthly Being – when we
reflect too how habits of Vice of all Kinds tend to retard this
growth, and how all our sufferings tend to extend & open it
out, and how all our Virtues & virtuous and loving Affections
tend to bind it, and as it were to inclose the fleeting
Retrospect as within a wall! – And again, what sublime
motives to Self-respect with humble Hope does not the Idea
give, that each Soul is a Species in itself; and what Impulses to
more than brotherly Love of our fellow-creatures, the Idea
that all men form as it were, one Soul! –

I have quoted this passage at length because it shows Coleridge
beginning to recognise how his various ideas about human perception and association lead naturally to a religious conclusion. It
also casts light on his view of morals in politics and illustrates one
of the fundamental ideas of the 'Ancient Mariner', that damage to
part is damage to the whole of creation.

As late as December 1813, at the height of the opium crisis,
Coleridge was praying for 'a living instead a reasoning Faith!'[11] and
a letter to Cottle in April 1814 expands on this theme. The letter
is in response to a question about Coleridge's view of the Trinity,
and its orthodoxy relates, no doubt, to Coleridge's acceptance of the
hopelessness of his 'passion after an earthly good' – which must refer
to Sara Hutchinson, and to the break with Wordsworth, and most
important, to his recognition of his inability to break the opium
habit. Now, Coleridge is prepared to recognise the insufficiency of
man's reason and accept the value of revelation:[12]

You ask me my views of the *Trinity*. I accept the doctrine, not
as deduced from human reason, in its grovelling capacity for
comprehending spritual things, but as the clear revelation of
Scripture.

This important concession marks an epoch in Coleridge's
religious development but, as we would expect, he was not for long
happy to relegate 'human reason', and before the letter is finished
Coleridge is trying to shed 'at least, a glimpse of light' by 'analogical
reasoning'. The triumphant tone of the conclusion of the letter does
not conceal an unresolved conflict between reason and revelation.[13]

In continuation of this reasoning, if God who is light, the Sun
of the Moral World, should in his union of Infinite Wisdom,
Power, and Goodness, and from all Eternity, have ordained
that an emanation from himself (for aught we know, an
essential emanation, as light is inseparable from the luminary
of day) should not only have existed in his Son, in the fulness
of time to be united to a mortal body, but that a like
emanation from himself (also perhaps essential) should have
constituted the Holy Spirit, who, without losing his ubiquity,
was more especially sent to the lower earth, *by* the Son, *at* the
impulse of the Father, then, in the most comprehensive sense,
God, and his Son, Jesus Christ, and the Holy Ghost, are ONE
– 'Three Persons in one God,' and/thus form the true Trinity
in Unity .... Yet this divine doctrine of the Trinity is to be
received, not because it is or can be clear to finite
apprehension, but, (in reiteration of the argument) because the
Scriptures, in their unsophisticated interpretation expressly state
it. The Trinity, therefore, from its important aspects, and
Biblical prominence, is the grand article of faith, and the
foundation of the whole christian system.

Even as Coleridge grew older and adopted a more orthodox
stand in religion, he could not abandon his belief in Reason, so that
finally this became for him an organ of faith, or as he said:[14]

Faith subsists in the *synthesis* of the reason and the
individual will. By virtue of the latter therefore it must be an
energy, and inasmuch as it relates to the whole moral man, it
must be exerted in each and all of his constituents or incidents,
faculties or tendencies;- it must be a total, not a partial; a
continuous, not a desultory or occasional energy. And by
virtue of the former, that is, reason, faith must be a light, a
form of knowing, a beholding of truth.

The struggles which accompanied these changes of belief were more deeply felt than those in other aspects of his thought, which may explain his silence until the appearance in 1825 of *Aids to Reflection*. In accordance with this unsureness, the work was first planned as Coleridge states in his offer to the publisher in a letter of 8 August 1823:[15]

Aids to Reflection: or Beauties and Characteristics of Archbishop Leighton, extracted from his various Writings, and arranged on a principle of connection under the three Heads, of 1. Philosophical and Miscellaneous. 2. Moral and Prudential. 3. Spiritual – with a Life of Leighton & a critique on his writings and opinions – with Notes throughout by the Editor.

During the planning and writing of the book, Leighton receded and Coleridge advanced to the foreground so that when the book appeared, its title page bore the following:[16]

Aids to Reflection in the formation of a manly character on the several grounds of Prudence, Morality, and Religion. Illustrated by select passages from our elder divines, especially from Archbishop Leighton

and the name of Coleridge as author was prominently and rightly displayed.

The book consists mainly of short paragraphs, called aphorisms and numbered, in three sections, entitled Prudential Aphorisms, Moral and Religious Aphorisms and Aphorisms on Spiritual Religion. These are rounded off by a conclusion and accompanied at intervals by longer notes. The peculiar form of the work does not make it easy to read consecutively, though there is a clear intention that the book should be considered as a whole. In the preface, Coleridge explains that it is a didactic work, generally intended for those who wish to study 'the principles of moral architecture' but '*especially* designed for the studious young at the close of their education or on their first entrance into the duties of manhood and the rights of self-government' and he summarises the objects of the book in the order of their comparative importance. First comes 'the value of the Science of Words'; second, 'the *distinct* characters of Prudence, Morality and Religion'; third, 'the momentous distinction between Reason and Understanding' and fourth, 'To exhibit a full and consistent Scheme of the Christian Dispensation'.[17]

Coleridge was obviously not displeased with the work in its final form and planned to follow *Aids to Reflection* with six disquisitions. These he lists in a letter to Hessey, the publisher, as:[18]

1. ON FAITH
2. ON THE EUCHARIST, doctrinally and historically.
3. On the PHILOSOPHY OF PRAYER.
4. On the Hebrew Prophets & the prophetic *Gift* (not more than four pages).
5. On the Church – & the true character of the Romish Church.
6. On the right and the superstitious Use of the Sacred Scriptures.

Possibly Hessey did not consider this an attractive proposition, but the work did not appear as planned, though *On the Constitution of Church and State,* published in 1830, is the fifth disquisition and two more, *The Essay on Faith* and *Confessions of an Inquiring Spirit,* which is disquisition six, were published posthumously by H. N. Coleridge, the former in the *Literary Remains* (1836) and the latter separately in 1840.

*On the Constitution of Church and State* was discussed in the chapter on political theory because it seemed more appropriate there, and indeed the work contains little theological discussion. However, both *On Church and State,* and to a lesser extent, the *Lay Sermons* demonstrate the importance which Coleridge attached to religion in worldly affairs.

The *Essay on Faith* is only a few pages long, and is pithier than much of Coleridge's prose. It opens: 'Faith may be defined as fidelity to our own being' and concludes:[19]

> Now as life is here the sum or collective of all moral and spiritual acts, in suffering, doing, and being, so is faith the source and the sum, the energy and the principle of the fidelity of man to God, by the subordination of his human will, in all provinces of his nature to his reason, as the sum of spiritual truth, representing and manifesting the will Divine.

The tension between the subjective and objective is evident here and, I think, Coleridge's sympathy, if not his intellectual consent, comes out clearly on the side of the subjective. Also in *Literary Remains,* volume 4, H. N. Coleridge prints a selection of marginalia found in religious works. The books in which they were found give an interesting sidelight into Coleridge's religious thinking, though this will be much enhanced when the new edition of marginalia is published. The list of books confirms our knowledge of Coleridge's admiration for Luther's *Table Talk*, for Archbishop Leighton, St Theresa and Richard Baxter. There are recordings, too, of his reading of early nineteenth-century religious controversy. Coleridge's comments on Daniel Waterland's *Vindication of Christ's Divinity* and William Sherlock's *Vindicaion of the Doctrine of the Trinity* show the way in which he used other writers to help him to clarify his arguments, but it is in the comments on Luther's *Table Talk* that we find the best indication of the developing of Coleridge's particular creed.

*Confessions of an Inquiring Spirit*, which appeared in 1840 as a separate volume, is written in the form of seven letters 'to a friend', who is promised a work:[20]

> in which the Writer submissively discloses his own private judgment on the following Questions:-
>
> I.   Is it necessary, or expedient, to insist on the belief of the divine origin and authority of all, and every part of the Canonical Books as the condition, or first principle, of Christian Faith?
>
> II.   Or, may not the due appreciation of the Scriptures collectively be more safely relied on as a result and consequence of the belief in Christ; the gradual increase – in respect of particular passages:- of our spiritual discernment of their truth and authority supplying a test and measure of our own growth and progress as individual believers, without the servile fear that prevents or overclouds the free honour which cometh from love? 1 *John* iv. 18

This concern for the revelation of the scriptures brings Coleridge full circle, for this is very much where he began his career as a religious commentator in his 'Lectures on Revealed Religion'. Although the Lectures depend to a considerable extent on writings of religious controversy, many of them borrowed from the Bristol Library, as we may surmise, for the express purpose,[21] there is still much which is truly Coleridgean – for instance, the refutation of Godwin in the third lecture. This appeared elsewhere in a political context[22] but is here developed extensively in one of the most fully imagined religious declarations in Coleridge's prose:[23]

> if we love not our friends and Parents whom we have seen – how can we love our universal Friend and Almighty Parent whom we have not seen. Jesus was a Son, and he cast the Eye of Tenderness and careful regard on his Mother Mary, even while agonizing on the Cross. Jesus was a Friend, and he wept at the Tomb of Lazarus. Jesus was the friend of the whole human Race, yet he disguised not the national feelings, when he foresaw the particular distresses of his Countryman ... Jesus knew our Nature – and that expands like the circles of a Lake – the Love of our Friends, parents and neighbours lead [s] us to the love of our Country to the love of all Mankind. The intensity of private attachment encourages, not prevents, universal philanthropy – the nearer we approach to the Sun, the more intense his Rays – yet what corner of the System does he not cheer and vivify?

To a certain extent the emphasis on the human goodness of Jesus reflects the Unitarian concept of Christ, but that combination of religious belief and moral behaviour is of central importance in Coleridge's thought. It shows him trying to unite the individual in the whole while preserving the identity of the individual, whereas he saw Godwin's system as heartlessly ignoring the individual in its pursuit of the benefit of the whole. This is a shaping principle in the political thought and here we see how firmly it is grounded in religious belief.

Other early statements are interesting mainly because they show a starting point from which Coleridge gradually moved to his mature position. The first lecture, which has among its subjects the origin of evil, offers:[24]

> the greatest possible Evil is Moral Evil. Those Pains therefore that rouse us to the removal of it become Good. So we shall find through all Nature that Pain is intended as a stimulus to Man in order that he may remove moral Evil. Activity is the proper Happiness of rational Beings – and we cannot conceive a man active without a motive – the only conceivable motive by which Nature can and does prompt to Activity is by making Inexertion unpleasant & the source of future Pain. The

narrow Limits of this Lecture make it inconvenient, or I
should not despair of proving that there is not one Pain but
which is somehow or other the effect of moral Evil.

Coleridge must quickly have learnt that this was too glib an
account of a difficult subject, and by the end of his life his position
was so different that he frequently excused the moral evil of his
opium addiction on the grounds that he had sought only the
alleviation of pain. Even the assurance behind the following was to
be tested to the utmost, although it remained a foundation stone of
Coleridge's religious belief:[25]

It was therefore necessary that Man should run through the
Course of Vice & Mischief since by Experience alone his Virtue
& Happiness can acquire Permanence & Security.

This was only to become true for Coleridge when he was ready
to accept the mediation of Christ, the Redeemer; at this stage, he
was emphatically opposed to this doctrine, and a major part of the
fifth lecture is devoted to a criticism of the doctrine, which he calls
a 'corruption'. The criticism is on orthodox Unitarian lines but its
manner is truly Coleridgean:[26]

you are told of the wondrous Power of the Cross, yet you
find that this wonder working Sacrifice possesses no efficacy
unless there be added to it everything that, if God be
benevolent, must be sufficient without it. This is the
mysterious cookery of the Orthodox – which promises to
make Broth out of a Flint, but when you are congratulating
yourself on the cheapness of your proposed Diet, requires as
necessary ingredients, Beef, Salt and Turnips! But the Layman
might say – I can make a Broth out of Beef, Salt and Turnips
myself. Most true! but the Cook would have no plea for
demanding his wages were it not for his merit on dropping in
the Flint.

The cook about whose role Coleridge is so scathing is, of course, the
priest, whose function as mediator of salvation Coleridge strongly
denies. In a footnote to his 'Lecture on the Present War', Coleridge
confidently predicts the end of the priesthood:[27]

Him the High Priests crucified; but he has left us a Religion,
which shall prove fatal to every HIGH PRIEST – a Religion,

of which every true Christian is the Priest, his own Heart the Altar, the Universe its Temple, and Errors and Vices its only Sacrifices. . . .

This was the optimism of the early French Revolution, of a young man whose high ideals had not yet been tempered by a sense of his own inadequacy.

Coleridge's early opposition to the priesthood was political; he saw in the established church an instrument of oppression. Both religious and political ideas were conditioned by revolutionary sympathies, and though at this stage, the political aspect was more prominent, the religious thought, influenced as it is by Unitarianism and subordinate to politics, is not without importance. Coleridge's ideals lead him into an unworldliness which he was unable to sustain for long but which throughout his life enabled him to see events not only in the light of their local and temporal consequences but as related to first principles. Nor was he in youth, or in maturity, afraid to speak out uncompromisingly:[28]

He who sees any real difference between the Church of Rome and the Church of England possesses optics which I do not possess – the mark of antichrist· is on both of them. Have not both an intimate alliance with the powers of this World, which Jesus positively forbids? Are they not both decked with gold and precious stones? Is there not written on both their Foreheads Mystery? Do not they both SELL the Gospel – Nay, nay, they neither sell, nor is it the Gospel – they forcibly exchange Blasphemy for the first fruits, and snatching the scanty Bread from the poor Man's Mouth they cram their lying legends down his Throat!

This comes from the end of the fifth lecture and the sixth and final lecture is no less forthright. This expression of Coleridge's belief in the religious value of a country life precedes his intimacy with Wordsworth and we must assume that this was one of the ideas, common to both, which drew the two men together:[29]

In the country, the Love and Power of the great Invisible are everywhere perspicuous, and by degrees we become partakers of that which we are accustomed to contemplate. The Beautiful and the Good are miniatured on the Heart of the Contemplator as the surrounding Landscape on a Convex

Mirror. But in Cities God is everywhere removed from our Sight and Man obtruded upon us – not Man, the work of God, but the debased offspring of Luxury and Want. At every step some Instance of bloated Depravity, or squallid wretchedness meets us till at last we have doubts of providential Benevolence – and selfish Man accuses God for Miseries, which, if he had been employing himself as God and Nature ordained, he would not have been present to behold.

Coleridge condemns the commercial man as insincere and selfish. Trade is dependent on the atrocities of the East India Company or of the slave trade and leaves an 'indelible stain on our national character'. Coleridge goes on to assert that 'Jesus Christ forbids to his disciples all property'. From here, the lecture survives only in incomplete notes, but Coleridge's gist is clear enough:[30]

> While I possess anything exclusively mine, the selfish Passions will have full play, and our Hearts will never learn that great Truth that the good of the Whole etc. ... Let us exert over own hearts a virtuous despotism, and lead our own Passions in triumph, and then we shall want neither Monarch nor General. If we would have no Nero without, we must place a Caesar within us, and that Caesar must be Religion!

The tension between the world and a religious life was to occupy Coleridge's thoughts again in his *Lay Sermons* and there he shows a more mature attitude to the relationship between the commercial and religious values, without lessening his stress on the value of religion as Caesar. Later still, in *On Church and State*, Coleridge conceded the need for some body to represent and minister to non-material needs, but even then he was adamant that the value of the established church in its social and political function should be considered separately from its religious dogma.

As a contrast to this, *Aids to Reflection* and *Confessions of an Inquiring Spirit* are almost entirely free from political considerations and concentrate on religion as a function of the individual rather than of society. This does not mean that Coleridge was writing as an isolated believer; on the contrary, as the first chapter of J. D. Boulger's book *Coleridge as Religious Thinker*[31] well demonstrates, much of Coleridge's theory is developed as a criticism of the more generally accepted thinking of his day. Without the political and social dimension *Aids* is much more closely linked to the developments in Coleridge's philosophical thought and the tension which underlies this book is found in almost all Coleridge's later religious and philosophical thought. Coleridge himself expressed it as a tension between reason and understanding, between subjective and objective. This, however, is only a formulation of a difficulty which Coleridge never solved, although the attempt offers much valuable insight into his religious and philosophical ideas.

The tension can be illustrated biographically, for it is reflected no less in the early Unitarianism than in the later Anglicanism. It is the tension between a concern for logical demonstrations of the truth of certain positions, the ruthless inquiry into all aspects of man to find a first cause, and the emotional need of a lonely man convinced of his own inadequacy for a redeeming God. Coleridge was fully aware of this tension and his attempt to reconcile the two into a religious whole shapes *Aids to Reflection*, and especially the distinction between reason and understanding, which Coleridge thought central to the book. In the introduction he announces as:[32]

> one main object of this volume to establish the position, that whoever transfers to the Understanding the primacy due to the Reason, loses the one and spoils the other.

In terms of religious debate, it is best seen as a tension between subjective faith and acceptance of objective fact (which Coleridge calls Revelation). To a man of Coleridge's intellectual capacity, the acceptance of the Bible as literal truth posed serious problems, which involved him in biblical scholarship as well as philosophical argument. To complicate matters, Coleridge could not accept the objective proof without the subjective, nor vice versa:[33]

> The most *momentous* question a man can ask is, Have I a Saviour? And yet as far as the individual querist is concerned, it is premature and to no purpose, unless another question has been previously put and answered, (alas! too generally put after the wounded conscience has already given the answer!) namely, Have I any need of a Saviour? For him who *needs* none, (O bitter irony of the evil Spirit, whose whispers the proud Soul takes for its own thoughts,) there *is* none, as long as he feels no need.

In terms of the classic dichotomy of religious debate this tension can

188

be summarised. How far is salvation purely the grace or gift of God and how far is it earned by man's works? Coleridge, following Luther, as he so often does, attempts a compromise, which is reflected in the above quotation. Thus, we see Coleridge struggling to reconcile and account for two quite separate strands of thought, making full use of the desynonymised terms 'understanding' and 'reason'. The difference between the two, which originally had a political context, is now cast in more theological terms. Understanding is the faculty common to man and beast too close an adherence to which has caused man so many religious problems. Reason, on the other hand, is the capacity of man for apprehension of the whole; it embraces will and faith and the knowledge of truth. This is the faculty which Coleridge looked to for a way of believing without sacrificing either subjective or objective values.

This theme unfolds as *Aids to Reflection* develops, aphorisms of differing lengths are interspersed with comments, which are generally longer, and occasionally Coleridge interrupts the flow of aphorism and comment to make longer notes: 'Reflections Introductory to Aphorism X', 'Elements of Religious Philosophy preliminary to the Aphorisms on Spiritual Religion' and most important, 'On the Difference in Kind of Reason and the Understanding' (this is announced in capitals). In addition to this, the work is liberally sprinkled with footnotes which Coleridge boldly defends:[34]

> P.S. In a continuous work, the frequent insertion and length of Notes would need an Apology: in a book like this of Aphorisms and detached Comments none is necessary, it being understood beforehand, that the sauce and the garnish are to occupy the greater part of the dish.

The abandoning of any attempt to organise the book into a coherent whole must have made it easier for Coleridge to finish the book, but it makes the work difficult for the reader to understand as a whole. This is partly because the most easily understood aphorisms tend not to be the ones central to the argument which Coleridge is developing about reason in religion. Furthermore, the mind becomes accustomed to short passages and cannot readily attune to such sustained reasoning as is found, for instance, in the fourteen pages of comment on the second aphorism of spiritual religion. Coleridge is careful to warn the reader of the dangers attendant on the aphoristic style:[35]

> It is a dull and obtuse mind, that must divide in order to distinguish; but it is still worse, that distinguishes in order to divide. In the former, we may contemplate the source of superstition and idolatry; in the latter, of schism, heresy, and a seditious and sectarian spirit.

The short sections of prudential and moral and religious aphorisms come before the much longer section on spiritual religion because Coleridge feels a man must be aware of religion before he can embrace the spiritual. In the section on moral and religious aphorisms, there is a long comment on the relationship of the individual will to the world as a whole:[36]

> the Will is pre-eminently the *spiritual* Constituent in our Being. But will any reflecting man admit, that his own Will is the only and sufficient determinant of all he *is*, and all he does? Is nothing to be attributed to the harmony of the system to which he belongs, and to the pre-established Fitness of the Objects and Agents, known and unknown, that surround him, as acting *on* the will, though, doubtless, *with* it likewise? a process, which the co-instantaneous yet reciprocal action of the air and the vital energy of the lungs in breathing may help to render intelligible.

This Coleridge expands to provide what he calls a 'negative conception' of God (a positive conception 'belongs to a more advanced stage: for spiritual truths can only be spiritually discerned'):[37]

> Now will Reason, will Common Sense, endure the assumption, that in the material and visible system, it is highly reasonable to believe a Universal Power, as the cause and pre-condition of the harmony of all particular Wholes, each of which involves the working Principle of its own Union – that it is reasonable, I say, to believe this respecting the Aggregate of *Objects*, which without a *Subject* (that is, a sentient and intelligent Existence) would be purposeless; and yet unreasonable and even superstitious or enthusiastic to entertain a similar Belief in relation to the System of intelligent and self-conscious Beings, to the moral and personal World? But if

in *this* too, in the great Community of *Persons*, it is rational to infer a One universal Presence, a One present to all and in all, is it not most irrational to suppose that a finite Will can exclude it?

Here we begin to glimpse how the unity of creation is not in Coleridge's view something imposed from without but is an expression of the individual nature of each created thing. This is later more fully developed in the *Theory of Life*, where it is, as here, accompanied by the idea that this unity can only be when perceived by a subject, and here that subject, the one universal Presence, is God – whom, in turn, we can know only with the consent of the human will. The means of apprehending this divine unity are more fully explored in the section on spiritual religion. This is where the distinction between understanding and reason is important. Eighteenth-century theologians had been concerned to offer 'proofs' of Christianity which were logically convincing; this they thought rational. Coleridge could not accept this; he thought such 'proofs' took the religious element away from religion; for him, the organ for apprehending divine truth is Reason. Here, following Kant, Coleridge distinguishes between two kinds of reason, one, abstract and speculative, the other, practical. The former in religious matters has only a 'negative voice'; in other words, nothing can be allowed as true for the human mind, which directly contradicts this reason. Coleridge then continues:[38]

if not the abstract or speculative reason, and yet a reason there must be in order to a rational belief – then it must be the *practical* reason of man, comprehending the Will, the Conscience, the Moral Being with its inseparable Interests and Affections – that Reason, namely, which is the Organ of *Wisdom*, and (as far as man is concerned) the source of living and actual Truths.

Reason has now been expanded to include a religious dimension, but essentially the reason/understanding distinction remains much as it was when it first appeared in a political context. The distinction is a critical one, a means of exposing what Coleridge felt were inadequacies in received ideas, either in politics or religion. The Coleridgean reason offers a means of combining intellectual qualities with other more spiritual attributes, conscience, will and

191

faith, specifically to create a medium of religious apprehension open equally to all. This is well expressed in a letter to C. A. Tulk:[39]

> in Reason there is and can be no *degree*. Deus introit aut non introit. – Secondly, in Reason there are no *means* nor ends; Reason itself being one with the ultimate end, of which it is the manifestation. Thirdly, Reason has no concern with *things* (i.e. the impermanent flux of particulars) but with the permanent *relations*; & is to be defined, even in its lowest or theoretical attribute, as the Power which enables man to draw *necessary* and *universal* conclusions from particular facts or forms – ex.gr. from any 3 cornered thing that the 2 sides of a Triangle are & must be greater than the third. – From the Understanding to the Reason there is no continuous *ascent* possible, it is a metabasis ἐις ἄλλο γένος, even as from the air to the Light. The true essential peculiarity of the Human Understanding consists in its capability of being irradiated by the reason – in it's recipiency – & even this is *given* to it by the presence of a higher power than itself.

The distinction between reason and understanding was, however, only one of the aims of *Aids to Reflection*. A major part of Coleridge's religious concern was, in reaction to his early Unitarianism, to establish the central nature of the doctrine of the Trinity. This, for Coleridge, turns on the doctrine of the redemption. It is interesting that this is dealt with in full in the same comment to the second aphorism on spiritual religion which was quoted above on the subject of reason; one discussion led to the other.

Coleridge boldly affirms the ground of belief in God:[40]

> this truth, the hardest to demonstrate, is the one which of all others least needs to be demonstrated; that though there may be no conclusive demonstrations of a good, wise, living, and personal God, there are so many convincing reasons for it, within and without – a grain of sand sufficing, and a whole universe at hand to echo the decision! – that for every mind not devoid of all reason, and desperately conscience-proof, the Truth which it is the least possible to prove, it is little less than impossible not to believe! only indeed just so much short of impossible, as to leave some room for the will and the

moral election, and thereby to keep it a truth of Religion, and the possible subject of a Commandment.

Coleridge concedes that the same ground cannot be said to apply in the case of the Trinity, and here he has recourse to revelation. The heat in the argument is a reminder of the old Unitarian days:[41]

> the case is quite different with a Christian, who accepts the Scriptures as the Word of God, yet refuses his assent to the plainest declaration of these Scriptures, and explains away the most express texts into metaphor and hyperbole, *because* the literal and obvious interpretation is (according to *his* notions) absurd and contrary to reason. *He* is bound to show, that it is so in any sense, not equally applicable to the texts asserting the Being, Infinity, and Personality of God the Father, the Eternal and Omnipresent ONE, who *created* the Heaven and the Earth. And the more is he bound to do this, and the greater is my right to demand it of him, because the doctrine of Redemption from sin supplies the Christian with motives and reasons for the divinity of the Redeemer far more *concerning* and coercive *subjectively*, that is, in the economy of his own soul, than are all the inducements that can influence the Deist *objectively*, that is, in the interpretation of Nature.

The impatience here is undoubtedly, in part, with Coleridge's own youthful self but it also reflects his inescapable commitment to the truth, for as he said in one of the shorter aphorisms:[42]

> He, who begins by loving Christianity better than Truth, will proceed by loving his own Sect or Church better than Christianity, and end in loving himself better than all.

Such an uncompromising attitude is amplified later in a footnote:[43]

> Tolerate no Belief, that you can judge false and of injurious tendency and arraign no Believer. The Man is more and other than his Belief: and God only knows, how small or how large a part of him the Belief in question may be, for good or for evil. Resist every false doctrine: and call no man heretic. The false doctrine does not necessarily make the man a heretic; but an evil heart can make any doctrine heretical.

This shows a genuine and lifelong tolerance of other men and emphasises how Coleridge considered the whole man above any

193

professed belief. His acceptance of Christian doctrine never narrowed his sympathies and thoughts to a prescribed pattern. No better indication of the peculiar nature of Coleridge's religious belief can be given than the description of Hyman Hurwitz, a Jewish neighbour in Highgate. Written in 1820, this seriously modifies any idea that Coleridge was, at that time anyway, an orthodox member of the Anglican community, and it undercuts his own professed belief in the central nature of the redemption of Christ:[44]

> a learned, un-prejudiced, & yet strictly *orthodox* Jew may be much nearer in point of faith & religious principles to a Learned & strictly orthodox Christian, of the Church of England, than many called Christians who hold a sincere Churchman & indeed every one who will not accept the hollow· Shell of the history of Christianity for the Religion itself, in supreme contempt. –

Coleridge's last work, *Confessions of an Inquiring Spirit*, in its title reflects this refusal to be tied down which makes the religious writing at once so difficult to follow and so interesting to study. This comparatively short work concentrates on an enquiry into the authority of the Bible, defending the critical function in Biblical studies. As has frequently been the case with Coleridge, before discussing the work itself it is necessary to discuss the question of plagiarism. In the case of the *Confessions*, this has been done for us by J. H. Green, Coleridge's disciple of his last years, in an introduction written for the second edition of 1849. Green examines parallels 'in the present work and in the theological writings of Lessing' and comments:[45]

> It would be perhaps as idle as it would be dishonest to deny that the agreements of the two authors are more than accidental; and yet it cannot but be apparent that the most striking parallelisms are in passages, which a plagiarist would have avoided as most easily exposing him to detection, and which he might have dispensed with as a worthless portion of the spoil, namely, as merely collateral to, and illustrative of, the main subject.

Green solves this paradox as follows:

> It is indeed highly probable that in developing this scheme and

194

during the process of mental growth, the salient points of the German author, whom he confessedly studied and admired, became so impropriated by, and amalgamated with, his own mind, that they were no longer remembered, or thought of, as outward and alien, and were indeed as little such as the light, the air, and the warmth, which have been incorporated in the growing plant. And if it may be admitted that to Coleridge's mind Lessing's spirit was seminative, excitant, and nutrient, it must also be borne in mind that these, or similar terms, can have no meaning, except as denoting an action upon that which has inward life and energy, and in respect of Coleridge imply the originality, for which every one, acquainted with the individual character of his religious views, would contend.

This reflects accurately the character of Coleridge's mind, 'inquiring' as he says and receptive. Coleridge was not a thinker who developed in isolation; arguably he never had the confidence, which Wordsworth, for instance, had, to do so. His thought involves the thought of those whom he knew and those whose work he studied. That Coleridge himself considered this a viable way of thought is well demonstrated by his refusal to cover his tracks when he 'borrowed' from other writers. It should not detract from the integrity and originality of Coleridge's thought as a whole.

Coleridge describes himself in the opening letter of *Confessions* as one:[46]

> who – groaning under a deep sense of infirmity and manifold imperfection – feels the want, the necessity, of religious support; – who cannot afford to lose any the smallest buttress, but who not only loves Truth even for itself, and when it reveals itself aloof from all interest, but who loves it with an indescribable awe, which too often withdraws the genial sap of his activity from the columnar trunk, the sheltering leaves, the bright and fragrant flower, and the foodful or medicinal fruitage, to the deep root ramifying in obscurity and labyrinthine way-winning – ... I should perhaps be a happier – at all events a more useful – man if my mind were otherwise constituted. But so it is: and even with regard to Christianity itself, like certain plants, I creep towards the light, even though it draw me away from the more nourishing warmth.

As this suggests, *Confessions* is a personal book, and the letter form enables Coleridge to make his position clear in a direct and personal way. The book applies the difference between objective and subjective grounds of faith to the Bible, and here the emphasis is very much on the subjective, as the opening of the second letter shows:[47]

> In my last Letter I said that in the Bible there is more that *finds* me than I have experienced in all other books put together; that the words of the Bible find me at greater depths of my being; and that whatever finds me brings with it an irresistible evidence of its having proceeded from the Holy spirit.

This does not mean that Coleridge is prepared to accept every word of the Bible as God-given; instead, he goes on to assert that only the Pentateuch can, on the evidence of the Bible itself, be described as the word of God, directly imparted to man. The rest of the Bible, written by holy men under God's influence, is rich in spiritual aid but cannot be taken for literal truth, except where we are expressly told in the Bible that the words are the word of God. Refusal to accept this, according to Coleridge, causes inconsistency and bigotry, and leads in the end to manipulation of the text to suit the pre-conceived ideas of the interpreter. Instead, Coleridge prefers a more whole-heartedly personal base for acceptance for the Bible:[48]

> The truth revealed through Christ has its evidence in itself, and the proof of its divine authority in its fitness to our nature and needs; – the clearness and cogency of this proof being proportionate to the degree of self-knowledge in each individual hearer.

This self-knowledge, which has always occupied a central position in Coleridge's thought, now is complemented by external facts:

> Christianity has likewise its historical evidences, and these as strong as is compatible with the nature of history, and with the aims and objects of a religious dispensation. And to all these Christianity itself, as an existing Power in the world, and Christendom as an existing Fact, with the no less evident fact of a progressive expansion, give a force of moral demonstration that almost supersedes particular testimony.

Coleridge cannot accept any curb on his critical faculty even in his attitude to the Bible and he boldly asserts (even today this would offend some, and in 1830 could be relied upon to cause disquiet in many orthodox Christians):[49]

> the more tranquilly an inquirer takes up the Bible as he would any other body of ancient writings, the livelier and steadier will be his impressions of its superiority to all other books.

This is expanded in *Table Talk*:[50]

> All religion is revealed; – *revealed* religion is, in my judgement, a mere pleonasm. Revelations of facts were undoubtedly made to the prophets; revelations of doctrines were as undoubtedly made to John and Paul; – but is it not a mere matter of our very senses that John and Paul each dealt with those revelations, expounded them, insisted on them, just exactly according to his own natural strength of intellect, habit of reasoning, moral and even physical temperament? ... You read the Bible as the best of all books, but still as a book; and make use of all the means and appliances which learning and skill, under the blessing of God, can afford towards rightly apprehending the general sense of it – not solicitous to find out doctrine in mere epistolary familiarity, or facts in clear *ad hominem et pro tempore* allusions to national traditions.

Nor was Coleridge unaware that known facts sometimes precluded acceptance of the Bible version and he specifically refers to Copernican astronomy in this respect.[51] We can only guess at his reaction to the Darwinian undermining of the Pentateuch version of creation, though the evidence suggests that once he had fully accepted the historical facts, he would have abandoned the Bible version for the common-sense version, without its affecting his Christianity. The following remark in the *Table Talk* shows how far Coleridge was prepared to go in this direction:[52]

> Whatever may be thought of the genuineness or authority of any part of the book of Daniel, it makes no difference in my belief in Christianity; for Christianity is within a man, even as he is a being gifted with reason; it is associated with your mother's chair, and with the first remembered tones of her blessed voice.

This seems like a *reductio ad absurdum* of the Coleridgean theory and is reducing God to the same status as a well-loved teddy bear. It demonstrates the weaknesses of Coleridge's dependence on interior religion, just as the many contradictions as to historical data have weaknesses in the other direction. Although in his published prose Coleridge tried to balance this internally proved belief with an acceptance of the historical evidences, and worked all his life to try to reconcile subjective and objective, private utterances such as letters and the notebooks show thqt Coleridge's real sympathy was with the self-found interior faith. A notebook entry in 1810 deals with the problem at length. He dismisses:[53]

> this perpetual Bustle about *evidences* – apologies – testimony &c
> – The true Guide is this – What are the great component
> Doctrines contained in Christianity, and the Books and from
> all historical evidences of the accompanying facts, and the
> critical evidences of the Authenticity of the Books themselves –
> in other words, take the old Symbolum Fidei, which was the
> Conductor of Christianity for so many years – 1. Natural
> Religion or rather Universal Religion – i.e. – that which
> Angels who never fell & Spirits of <the> good purified from
> the Fall possess for themselves and relatively to themselves, in
> common with Mankind – that which would have been
> Religion tho' Adam had retained his perfection/– 2. the
> additions that rise of necessity out of the fallen state of the
> will – the natural Striving against perfect obedience –/ 3. the
> completion of this Religion by the system of Redemption/ –
> 1. God-Reason+Free-will=Conscience – Progression,
> Immortality. 2. Weakness, Sin, Remorse – Humiliation, Sense
> of the necessity of Help from above, Doubt of the imperfection
> of Repentance as an Atonement, Sense of the incapability of a
> genuine Repentance without that Help – in short, the throes
> of Creation groaning for the Saviour its highest State Faith in
> the super-sensual Obligation to Integrity (see Job–) 3. – Joyful
> acceptance of the Redemption, and earnest endeavours to
> realize the *conditions* of it –

A letter to J. H. Green written 29 March 1832 summarises Coleridge's position:[54]

> My principle has ever been, that Reason is *subjective*
> Revelation, Revelation *objective*– and that *our* business is

not to *derive* Authority from the *mythoi* of the Jews & the first Jew-Christians (i.e. the O. and N. Testament) but to *give* it to them – never to assume their stories as facts, any more than you would Quack Doctors' affidavits on oath before the Lord Mayor – and verily in point of Old Bailey Evidence this is a flattering representation of the Paleyian Evidence – but by *science* to confirm the *Facit*, kindly afforded to beginners in Arithmetic. If I lose my faith in *Reason*, as the perpetual revelation, I lose my faith altogether. I must deduce the objective from the subjective Revelation, or it is no longer a revelation for me, but a beastly fear, and superstition.

This was Coleridge's mature position and represents a change from the beliefs of his youth only in so far as he is now prepared to recognise revealed religion as a medium for subjective truth, rather than its antithesis:[55]

Of the evil arising from all Revealed Religions, in as much as by attempting to given [*sic*] motives to Reason & Goodness beyond & alien to Reason and Goodness, it weakens and degrades the Souls of men by an unnatural Stimulus; and at all events so perverts the visual nerve of the mind that we still look at Virtue asquint.

To the extent that he abandoned this position to recognise the redemption of Christ on the Cross, Coleridge accepted an objective ground for religion. In an attempt to reconcile his ideas with those of the established church, he accepted also the authority of the Bible but only as it accorded with his own response to it. Coleridge never did and never pretended to subjugate the self to a divine rule. This is expressed most positively and movingly in the following notebook entry:[56]

Blessed be God! That which makes us capable of vicious self-interestedness capacitates us for disinterestedness – ... and this, too, that I am capable of loving my neighbour as myself, empowers me to love myself *as* my neighbour – not only as much, but in the same way & the very same feeling. – Great Privilege of pure Religion! by directing Self-love to our self under those relations, in which it alone is worthy of our anxiety, it annihilates Self, as a notion of diversity, – Extremes meet –

This is confirmed in the conclusion to *Confessions of an Inquiring Spirit*:[57]

> Revealed Religion (and I know of no religion not revealed) is
> in its highest contemplation the unity, that is, the identity or
> coinherence, of Subjective and Objective. It is in itself, and
> irrelatively, at once inward Life and Truth, and outward Fact
> and Luminary. But as all Power manifests itself in the
> harmony of correspondent Opposites, each supposing and
> supporting the other, – so has Religion its objective, or historic
> and ecclesiastical pole. In the miracles, and miraculous parts of
> religion – both in the first communication of divine truths,
> and in the promulgation of the truths thus communicated –
> we have the union of the two, that is, the subjective and
> supernatural displayed objectively – outwardly and
> phenomenally – *as* subjective and supernatural.

# 8

# Philosophical Writings

Coleridge as philosopher stands next to Coleridge as poet and critic in posterity's interest; yet he published no specifically philosophical work. His reputation rests rather on the philosóphical cast of the *Biographia* and on Coleridge's own estimate of himself as a philosopher, which in turn depended on his projected *Opus Maximum*. This was never finished; even J. H. Green, Coleridge's literary executor charged with final preparation of the text for posthumous publication, failed to organise the extensive papers into a whole. To a cynical critic the *Opus Maximum* represents yet another instance of Coleridge's inability to complete a project and when it is referred to in the *Biographia*,[1] the reader may well feel that Coleridge is using the great work of the future to disguise his present difficulties, thus frustrating his readers just as they approach the crux of the matter. In reality, the picture is somewhat different. The work, which had many titles, possibly first occurred to Coleridge as early as 1803:[2]

> Seem to have made up my mind to write my metaphysical works, as *my Life*, & *in* my Life – intermixed with all the other events/or history of the mind & fortunes of S. T. Coleridge.

This format was pre-empted by the *Biographia*, which for that reason provides the best account of the development of Coleridge's philosophical ideas. Another notebook entry a little later on gives a list of projected works which includes:[3]

On Man and the probable Destiny of the Human Race. – *My last & great* work. – always had in mind,

The History of Logic a Compendium of Aristotelian Logic prefixed       7th

History of Metaphys. in Germany     8th
Organum verè Organum

None of this work was ever prepared for publication but, as
Coleridge said in the note added later, 'always had in mind'. This
is true to such an extent that in many ways little is lost in not
having the dream realised in published form. Undoubtedly, from its
first conception Coleridge's thought was all preliminary and in a
practical way preparatory to this *Opus Maximum*. This is instanced
by his persistent desire to have the meaning of his terms understood
exactly, so that he can use them to explain the central tenets in his
great work. Those who knew Coleridge in his later years must have
been listening to more preparations on Thursday evenings at
Highgate, and the class of gentlemen pupils who attended at
Highgate in the winter of 1822-3 seem to have taken down the
manuscript of the long projected *Logic*, as dictated by Coleridge.[4]
Notebooks and letters give further examples of the thought which
Coleridge devoted to his master work, and provide an insight into
his hopes that these fragments would one day be published as a
systematic whole. That Coleridge never arrived at this grand
conclusion to a life's work is symptomatic of his thought process, a
feature of which he himself was well aware. The following passage
in a letter to his son Hartley helps us to realise why this failure to
produce a finished article does not necessarily mean that Coleridge's
thinking was incomplete:[5]

> We proceed – (at a tortoise or pedicular Crawl, you will say –
> but believe me, dear Boy! there is no other way of attaining a
> clear and productive Insight, and that all impatience is an
> infallible Symptom that the Inquirer is not seeking *the* Truth
> for Truth's sake, but only *a* truth or something that may pass
> for such, in order to some alien *End* ... There is no way of
> arriving at any sciential End but by finding it at every step.
> The End is in the Means: or the adequacy of each Mean is
> already it's end. Southey once said to me: You are nosing
> every nettle along the Hedge, while the Greyhound (meaning
> himself, I presume) wants only to get to sight of the Hare, &
> FLASH! – strait as a line! – he has it in his mouth! – Even so,
> I replied, might a Cannibal say to an Anatomist, whom he
> had watched dissecting a body. But the fact is – I do not care
> two-pence for the *Hare*; but I value most highly the

excellencies of scent, patience, discrimination, free Activity; and find a Hare in every Nettle, I make myself acquainted with.

For readers who must catch the hare the process is naturally frustrating but to a sympathetic mind this, as Kathleen Coburn points out, is one of the distinguishing virtues of Coleridge's thinking:[6]

> The very comprehensiveness of his thought has an organic character that makes it a never-ending process of 'involution and evolution'. Because of his unceasing effort to grasp knowledge whole and the ever-widening circles of awareness that make him accept the fact that this is impossible, because of the relentless drive of his need to integrate the multitude of the parts of experience into a unity, not merely as an abstract pattern for a philosophical system but as a basis for understanding man's life, because, indeed, of the interdependence of all the parts in the picture of the whole, we are defeated when we try, from less commanding heights, to make clear to ourselves his meaning.

The *Biographia* contains Coleridge's first published philosophical writing of any length, but long before that appeared in 1817, Coleridge had been studying philosophy systematically. At school, if Lamb's memory is accurate, Coleridge was already versed in the Neo-platonists and at university his interest developed to include the seventeenth-century Cambridge platonists. Early manhood saw the acceptance of Hartley and then of Berkeley, but not until he settled at Greta Hall is there evidence of Coleridge thinking philosophically for himself. In his 'Dejection' ode, Coleridge suggests that he turned to abstruse research as a consolation for the failure of his marriage, but while some critics have agreed with this, others have attributed the interest in philosophy to the visit to Germany. In fact, Coleridge's mind had long been receptive to philosophical thinking and it seems merely that at this point in his life circumstances favoured his studies. The return from Germany in 1799 was followed by twelve months' wandering, some of it spent in London writing for the newspapers. In 1800 he, Sara and Hartley settled at Greta Hall, which gave him for the first time the opportunity to study the contents of the big box of books he had brought back from Germany. Furthermore, in the first months of 1801 he was unwell, which, confining him to his room, enabled him to concentrate still more on his studies. One of the first fruits of this appears in the four letters on Locke and Descartes sent to the Wedgwoods.

The avowed intention of these letters is to establish that Locke owed much to Descartes, despite his criticism of the French philosopher. Coleridge goes so far as to say:[7]

> there is no Principle, no organic part, if I may so express myself, of Mr Locke's Essay which did not exist in the *meta-physical* System of Des Cartes

In reality though, the impulse behind these letters is the demolition of Locke, whose influence in English thought at that time was considerable and, in Coleridge's view, pernicious. In Locke's place, Coleridge would place as useful English philosophers Berkeley, Butler, and Hartley, though Bacon too is given prominence. In his attempt to undermine Locke's authority, Coleridge overstates his dependence on Descartes, but even allowing for this, experts in the field, according to the notes in the *Collected Letters*,[8] feel that Coleridge deserves credit for being one of the first English thinkers to trace any connection between Locke and Descartes. It has frequently been remarked, and rightly, that much in Coleridge's work is written as a reaction to eighteenth-century thought, and here it is especially interesting that Coleridge had looked first to accepted thinkers and rejected them only after serious study. Coleridge is aware of a certain risk in this:[9]

> I hazard the danger of being considered one of those trifling men who whenever a System has gained the applause of mankind hunt out in obscure corners of obscure Books for paragraphs in which that System may seem to have been anticipated; or perhaps some sentence of half [a] dozen words, in the intellectual Loins of which the System had lain snug in *homuncular* perfection.

It is a process to which Coleridge has often been subjected; but despite this hint of special pleading, the charge should be dismissed here. Rather, we can see that Coleridge felt a dissatisfaction with accepted thought, which in the fourth letter he discusses in some detail, and turned to the source of these ideas, Locke, and then Descartes, to see if he could analyse why he felt this shortcoming.

The result of all this was that Coleridge in his philosophical writing especially, but also to a lesser extent in his criticism, had to work outside the accepted framework and, as Owen Barfield puts it, this had important consequences for his method and style:[10]

> Speaking, as he had to do, to his already empirically minded English contemporaries, he had so to speak, to lay down his track as he went along, and caterpillar wheels are slow compared with ordinary wheeled traction. But then they can go into much cruder places.

In June 1803 Coleridge's philosophical studies enabled him to form so clear an idea of the great work that he could describe it minutely to Godwin, giving him to understand, surely inaccurately, that it was 'ready to go to the Press'. Twelve chapters deal with the history of philosophy and special attention is devoted to Plato, Aristotle, Raymund Lully, Peter Ramus, Bacon, Descartes and Condillac, and then follows Coleridge's:[11]

> own Organum verè Organum - which consists of a $\Sigma \nu \sigma \tau \eta \mu a$ of all *possible* modes of true, probable, & false reasoning, arranged philosophically, i.e. on a strict analysis of those operations & passions of the mind, in which they originate, & by which they act, with one or more striking instances annexed to each from authors of high Estimation - and to each instance of false reasoning, the manner in which the Sophistry is to be detected, & the words, in which it may be exposed. - The whole will conclude with considerations of the value of the work, & its practical utility -

The letter is worth reading as a whole for the closely detailed description it gives of the work, but even this short extract reveals much of interest. To take the last point first, Coleridge considers his work will be useful to scientists, medical men, politicians, churchmen and lawyers and clearly he had no thought that such a work as he describes would be taken by later students to be mere abstract quibbling. Second, there is the combination of the detailed treatment of previous thinkers with Coleridge's own system, which is to be a combination of all 'modes of reasoning' subjected to a 'strict analysis of these operations & passions of the mind in which they originate'. This is very important for an understanding of Coleridge's thought, which comprises two strands - the critical, which depends on a response to the thought of others, and a self-inquiring strand, which relies on psychological insight, mainly into Coleridge's consciousness of his own mind. The two had long been vital to Coleridge, the former reflected in his eager criticisms of other thinkers and the latter reflected both in private utterances and, maybe surprisingly, in the outburst in defence of the use of 'I' in his preface to *Poems on Various Subjects*.[12] It is the critical strand which offers most difficulties for reader and philosopher alike. To the former, the list of names, many unfamiliar, to which Coleridge refers is in itself awe-inspiring; to the latter the problem is whether Coleridge evolved his own system or, rather, depended on an amalgam of the ideas of others, not always accurately represented. I would tentatively suggest that the problems of both might be eased if more attention were paid to the second strand in Coleridge's thought. Certainly it is beyond the scope of this chapter to consider in any depth Coleridge's relation to the many philosophers whom he read and studied. Instead, making here the proviso that much of Coleridge's thought relies heavily on other thinkers, I shall concentrate on what Coleridge actually wrote.[13]

When the *Biographia* appeared in 1817, the *Logosophia*, as it was often called in this middle period, was a long cherished project and Coleridge felt able to promise a prospectus at the end of the second volume. The *Biographia* too is influenced by this other work. The philosophical chapters (5-13) are a retrospective not so much of British philosophy but of Coleridge's reaction to it; and the culminating distinction between imagination and fancy clearly looks forward to a work which will enlarge on the function of the imagination. The 1818 version of *The Friend* also illustrates how all publications were coloured by and then seen to make a contribution to the great philosophical study. The portion of *The Friend* with which this chapter is concerned, the 'Essay on Method' was incorporated into the 'rifacciamento' of *The Friend* after its publication in the work for which it was commissioned, the *Encyclopaedia Metropolitana*. Originally Coleridge was asked by the publisher, Curtis at the firm of Rest Fenner, to make considerable contributions to the *Encyclopaedia* and to oversee its production. In fact, the introduction or 'A Preliminary Treatise on Method' was all that appeared. Coleridge describes this version:[14]

they have sent the world an Essay, which cost me four

months' incessant labor, and which I valued more than all my
other prose writings taken collectively, so bedeviled, so
interpolated and topsy-turvied, so utterly unlike my principles
or from endless contradictions any principle at all, that it
would be hard to decide whether it is in it's present state more
disreputable to me as a man of letters or dishonourable to me
as an honest man - and on my demanding my MSS ... I
received the modest reply - that they had purchased the goods,
and should do what they liked with them.

Eventually Coleridge did retrieve 'his manuscript 'cut up into snips
so as to make it almost useless'.[15] This chopping up of the original
and re-piecing seems to be Coleridge's chief objection to the way in
which it was edited. He suspected John Stoddart of the revision, of
whom he said:[16]

Had the Paradise Lost been presented to him in Mss, he
would have given the same opinion, & pulled it piecemeal &
rejoined it in the same manner.

Coleridge's concern at the joint violation of both form and meaning
shows how much he cared about the formal unity of his prose,
confuting the criticism that it is unthinkingly shapeless. Coleridge
restored the essay and incorporated it in the 1818 version of *The
Friend*. In 1934 Alice D. Snyder published an edition of the treatise
as it appeared in the *Encyclopaedia*. There are two main differences
between the two versions. First, as A. D. Snyder remarks, the
treatise demonstrates the:[17]

need to argue for method in arranging the subject matter of
an encyclopaedia, and to explain the particular method used in
the *Metropolitana*

and second, the style and tone of the work reflect the wider
readership for which it was intended. Coleridge here reveals some
of his central thoughts in a style which is much less obscure than
usual. The following, for instance, enlightens with a homely
example:[18]

The idea may exist in a clear, distinct, definite form, as that of
a circle in the mind of an accurate Geometrician; or it may be
a mere *instinct*, a vague appetency towards something which
the Mind incessantly hunts for, but cannot find, like a name

which has escaped our recollection, or the impulse which fills the young Poet's eye with tears, he knows not why.

In *The Friend* however, the 'Essay on Method' appears in its most truly Coleridgean form and this chapter will concentrate on that version.

As the rifacciamento of *The Friend* appeared, Coleridge was preparing his *Philosophical Lectures*. These were delivered alternately with a literary series from December 1818 to March 1819. Although not published until 1949, the lectures were recorded verbatim, as a letter to Southey reveals:[19]

> Mr Frere *at a heavy expence* (I was astonished to learn thro' Mr Gillman from the Scribe himself, at how heavy an expence!) has had my lectures taken down in short-hand. It will be of service to me: tho' the Publication must of course contain much that could not be delivered to a public Audience who, respectable as they have been (scant, I am sorry to add), expect to be kept awake. – I shall however, God granting me the continuance of the power and the strength, bring them out – first, because a History of *Philosophy*, as the gradual evolution of the instinct of Man to enquire into *the Origin* by the efforts of his own reason, is a desideratum in Literature – and secondly, because it is almost a necessary Introduction to my *magnum opus*, in which I had been making regular and considerable progress till my Lectures – and shall resume, immediately after.

Possibly the course was offered with a view to making some profit from work in progress. If so, Coleridge must have been very disappointed at the response. Miss Coburn in her introduction to the lectures points out that there were many unfavourable circumstances: advertising was poor, the start had to be postponed on account of mourning for Queen Charlotte, as had the second lecture because it fell on a Bank Holiday; the Christmas season and cold wet evenings probably kept people indoors; and both Hazlitt and Thelwall were also offering courses at the same time; but the overriding cause must have been that Coleridge, despite his success as a lecturer on Shakespeare (and the alternate literary series must further have depressed audience interest), had no reputation as a philosophical lecturer. Neither *The Friend* only just re-published nor the *Biographia* made such impression on the reading public and the reputation of *Aids to Reflection* and the Highgate Thursdays was still in the future. In financial terms, one of the most successful lectures failed by more than half to cover expenses. Despite this and, as the notebooks reveal, worn out and dispirited at his effort, Coleridge finished both this course of fourteen lectures and the literary series. Considering that in uncongenial weather he had to journey from Highgate to the Crown and Anchor in the Strand by stage and hackney coach only to be faced by an audience clearly insufficient to defray costs, this displays a perseverance for which Coleridge is seldom credited.

Also about this time, Coleridge seems to have written the *Hints towards the formation of a more comprehensive Theory of Life*. This was published posthumously in 1848 under Coleridge's name and edited by Seth B. Watson. The intention was clearly to make capital out of Coleridge's posthumous reputation but at the end of the volume there is a note suggesting that, after all, Dr. J. Gillman may have been a co-author. It is difficult now to be sure of the exact date and manner of composition. E. H. Coleridge surmised that it was intended as an introduction to a proposed history of scrofula by Gillman, and letters to C. A. Tulk in 1817-18 suggest that this is the likely period of composition. A. D. Snyder in her *Coleridge on Logic and Learning*[20] discusses what is known of the work and concludes that the balance of probability is that Coleridge was the main author. Certainly the central philosophy of life is of a piece with the rest of his work.

For the rest, all is manuscript, little of it as yet available to the public, although in 1929 A. D. Snyder's book made available much of the material which Coleridge prepared towards a work on Logic designed to serve as a preface to the great work itself. This edition is valuable for the insight it gives into the progress of Coleridge towards this goal, but because of the fragmentary nature of the papers little emerges that can be considered a coherent whole. So, we must suppose, it will be with the remainder of the unpublished material, although the Collected Coleridge edition of the manuscripts will undoubtedly add to what is known of Coleridge's thinking in his later years. The publication of the later notebooks, too, will provide an opportunity to examine Coleridge's philosophical studies in more depth. As it is, we have to rely on the letters for occasional hints of the progress of the great work. As early as 1803 Coleridge had been able to describe the work minutely to Godwin and again in 1814 in a long letter to Stuart, he talks of:[21]

> my most important Work, which is printing at Bristol, two of my friends having taken upon them the risk ... The Title is: Christianity the one true Philosophy – or 5 Treatises on the Logos, or communicative Intelligence, Natural, Human, and Divine: – to which is prefixed a prefatory Essay on the Laws & Limits of Toleration & Liberality illustrated by fragments of *Auto*-biography –.

Again there is a likeness to the *Biographia* and possibly the need to provide a preface to the *Sibylline Leaves* provided a necessary spur to publish something along the lines he had long been planning. If so, the literary context would explain the critical bias of what seems originally to have been intended as a philosophical work.

By the end of 1822, Coleridge has divided the great work into two parts, first the Logic and second:[22]

> the greater Work on Religion, of which the first half, containing the Philosophy or *ideal* Truth, Possibility and a priori Probability of the Articles of Christian Faith, was completed Sunday last.

How far these works were 'completed' it is impossible to say without a thorough study of the manuscripts, but it can be safely stated that no Coleridgean work was ever finished in the sense that there was no more to be said on the subject. So well aware of this was Coleridge that it would have been impossible for him to complete any major work without the intervention of a third party (often an importunate publisher) to take the work off his hands and call it done. On the other hand, J. H. Green, after Coleridge's death, looked at all the manuscripts and decided that none were fit for publication, so the completeness which Coleridge suggests means 'ready to go to press' was a delusion. As the years wore on, the Christian aspect of the great work became more important and Coleridge in the last entry his nephew recorded in his *Table Talk*, a fortnight before his death, admitted:[23]

> Hooker wished to live to finish his Ecclesiastical Polity: – so I own I wish life and strength had been spared to me to

complete my Philosophy. For, as God hears me, the
originating, continuing and sustaining wish and design in my
heart were to exalt the glory of his name and, which is the
same thing in other words, to promote the improvement of
mankind. But *visum aliter Deo,* and his will be done.

When we consider the work had been 'had in mind' for nearly
thirty years, it seems impossible that 'life and strength' were what
Coleridge lacked. Instead, I think we may regard the *Opus
Maximum* as an impossible dream, rather like the potion in *Alice in
Wonderland.* The combination of the flavours of: 'cherry-tart,
custard, pine-apple, roast turkey, toffee, and hot buttered toast' may
be very desirable but it is clearly a culinary impossibility. So
Coleridge's dream of 'uniting all knowledge into harmony' eluded
him, not because life is too short, but because it is beyond a man's
capacity. In the attempt, however, Coleridge cast new light on
many philosophical problems (not least because of his study of
German thinkers) and illuminated a new way of thinking which
could unite contraries and yet preserve their contrariety.

Towards the end of his life, Coleridge commented:[24]

The metaphysical disquisition at the end of the first volume of
the 'Biographia Literaria' is unformed and immature; – it
contains the fragments of the truth, but it is not fully thought
out.

The thought in these chapters is immature only in the sense that
Coleridge, who was in his forties when they were written, still had
a great deal of philosophical study before him, but it is not
unformed or fragmentary except is so far as Coleridge pursued the
same thought further in later years. Possibly because these chapters
offer a résumé of Coleridge's philosophical development establishing
a new position from which to work forward, they make an
excellent introduction to Coleridge the philosopher. Not all the
chapters from 5 to 13 are philosophical; chapter 10 is largely
autobiographical, while the short chapter 11 seems to dissuade the
would-be author from making writing his sole means of financial
support. What remains is a fairly coherent whole, moving forward
from the opening critique of the law of association to establish
Coleridge's own position, especially with reference to the distinction
between imagination and fancy. A good deal of Coleridge's atten-

tion on the way is given to a refutation of the materialist school of philosophy, especially of Hartley's law of association, this having been one motive for the attempt to find an alternative system. In Chapter 9, Coleridge acknowledges those thinkers whom he has found helpful: Kant, Fichte, Boehme, and Schelling are mentioned here. Also in these chapters Coleridge first expresses the desire to reconcile opposites, in a move towards what he was later to call his polar logic. The fifth chapter opens with a well-recognised division:[25]

> Our various sensations, perceptions, and movements were classed as active or passive, or as media partaking of both. A still finer distinction was soon established between the voluntary and the spontaneous.

From a study of Coleridge's religious belief we know that his preference was, in maturity, for the active and voluntary, or rather, that he could accept nothing that denied free-will, but at the same time he cannot deny the value of the passive and spontaneous as he illustrates in two very forceful metaphors:[26]

> Let us consider what we do when we leap. We first resist the gravitating power by an act purely voluntary, and then by another act, voluntary in part, we yield to it in order to land on the spot, which we had previously proposed to ourselves. Now let a man watch his mind while he is composing; or to take a still more common case, while he is trying to recollect a name; and he will find the process completely analogous. Most of my readers will have observed a small water-insect on the surface of rivulets, which throws a cinque-spotted shadow fringed with prismatic colours on the sunny bottom of the brook; and will have noticed, how the little animal *wins* its way up against the stream, by alternate pulses of active and passive motion, now resisting the current, and now yielding to it in order to gather strength and a momentary *fulcrum* for a further propulsion. This is no unapt emblem of the mind's self-experience in the act of thinking. There are evidently two powers at work, which relatively to each other are active and passive; and this is not possible without an intermediate faculty, which is at once both active and passive. (In philosophical language, we must denominate this intermediate faculty in all its degrees and determinations, the

IMAGINATION. But, in common language, and especially on the subject of poetry, we appropriate the name to a superior degree of the faculty, joined to a superior voluntary controul over it.)

This relates closely to the discussion of imagination and fancy, making it clear that it is impossible to isolate completely this part of the work. The whole of the philosophical part of the *Biographia* is related, however distantly, to the literary critical aim of the whole work. It is only because the discussion is also most useful for an understanding of Coleridge's philosophical position that it has been lifted from the *Biographia* for separate treatment. At the same time it is important to see how Coleridge's investigation into the creative mind (his own and Wordsworth's) led him deeper into a philosophical inquiry into the nature of perception and the nature of the perceived.

Already Coleridge's discussion of two aspects of the mind is leading him to a theory of a third aspect, the 'intermediate Faculty', but before he allows himself to suggest further thought about this third aspect, he further elaborates on another dualism, subjective and objective. This comes in Chapter 12, which although headed merely as a chapter of 'requests and premonitions concerning the perusal or omission of the chapter that follows', really contains the meat of Coleridge's philosophical argument in the *Biographia*. It is a long chapter and needs close concentration but it is not especially obscure or difficult to follow, and for an understanding of Coleridge's thought it is central. First of all, Coleridge makes a plea for the philosophic way of knowing; accepting that this is not for all men, still, he explains, it cannot be easily intelligible. Moreover, any one philosophical system seems to Coleridge to be inadequate for:[27]

> The deeper ... we penetrate into the ground of things, the more truth we discover in the doctrines of the greater number of the philosophical sects.

so that:

> The spirit of sectarianism has been hitherto our fault, and the cause of our failures. We have imprisoned our own conceptions by the lines, which we have drawn, in order to exclude the conceptions of others.

From this Coleridge moves to establish a position which will enable him to embrace all ways of knowing and all knowledge:[28]

> The postulate of philosophy and at the same time the test of philosophic capacity, is no other than the heaven-descended KNOW THYSELF!

From this follows Coleridge's discussion of the subjective and the objective:[29]

> All knowledge rests on the coincidence of an object with a subject ... For we can *know* that only which is true: and the truth is universally placed in the coincidence of the thought with the thing, of the representation with the object represented.

And Coleridge proceeds to illuminate the two sides of this equation in a paragraph worth noting for its lucid clarity as well as because, on that account, it offers a useful key to Coleridge's thought:

> Now the sum of all that is merely OBJECTIVE we will henceforth call NATURE, confining the term to its passive and material sense, as comprising all the phenomena by which its existence is made known to us. On the other hand the sum of all that is SUBJECTIVE, we may comprehend in the name of the SELF or INTELLIGENCE. Both conceptions are in necessary antithesis. Intelligence is conceived of as exclusively representative, nature as exclusively represented; the one as conscious, the other as without consciousness. Now in all acts of positive knowledge there is required a reciprocal concurrence of both, namely of the conscious being, and of that which is in itself unconscious. Our problem is to explain this concurrence, its possibility and its necessity.

The coalescence of subjective and objective is never so complete that the individual mind does not make distinctions, betraying a preference for one over the other. When Coleridge discusses the two, first in one order and then in reverse he shows his inclinations. Beginning with the objective he works it round to the following:[30]

> The theory of natural philosophy would then be completed, when all nature was demonstrated to be indentical in essence with that, which in its highest known power exists in man as

intelligence and self-consciousness; when the heavens and the earth shall declare not only the power of their maker, but the glory and the presence of their God, even as he appeared to the great prophet during the vision of the mount in the skirts of his divinity.

Next Coleridge propounds his ten theses. There is not space to discuss them all here, but I should like to emphasise themgression of thought which unites the theses into a whole. This is especially important since the substance of many of the thoughts in them owes a debt to Schelling, and unless the Coleridgean use to which these ideas are put is kept firmly in mind, it is too easy to dismiss the theses as unimportant for a study of Coleridge's thought. He begins by reaffirming:[31]

Truth is correlative to being. Knowledge without a corresponding reality is no knowledge; if we know, there must be somewhat known by us. To know is in its very essence a verb active.

Coleridge then seeks for the principle on which our knowledge can rely for a certainty of its truth. Carefully examining his steps in each thesis, he finally returns to self-consciousness, 'not a kind of *being* but a kind of *knowing*'. The theses, however, as Coleridge reminds us, relate only to:[32]

one of the two Polar Sciences, namely, to that which commences with and rigidly confines itself within the subjective, leaving the objective (as far as it is exclusively objective) to natural philosophy, which is its opposite pole.

This other pole also pays homage to self-consciousness:[33]

even when the Objective is assumed as the first, we yet can never pass beyond the principle of self-consciousness. Should we attempt it, we must be driven back from ground to ground, each of which would cease to be a Ground the moment we pressed on it. We must be whirl'd down the gulf of an infinite series. But this would make our reason baffle the end and purpose of all reason, namely, unity and system. Or we must break off the series arbitrarily, and affirm an absolute something, that is in and of itself at once cause and effect (*causa sui*), subject and object, or rather the absolute identity of both. But as this is inconceivable, except in a self-consciousness, it follows, that even as natural philosophers we must arrive at the same principle from which as transcendental philosophers we set out; that is, in a self-consciousness in which the principium essendi does not stand to the principium cognoscendi, in the relation of cause to effect, but both the one and the other are co-inherent and identical. Thus the true system of natural philosophy places the sole reality of things in an ABSOLUTE, which is at once causa sui et effectus, πατὴρ αὐτοπάτωρ υἱὸς ἑαυτοῦ – in the absolute identity of subject and object, which it calls nature, and which in its highest power is nothing else than self-conscious will or intelligence.

Coleridge is moving to a position where he can present his 'tertium aliquid', the interaction of both poles, and this brings him to his definition of the imagination. With the help of Kant he propounds two forces:[34]

the transcendental philosophy demands; first, that two forces should be conceived which counteract each other by their essential nature; not only not in consequence of the accidental direction of each, but as prior to all direction, nay, as the primary forces from which the conditions of all possible directions are derivative and deducible: secondly, that these forces should be assumed to be both alike infinite, both alike indestructible. ... The counteraction then of the two assumed forces does not depend on their meeting from opposite directions; the power which acts in them is indestructible; it is therefore inexhaustibly re-ebullient; and as something must be the result of these two forces, both alike infinite, and both alike indestructible; and as rest or neutralisation cannot be this result, no other conception is possible, but that the product must be a tertium aliquid ... which can be no other than an interpenetration of the counteracting powers, partaking of both.

Then realising that he has already over-taxed his reader's patience, he abruptly brings the chapter and the first volume to an end with the distinction between imagination and fancy. In default of the Logosophia, we miss a development of this discussion. The terms

216

'imagination' and 'fancy', clearly used in accordance with this distinction, do, however, together with the distinction between reason and understanding, play an essential rôle in Coleridge's philosophical development.

The 'Essay on Method' in *The Friend*, written at the time of the lectures and shortly after the *Biographia*, like that work founds its enquiry on literary critical studies. It is entirely consistent with Coleridge's thought that he should distinguish 'the man of education' from the 'ignorant man' by his use of language. Not the words themselves constitute the difference:[35]

> It is the unpremeditated and evidently habitual arrangement of his words, grounded on the habit of foreseeing, in each integral part, or (more plainly) in every sentence, the whole that he then intends to communicate.

So with the man of education, with the other, however:

> We immediately perceive, that his memory alone is called into action; and that the objects and events recur in the narration in the same order, and with the same accompaniments, however accidental or impertinent, as they had first occurred to the narrator.

It seems that fancy is being further defined here, and by implication imagination is being aligned to method and it comes as little surprise to find on the next page, that the difference between the well-disciplined and uncultivated understanding is found in Shakespeare. At this stage Coleridge's method is primarily literary critical, but its philosophical base soon becomes apparent:[36]

> Method, therefore, must result from the due mean or balance between our passive impressions and the mind's own re-action on the same. (Whether this re-action do not suppose or imply a primary act positively *originating* in the mind itself, and prior to the object in order of nature, though co-instantaneous in its manifestation, will be hereafter discussed.)

Thus, the debate about the balance between the active and passive is continued, and method is seen not to be fixed but '*a Way*, or *path of Transit*' so that:[37]

> The term, Method, cannot therefore, otherwise than by abuse,

be applied to a mere dead arrangement, containing in itself no principle of progression.

Method may have begun as an arrangement for an encyclopaedia but in true Coleridgean fashion it has quickly become a fundamental principle. It is important, first, because Coleridge himself considered method as a reflection of the essence of thought and, second, because it describes so well his own thinking process, constantly growing and never finished. The essays, numbered 4-11 in Section the Second of *The Friend*, beginning with the conversational differences between an educated and an uneducated man, range over the universe, taking material from such diverse subjects as botany, electricity, Greek philosophy, engineering experiments, and, of course, to begin with, Shakespeare. All is included, as befitted an encyclopaedia but also because Coleridge wanted to demonstrate that his method could embrace all things. Method is important to Coleridge because otherwise he fears the search for knowledge will diminish into the mere accretion of detail. Here is part of a criticism of Bacon:[38]

> For though Bacon never so far deviates from his own
> principles, as not to admonish the reader that the particulars
> are to be thus collected, only that by careful selection they
> may be concentrated into universals; yet so immense is their
> number, and so various and almost endless the relations in
> which each is to be separately considered, that the life of an
> ante-diluvian patriarch would be expended, and his strength
> and spirits have been wasted, is merely polling the votes, and
> long before he could commence the process of simplification,
> or have arrived in sight of the law

Coleridge is aware of the importance of classification, but he feels that it must take a subordinate role in the search for knowledge. Coleridge follows his assertion that the relations between objects are the prime materials of method by showing that there are two kinds of relation, of law and theory; theory is valuable, as it allows a study of cause and effect, but 'a *perfect* Method can be grounded' only on law because:[39]

> to *Law*, as the absolute *kind* which comprehending in itself the
> substance of every possible degree, not by generalization but by
> its own plenitude. As such, therefore, and as the sufficient cause

of the reality correspondent thereto, we contemplate it as exclusively an attribute of the Supreme Being, inseparable from the idea of God: adding, however, that from the contemplation of law in this, its only perfect form, must be derived all true insight into all other grounds and principles necessary to Method.

This is the anchor point of knowledge to which Coleridge referred in the *Biographia* and it is even more pervasive here, and in Coleridge's later thought. Method is seen to be a way of bringing the sciences within the framework of religion:[40]

> Religion therefore is the ultimate aim of philosophy, in consequence of which philosophy itself becomes the supplement of the sciences, both as the convergence of all to the common end, namely, wisdom; and as supplying the copula, which modified in each in the comprehension of its parts to one whole, is in its principles common to all, as integral parts of one system. And this is METHOD, itself a distinct science, the immediate offspring of philosophy, and the link or *mordant* by which philosophy becomes scientific and the sciences philosophical.

There is something circular about this argument: Law which reveals Divinity is the ground of 'all perfect Method' and the end of this same method is, equally, religion. Whereas to the critic this might seem to reduce the value of the argument, to Coleridge himself it illustrated the unity of means and end. It is in fact the cornerstone of Coleridge's theory of method that the seeker after truth must have an intuition of truth on which to found his search. This is because all matter partakes of the same bi-polar nature producing the inevitable *tertium aliquid*. Hence, Coleridge's need for the Trinity in religion and, granted that, his ability to see the creation, the creator and all created things not unified as in pantheism but inextricably linked in one system.

In order to apprehend this universal law, the seeker must first approach the method of the law in the individual case. Coleridge illustrates this from electricity, which was discovered in 1798 after the essential facts had been known for centuries. According to Coleridge the belated discovery was possible only because a law had been found to replace accumulated and useless theories which had tried to account for the nature of electricity in the qualities of the two reacting substances; but success came from:[41]

> those, namely, who, since the year 1798, in the true spirit of experimental dynamics, rejecting the imagination of any material substrate, simple or compound, contemplate in the phaenomena of electricity the operation of a law which reigns through all nature, the law of POLARITY, or the manifestation of one power by opposing forces:

Coleridge also finds support for his law of polarity among the philosophers. Plato is called to give evidence, and Bacon, perhaps surprisingly, is placed by his side. The two stand for opposite sides of the same coin according to Coleridge:[42]

> Plato so often calls ideas LIVING LAWS, in which the mind has its whole true being and permanence; ... Bacon, vicè versâ, names the laws of nature, *ideas*; and represents what we have, in a former part of this disquisition, called *facts of science* and *central phaenomena*, as signatures, impressions, and symbols of ideas.

Now Coleridge is into the heart of the matter, pausing at the end of the ninth eassay to pay homage to:[43]

> that grand prerogative of our nature, A HUNGRING AND THIRSTING AFTER TRUTH, as the appropriate end of our intelligential, and its point of union with, our moral nature.

This brings us back from the realms of abstruse philosophising to the world of social action. Here is the same spirit which selected the *Watchman* motto and in later days refused to admit that truth should bow down to religion. This is the spirit which gives strength to Coleridge's claims for unity of thought, for this belief not only in the spiritual value but in the practical worth of truth pervades his political and his critical utterances, shapes his finest poetry and supports his most rarified philosophy. This is why 'To know ... is a verb active' and why this difficult philosophical scheme belongs in such a work as *The Friend*, for as Coleridge says in the conclusion to these essays:[44]

> This elevation of the spirit above the semblances of custom and the sense to a world of spirit, this life in the idea, even in

the supreme and godlike, which alone merits the name of life, and without which our organic life is but a state of somnambulism; this it is which affords the sole sure anchorage in the storm, and at the same time the substantiating principle of all true wisdom, the satisfactory solution of all the contradictions of human nature, of the whole riddle of the world. This alone belongs to and speaks intelligibly to all alike, the learned and the ignorant, if but the *heart* listens. For alike present in all, it may be awakened, but it cannot be given. But let it not be supposed, that it is a sort of *knowledge*: No! it is a form of BEING, or indeed it is the only knowledge that truly *is*, and all other science is real only as far as it is symbolical of this.

The vehicle for this knowledge is reason and for Coleridge the clear apprehension of reason as opposed to understanding is 'the groundwork of all true philosophy'. Reason, 'that intuition of things which arises when we possess ourselves, as one with the whole', is opposed to understanding, which only gives abstract knowledge. Coleridge is careful to emphasise that it is the misuse of understanding rather than understanding itself which causes men to misapprehend the truth for:[45]

it is by this abstract knowledge that the understanding distinguishes the affirmed from the affirming. Well if it distinguish without dividing! Well! if by distinction it add clearness to fulness, and prepare for the intellectual reunion of the all in one, in that eternal reason whose fulness hath no opacity, whose transparency hath no vacuum.

The understanding is of value in assessing the particular laws which in combination with the universal laws maintain that balance of one and whole which was so important to Coleridge:[46]

we behold – first, a subjection to universal laws by which each thing belongs to the Whole, as interpenetrated by the powers of the Whole; and, secondly, the intervention of particular laws by which the universal laws are suspended or tempered for the weal and sustenance of each particular class, and by which each species, and each individual of every species, becomes a system in and for itself, a world of its own –

In man's case, such an intervening particular law allows the understanding to be suspended while miraculous revelation enables him to rise above classification and abstract knowledge to an apprehension of the one and the whole. Coleridge comments that often what have seemed to be particular laws have later, in fuller knowledge, emerged as part of the universal law, and he clearly hopes that this might be the case here too:[47]

> that what we now consider as miracles in opposition to ordinary experience, we should then reverence with a yet higher devotion as harmonious parts of the great complex miracle when the antithesis between experience and belief would itself be taken up into the unity of intuitive reason.
>
> And what purpose of *philosophy* can this acquiescence answer? A gracious purpose, a most valuable end: if it prevent the energies of philosophy from being idly wasted, by removing the opposition without confounding the distinction between philosophy and faith. The philosopher will remain a man in sympathy with his fellow men. The head will not be disjoined from the heart, nor will speculative truth be alienated from practical wisdom. And vainly without the union of both shall we expect an opening of the inward eye to the glorious vision of that existence which admits of no question out of itself, acknowledges no predicate but the I AM IN THAT I AM!

The philosophical lectures offer a pronounced contrast to the philosophical writing in the *Biographia* and *The Friend*, for their scope is much more limited. Coleridge's plan was mainly historical and this series is markedly different from the surviving record of literary lectures, not only in its completeness but also in its concentration on the announced course. Here and there Coleridge takes flight, but all the time the lecturer has managed to keep more or less to his prescribed topics. It seems as though Coleridge's whole heart was not in the task. Miss Coburn notices in the introduction to the lectures[48] that Coleridge's notes for the lectures have a vivacity and particularity missing in the reported lectures. Possibly Coleridge lacked confidence to develop his ideas for an audience to whom he had boldly stated in the prospectus:[49]

> were it in my power to select my auditors, the majority

would, perhaps, consist of persons whose acquaintance with the History of Philosophy would commence with their attendance on the Course of Lectures here announced.

We miss not only the ramblings and repetitions of the Shakespeare courses, but also those flashes of insight which more than compensate for any Coleridgean abstruseness. Coleridge may have regarded the philosophy lectures as a business venture, and his preparation shows an a-typical thoroughness. Much of the historical material Coleridge derived from a German critic of philosophy, Tenneman, and for the later lectures Coleridge borrowed extensively from his own works - from the recently published *Biographia* and *The Friend*, even from the pamphlet on the Cotton Factory Bill as well as from the manuscript 'Theory of Life'. While this shows a sensible economy of effort, especially in view of the concurrent literary series, the lectures are a little disappointing if we look in them for quintessential Coleridge on philosophy.

However, although Coleridge's avowed intention was to confine himself to a history of philosophy, occasionally he did develop theories of his own as they arose from the historical survey. For instance, Coleridge remarks of the early Greeks, 'they all took for granted the identity of God and the world' and adds that the concept of a creator separate from his creation 'was an idea so bold that it does not appear that it ever did suggest itself to any human mind unassisted by revelation'. Coleridge then quotes from an eighteenth-century translation of the Bhagavad-gitā and deduces that man is not happy with a pantheistic fragmentation of creation (and therefore of its creator) and so constantly strives for a unity. The striving is not successful:[50]

for that, be assured, is the utmost height human nature has arrived at by its own powers; that first of all the highest and best of man felt by an impulse from their reason a necessity to seek an unity; and those who felt wisely, like Plato and Socrates, feeling the difficulties of this, looked forward to that Being, of whom this necessity and their reason was a presentiment, to instruct them, and expected with reverence and hope that an instructor would come. But with regard to the others, it fell into a multitude of forms so that at length the theologists themselves were weary of counting them, and it has become a matter of dispute whether there were twenty, thirty, forty, or fifty thousand of the Roman and Greek deities.

This brief argument occupies only five pages of Lecture 3 but includes the ancient civilisations of Greece, Rome and India, and by implication the advent of Christianity to the Jews. It spans several centuries and thousands of miles yet it has a unity far deeper than any imposed by chronology; this is the unity of a central idea, the only unity of which Coleridge ever acknowledged the existence. This is, to be more specific, a unity coming from religious belief, which enabled him to see 'multeity in unity' and equally made it impossible not to see a central unity behind man's developing ideas. To a certain extent, the impersonal history of the early philosophers is coloured by this Christian retrospect, a point which Coleridge makes explicitly at the close of the second lecture:[51]

> in all that makes Greece Greece to us, we find it the great
> light of the world, the beating pulse, that power which was
> predetermined by Almighty Providence to gradually evolve all
> that could be evolved out of corrupt nature by its own reason;
> while on the opposite ground there was a nation bred up by
> inspiration in a childlike form, in obedience and in the exercise
> of the will. Till at length the two great component parts of
> our nature, in the unity of which all its excellency and all its
> hopes depend, namely that of the will in the one, as the higher
> and more especially godlike, and the reason in the other, as the
> compeer but yet second to that will, were to unite and to
> prepare the world for the reception of its Redeemer.

This is an anticipation of the lecture 'On the Prometheus of Aeschylus' where the argument is developed in more detail and with reference to the specific mythology of the Greek drama. It is an argument to which Coleridge refers again at the opening of Lecture 5, observing that men are prepared to recognise the hand of God in the pre-Christian history of Judaism, but that:[52]

> if you presume that the same Providence is at the same time
> working over the whole of the world as far as we know it
> and that Christianity was not welcomed in one direction only,
> but that from North to South and from South to North, from
> East to West and from West to East the whole march of
> human affairs tended to that one centre in which all men were

equally concerned and interested, and apply this principle in any particular, there is immediately a sort of sudden connexion in their minds that you have introduced something between Christianity and the world that they have not been accustomed to; they raise a sort of paganism as an objection; a kind of heathenism is felt.

Coleridge points out that the early Christian felt differently and his treatment of Plato (and platonism, which Coleridge saw as deriving from Plotinus and other early Christian neo-platonists) is coloured by a sense that he constitutes a preparation for Christianity. In accordance with this, Coleridge suggests the need for something more than philosophy:[53]

to feel that philosophy itself can only point out a good which by philosophy is unattainable; to feel that we have a disease, to believe that we have a physician, and in the conjoint action of these to exert that total energy of soul from which it is as impossible that evil or aught but good can follow (if it be indeed total) as that a fountain should send forth sands or a fire produce freezing around it ... Then only will true philosophy be existing when from philosophy it is passed into that wisdom which no man has but by the earnest aspirations to be united with the Only Wise, in that moment when the Father shall be all in all.

As the lectures move from the philosophers of the ancient world to those of modern Europe, the religious dimension becomes more apparent. In the second half of the course, Coleridge relies on his own writings and here he more frequently enlarges his thoughts on the philosophies under discussion. The description of earlier thinkers, too, is often revealing of Coleridge's own thought. The following is a description of William of Occam:[54]

He defined faith according to its proper nature. He said that it was an anticipation of knowledge by the moral will. That it was indeed below science, for that was what we were to enjoy as the reward of faith; but far above opinion: which therefore was not attainable in its height by reason but which was constantly tricked by it, and though ever flying before, still in its latter steps reached it; and consequently that a doctrine of faith that was against nature was absurd, and a faith that was not admitted to be above reason ceased to be faith altogether, inasmuch as it became one and the same with reason.

The treatment of the materialist philosophers also reveals a Coleridgean bias. Whereas Locke, Hobbes (who is only mentioned in passing) and Descartes are all fiercely criticised for ignoring the essential nature of mind in their attempt to reduce all thought to sense-impressions, earlier exponents of a mechanical rather than an idealist attitude to matter receive more balanced treatment. Democritus, who propounded an early theory of atoms:[55]

chose materialism instead of Spinosism, and therein he made the better choice, because by leading men more to exercise their senses, and to acquire experience concerning the bodies in nature and her operations, he then led us to science;

Similarly, the scheme of Anaxagoras:[56]

was better than the Eleatic School, the Idealists, because it left a world of observation open to the mind and was at least neutral if not favourable to experimental philosophy.

Here we see Coleridge's true attitude to objective and subjective, to the analysis of understanding and the apprehension of reason. What Coleridge was trying to show was the need for balance, for what he calls in these lectures, 'subordination not exclusion'. Notebooks and letters, his interest in Poole's tannery and Davy's chemistry attest to his study of the world without; it is only in combination with this that his philosophy of self-consciousness gives a perception of the truth. It is because Coleridge felt that the balance was overturned by the eighteenth-century philosophers that he is so strongly critical of their thought. The thirteenth lecture is devoted to a discussion of this subject, especially as it is treated by Locke, Bacon and Descartes. Here Coleridge asserts the importance of a proper use of the terms of philosophy:[57]

As society introduces new relations it introduces new distinctions, and either new words are introduced or new pronunciations. Now the duty of the philosopher is to aid and complete this process as his subject demands.

Then follow definitions of body, matter and finally the truly

Coleridgean: 'the mind may be defined as a subject which is its own object'.[58]

This recalls the familiar 'know thyself', which Coleridge refers to in the course of a discussion of the evil of witch-hunting:[59]

> The sole prevention, in reality, is the recurrence to our highest philosophy – know thyself: study thy own nature, but above all do no evil under the impression that you are serving God thereby.

This illustrates again how for Coleridge the study of philosophy was no abstract matter, but related closely to man in society. The definition of terms is never far removed from the moral dimension which, based on self-knowledge, should operate throughout society. This is why Coleridge's philosophical lectures are most interesting when they are least historical. When Coleridge confines himself to chronology and brief lives, the lectures do not come alive; when these are subordinate to a critical attention to the import of a philosopher's contribution to the development of man's thought, Coleridge shows a glimpse of his stature as a thinker. It is perhaps a matter of regret that, given Coleridge's avowed intention to address an audience ignorant of formal philosophy, these glimpses are not more frequent, for in the lectures Coleridge achieves an unusual clarity of thought and lucidity of expression.

The brief *Hints towards the Formation of a More Comprehensive Theory of Life* are illuminated by what seems to be a contemporary correspondence with C. A. Tulk and there is a useful summary of the fundamental issue in the second letter:[60]

> the two great Laws (causae effectivae) of Nature would be Identity – or the Law of the Ground: and Identity in the difference, or Polarity = the Manifestation of unity by opposites.

Because of the uncertainty about its authorship, the *Theory of Life* has not until recently received much critical attention. The scientific content, which in the light of post-Darwinian biology seems very wide of the mark, has tended to draw attention away from the more philosophical aspect of the work. As Craig Miller comments in an early article on the *Theory of Life*:[61]

> At times his ideas appear nonsensical, as when he tries to make the Vermes the mid-point between the endoskeletons and

exoskeletons; at other times he appears inconsistent, as when he seems to give certain 'moral qualities' to fishes. He underestimates the complexity of even the simplest forms of life, and he oversimplifies as well as poetizes the evolutionary process.

Despite this, there is a good deal in the *Theory of Life* which is of interest not only to students of Coleridge but also to historians of the development of Victorian attitudes to nature. Darwin's *Origin of Species* was published in 1859 and, as its title suggests, it was an attempt to understand how different varieties of life arose. Coleridge's solution to the problem now seems outdated and inadequate but it is significant that forty years before Darwin's work was published Coleridge was one of those who turned his attention to the same problem. At the same time this excursion into biology, probably an interest shared with Gillman, displays Coleridge's own philosophical preoccupations in yet another guise, adding another dimension to his thinking. Here is a brief example. He defines life:[62]

> *absolutely*, as the principle of unity in *multeity*, as far as the former, the unity to wit, is produced *ab intra*; but *eminently* (*sensu eminenti*), I define life as *the principle of individuation*, or the power which unites a given *all* into a *whole* that is presupposed by all its parts. The link that combines the two, and acts throughout both, will, of course, be defined by the *tendency to individuation*.

This 'tendency to individuation' is Coleridge's answer to the creation of different species, and it is according to degrees of individuation that the various forms of life can be arranged. Metals display it in the minimum, lichens slightly more, insects more still and so on until man is reached:[63]

> By Life I everywhere mean the true Idea of Life, or that most general form under which Life manifests itself to us, which includes all its other forms. This I have stated to be the *tendency to individuation*, and the degrees or intensities of Life to consist in progressive realization of this tendency.

This reminds the reader of Coleridge's insistence on respect for the individual in his political writings, of his refusal to see society in terms other than a combination of individuals. As is so often the case with Coleridge, in the most surprising places we are reminded that however imperfect their expression in various forms, there is a body of consistently held ideas underlying his work.

The 'tendency to individuation' is not all the answer and Coleridge next asks:[64]

> What is the most general law? I answer – polarity, or the essential dualism of Nature, arising out of its productive unity, and still tending to reaffirm it, either as equilibrium, indifference, or identity.

Now we recognise a continuation of the line of thought in the *Biographia*, a reminder that all the works considered in this chapter were produced within four years, a period which also saw much other activity, including the *Lay Sermons*, the literary lectures and editions of most of the poetry. This concentrated activity explains why it is in the works of these years that we can most clearly see Coleridge's central ideas, those for which he hoped to find a vehicle in his great work, but which the reader instead finds, if he cares to look, affirmed over and over again in the most diverse settings, a nice example of 'unity in multeity'. It is in these works, in which Coleridge takes a retrospective view of his earliest thoughts and traces the development which brought him from Hartleian neces-sarianism and Unitarianism to a full awareness of Free Will and the Christian Trinity, that all the facets of Coleridge's mind are given balanced play in his thought. There is, too, a buoyancy in these central works, perhaps a reflection of the fact that after the dark Bristol days following the break with Wordsworth, Coleridge had pulled through to the comparative serenity of Highgate. In the treatment of life, Coleridge seems more confident than anywhere else, perhaps because the nature of his object enabled him to expand his theme of the 'unity in multeity', as he says:[65]

> Life, then, we consider as the copula, or the unity of thesis and antithesis, position and counterposition, – Life itself being the positive of both; as, on the other hand, the two counterpoints are the necessary conditions of the *manifestations* of Life.

Coleridge then goes on to regret:[66]

> we cannot force any man into an insight or intuitive possession of the true philosophy, because we cannot give him

abstraction, intellectual intuition, or constructive imagination, because we cannot organize for him an eye that can see, an ear that can listen to, or a heart that can feel, the harmonies of Nature, or recognize in her endless forms, the thousand-fold realization of those simple and majestic laws which yet in their absoluteness can be discovered only in the recesses of his own spirit, – not by that man, therefore, whose imaginative powers have been *ossified* by the continual reaction and assimilating influence of mere *objects* on his mind, and who is a prisoner to his own eye and its reflex, the passive fancy!

This is a continuation of the discussion of the active imagination in the *Biographia*, and it is in terms of that discussion that the *Theory of Life* has its greatest value. When Coleridge turns to discuss actual behaviour in the animal kingdom he invites the reader's impatience by an attempt to permeate the entire created world with man's moral insights. Given the Christian basis of Coleridge's thought, the reader can accept as something more than whimsical:[67]

The arborescent forms on a frosty morning, to be seen on the window and pavement, must have *some* relation to the more perfect forms developed in the vegetable world.

but no such allowances can make us take seriously an arrangement of the species which relies on such observations as: 'the fish sinks a step below the insect, in the mode and circumstances of impregnation.'[68] The *Theory of Life* is throughout an odd combination of misplaced scientific observations, possibly reflecting Gillman's interests, and truly Coleridgean thoughts about the nature of life. The reader must resist the temptation to discredit the latter on account of the former.[69]

For the rest of Coleridge's life we know that he continued to work on his *Opus Maximum* to develop his ideas on those problems which he considered fundamental, but for his findings on these subjects we have to delve deep and it is impossible to do more than suggest some of the thoughts of these late years until the Collected Coleridge gives us a more coherent picture of the philosophical fragments. In *Coleridge on Logic and Learning*, A. D. Snyder has given a useful summary of what exists of Coleridge's *Logic* and reprints related notebook entries. In many cases scholarship has overtaken this work, published in 1929, especially as far as the notebooks are concerned, but as an insight into Coleridge's work on *Logic* it remains unique. Here we find that Coleridge had at least begun work on the project which in the letter to Godwin in 1803 was announced as ready for printing. Lengthy extracts from this early attempt at a *Logic* confirm the tendency of Coleridge's thought and in many ways show a parallel development in historical form to the first half of the *Philosophical Lectures*. The later manuscript, which A. D. Snyder dates 1822-3, is the fruit of Coleridge's philosophical class at Highgate, but her book publishes only a brief survey with a few quotations so that it is difficult to judge exactly what Coleridge said. Such quotations as there are make it clear that there are no striking departures from Coleridge's published thoughts.

Using a sextant as an illustration, following a habit of recourse to mathematical metaphors for philosophical ideas, Coleridge discusses various modes of apprehension, the last being the construction of the sextant itself. From this Coleridge turns to the mind:[70]

> the investigation into the composition and constitution of the mind itself, yet remains the weightiest and worthiest of all contemplations if the Poet have said rightly,
>
> De coelo descendit γνῶθι σεαυτόν
>
> and the knowledge of our intellectual nature is the substance and life of all our knowledge and the ground of intelligibility of all other objects of knowledge.

Similarly, the following quotation is clearly related to the distinction first made in the *Lay Sermons* and *The Friend*, although it develops the point in a specific way:[71]

> We may commence this inquisition by defining the Reason (I mean solely in reference to the logical process) as the Source of Principles, the Understanding as the faculty of Rules

Thus, it seems likely from what evidence there is[72] that the tendency of Coleridge's later thought was to amplify and confirm the ideas set out in his published works. Coleridge's philosophical flowering seems to have come like his poetic outburst, all at once. Later works develop thinking which almost always relates back to this second creative period, when all Coleridge's central philosophical concepts seem to have found their fullest expression.

Coleridge's late published prose concentrates on Christian theology and in so far as there is any real development of thought towards the end of Coleridge's life, it is in the more explicit handling of the role of God the creator in Coleridge's scheme of life. However, a discerning reader might have found this too as a germinating thought in the first of the prose works of the central period, the *Biographia*.

# Conclusion

All the various Coleridges and they are more numerous than is sometimes realised are one Coleridge.[1]

By now I hope that the reader will have recognised how inadequate is any subdivision of Coleridge's work into categories. Really, Coleridge's thought is such that there is as much of almost any aspect of it implied in each work as in any other. This is not because Coleridge could not organise his thinking clearly but because his central ideas involved a way of looking at life which is more fundamental than the philosophical, the political or the religious. His system offered a method for seeing the world in all the many aspects which interested him that transcends or removes such subdivisions. Consequently, in writing of Coleridge as political scientist, one feels a weakness, a lack of commitment to political solutions; equally, his religion seems not quite wholly religious and his philosophy has proved too unphilosophical for many a critic. Even the literary criticism, it has been argued, is marred by non-critical excrescences. To a specialist in any of these fields, these seem severe shortcomings, but to a student of Coleridge they are a reflection of a mind that refused to be condemned to narrow categories because, he felt, this was untrue to reality:[2]

> My system if I may venture to give it so fine a name, is the only attempt I know, ever made to reduce all knowledges into harmony. It opposes no other system, but shows what was true in each; and how that which was true in the particular, in each of them became error, *because* it was only half the truth. I have endeavoured to unite the insulated fragments of truth, and therewith to frame a perfect mirror.

If it is possible to sum up Coleridge's thought, the two words which

233

most accurately reflect the character of his writing, both poetry and prose, are 'critical' and 'moral'. Both are based on self-knowledge, and the two were inextricably linked as part of the process whereby Coleridge delineated and attacked the questions which he considered central. The solution involved a third component, for as he explained in the Appendix C to *The Statesman's Manual*, the world in its relation to the human soul is 'a mystery ... of which God is the only solution.'[3] For Coleridge this is not a mere pulpit platitude but the hard-won result of the scrutiny of many other ideas. The problem of the nature of man and of the world around him had long occupied his thoughts, and from relatively early on there had been a religious dimension which, if recognised, helps us to understand Coleridge's system:[4]

> a Symbol ... is characterized by a translucence of the Eternal through and in the Temporal. It always partakes of the Reality which it renders intelligible; and while it enunciates the whole, abides itself as a living part of that Unity, of which it is the representative.

Coleridge had had this in mind long before it appeared as a definition, as can be seen from the notebook entry of 1805:[5]

> The best, the truly lovely, in each & all is God. Therefore the truly Beloved is the symbol of God to whomever it is truly beloved by!

These are complex ideas and represent much thought, including the study of other men's thinking. The pantheism of an identity of Created and Creator was unacceptable to Coleridge, the materialism of a total separation was abhorrent. Here is his own compromise between the two: the created world is a symbol, partaking of the 'Reality which it renders intelligible'. Of the Divinity the loved one becomes such a symbol because the love felt is symbolical in the same way.

To Coleridge the most powerful symbol of the mind of God was the mind of man. This is why introspection is such a valuable activity; by knowing ourselves we come symbolically to know God. Imagination is the key to this:[6]

> The primary Imagination I hold to be the living power and prime agent of all human Perception, and as a repetition in the finite mind of the eternal act of creation in the infinite I AM.

This enables us to make another connection. The secondary imagination, which is that which operates in poetry and other fine arts, can give us an insight into the primary imagination, which in turn enables us to apprehend the nature of the Divine. As it is in the world of literary criticism, so it is in the world of action, for as A. J. Harding suggests:[7]

> What ultimately matters about Christian charity may be not its beneficial effects on mankind and the animal world in general, but the fact that whoever achieves it is thereby brought a very little closer to resembling God's own nature.

Hence the word 'moral' is always reappearing not only in unexpected places but also in unexpectedly central ways:[8]

> Every man who admits that he may be deceived admits at the same time that there is a something upon which he cannot be deceived. Doubtless *that* he will not find in his own individual reasoning, but he will find it in that principle which is above reasoning, in his moral nature, (and as long as he remains in any degree what he ought to be) in the contradiction which he finds in certain errors within his own moral nature.

For as J. H. Muirhead remarks, in Coleridge's religious discussions: 'morality [is] the surest test in the end of theoretic validity.'[9] This emphasis on the moral helps to explain why Coleridge only accepted with reluctance and initially without conviction that revelation is the only means by which man may perceive God the Father, God the Son and God the Holy Ghost.

Once he has accepted it, Coleridge is certain that this revelation, this given fact has to be the starting point, the organising force which enables us to embark on the process of exploration of the mind within, the created world without, which will in turn confirm our knowledge of the 'infinite I AM.' In a sense the only significant development in Coleridge's thought towards the end of his life was the degree to which, returning to the orthodoxy of the established church, he was able to accept revelation, so that in the last months of his life he could summarise all knowledge as follows:[10]

> Assume the existence of God, – and then the harmony and fitness of the physical creation may be shown to correspond

with and support such an assumption; – but to set about *proving* the existence of a God by such means is a mere circle, a delusion. It can be no proof to a good reasoner, unless he violates all syllogistic logic, and presumes his conclusion.

But it is impossible to summarise Coleridge, for as he often remarked, in the pursuit of knowledge the means is the end. There is a clear warning in *The Friend*:[11]

> The reader, who would follow a close reasoner to the summit and absolute principle of any one important subject, has chosen a Chamois-hunter for his guide. Our guide will, indeed, take us the shortest way, will save us many a wearisome and perilous wandering, and warn us of many a mock road that had formerly led himself to the brink of chasms and precipices, or at the best in an idle circle to the spot from whence he started. But he cannot carry us on his shoulders: we must strain our own sinews, as he has strained his; and make firm footing on the smooth rock for ourselves, by the blood of toil from our own feet.

This communication of knowledge, the means as well as the end, is the major impulse behind Coleridge's writings and, by implication, the answer to the problem of why God created the world.

Coleridge's was a life in which there was much change; the world retreated from its pre-revolutionary optimism to the repressive conservatism of post-Napoleonic Europe; he himself was transformed from the eager youth who vaulted over the gate to Racedown into the semi-invalid sage of Highgate. To an important extent, though, he ended where he began: the various changes en route, the period of Hartley's influence, of Unitarianism, of revolutionary sympathy were those 'mock roads', 'idle circles' which he wished to prevent his readers following. What Coleridge arrived at in the end was a philosophy true to himself, and it is fitting that it should receive its finest expression in the *Biographia*. But Coleridge would not be Coleridge if his interest were only self-sustained. An equally important side of his nature was outward looking, concerned for others. This never changed, it made him, as a man, loved and lovable, and as a writer it gave him his deepest integrity, so that in a letter written in 1828 he could quote the motto of one of his earliest publications. It is quite proper that in

Christian terms, quoting the New Testament, he should phrase his support for a secular University in a letter to a Jewish professor:[12]

The Word in whom is Life and that Life the Light of Men fixed for every Recipient of that Light of Life in all ages the End and Aim of his Labors – that all may know the Truth and that the Truth may make them free.

# Notes

## Introduction

1   *CL* 5, p.395.
2   W. Hazlitt, review of *Lay Sermon* by S. T. Coleridge, *Edinburgh Review*, 28 December 1816. In *Complete Works* of W. Hazlitt, ed. P. P. Howe, vol. 16, pp.99–114, p.102.
3   N. Fruman, *Coleridge, the Damaged Archangel*, 1972, p.209.
4   *CN* 2, 2375, 21.555.
5   *ShC* 2, p.11.
6   T. McFarland, 'Coleridge's anxiety' in *Coleridge's Variety*, ed. J. Beer, 1974, pp.134–65, pp.162–4.
7   *EOT* 3, p.757.
8   *CCF* 1, p.47.
9   W. Pater, *Appreciations*, 1915, p.72.
10  *CL* 3, p.282. A Hortus siccus was a kind of artificial garden made of dried flowers.
11  G. Whalley, 'Coleridge unlabyrinthed', *University of Toronto Quarterly*, vol. 32, July 1963, pp.325–45, p.344. The article is well worth reading as a whole as an introduction to Coleridge's works in their various editions.
12  *CN* 3, 3401, 13.34.
13  *CL* 4, p.598.
14  *CCF* 1, p.1.
15  There is some reference to language in the chapters on poetry and criticism and the notebooks provide useful insights into Coleridge's study of foreign languages and etymologies. Some reference to science in the philosophy chapter could be augmented by reference to the section on science, pp.393–9 in R. F. Brinkley, *Coleridge on the Seventeenth Century*, 1955. A. D. Snyder in *Coleridge on Logic and Learning*, 1929, discussed Coleridge's views on education and there is also W. J. Walsh, *The Use of the Imagination*, 1959.
16  *CN* 3, 3325, 21¼.19.

238

Chapter 1  Life

1  I. A. Richards, *Coleridge on Imagination*, 1934, p.ix.
2  D. P. Calleo, *Coleridge and the Idea of the Modern State*, NY and London, 1966, p.1.
3  T. McFarland, 'Coleridge's anxiety' in *Coleridge's Variety*, ed. J. Beer, 1974, pp.134-65, p.150; N. Fruman, *Coleridge, the Damaged Archangel*, 1972, p.22; M. Lefebure, *Samuel Taylor Coleridge: A Bondage of Opium*, 1974, pp.73-4.
4  *CL* 1, p.354. The series of autobiographical letters to Poole (nos.174, 179, 208, 210, 234 in *CL* 1) provide useful source material on Coleridge's childhood, but they must be read with attention to the fact that they are the personal reminiscences of an idiosyncratic genius.
5  *CL* 1, p.389.
6  *CP* 1, p.242.
7  *BL* 1, p.4.
8  Charles Lamb, *Works*, ed. T. Hutchinson, 1924, vol. 2, p.498.
9  *CL* 1, p.15.
10  *CL* 1, p.17.
11  *CL* 5, p.140.
12  Parson Woodforde's diary provides a useful if slightly earlier insight into rural ecclesiastical mores (Oxford, World's Classic, 1975).
13  E. S. Shaffer, '*Kubla Khan' and the Fall of Jerusalem*, 1975, is useful on the Unitarian influence on Coleridge's early maturity.
14  E. L. Griggs, 'Robert Southey's estimate of Samuel Taylor Coleridge', *Huntington Library Quarterly*, vol. 9, 1945, pp.61-94, p.75.
15  *CL* 1, pp.67-8.
16  Many works, too numerous to mention here, treat of Coleridge's friends. G. Yarlott's chapter 'Wanted: A sheet anchor' in *Coleridge and the Abyssinian Maid*, 1967, is a useful discussion on the nature of Coleridge's dependence on his friends.
17  *CL* 1, p.84. J. R. MacGillivray, 'The Pantisocracy scheme and its immediate background', in *Studies in English*, Toronto, 1931, pp.131-69, is very useful on the intellectual background to the venture.
18  *CL* 1, p.133.
19  *CN* 1, 6.1.8.
20  *CL* 1, p.145.
21  *CL* 1, p.165.
22  *CL* 1, p.166.
23  *CL* 1, p.236.
24  *CL* 1, p.482.
25  *CL* 1, p.495.

26    *CL* 1, p.483.
27    *CL* 1, p.477.
28    *CL* 1, p.584.
29    *CL* 2, p.662.
30    *CL* 6, p.894.
31    *CL* 1, p.491.
32    *PhL* p.150.
33    *CL* 2, p.918.
34    Cf. K. Coburn, 'Poet into public servant', *Transactions of the Royal Society of Canada*, 54, series 3, June 1960, section 2, pp.1-11; D. Sultana, *Samuel Taylor Coleridge in Malta and Italy*, 1969; A. Hayter, *A Voyage in Vain*, 1973.
35    *CN* 2, 2935, 11.125.
36    *CL* 3, pp. 125-6.
37    *CL* 5, pp.249-51.
38    *CN* 3, 4001, M.2.
39    *CL* 3, p.463.
40    *CL* 3, pp.480-6.
41    *CL* 3, p.486.
42    *CL* 6, p.918.
43    T. Carlyle, *Life of Sterling*, 1885, pp.46-7. The chapter on Coleridge is well worth study as a whole.
44    *CP* 1, pp.491-2.
45    *CN* 3, 4188, M.2.

Chapter 2    Plays

1    *CL* 3, pp.430-1.
2    *CL* 3, pp.436-7.
3    R. M. Fletcher, *English Romantic Drama 1795-1843*, NY, 1966, p.71.
4    Ibid., p.70.
5    *CL* 3, p.432n. The 1873 edition of *Osorio* publishes as well as the original play parallel passages from one of these editions of *Remorse*. J. D. Campbell has some interesting comments on Pople's editions in *Athenaeum*, 3285, 5 April 1890, pp.445-6. The 1873 edition usefully prints a cast list and reviews of the 1813 production.
6    *CL* 1, p.304.
7    R. M. Fletcher, op.cit., p.24.
8    *Bertram*, or 'The Castle of Aldobrand. A Tragedy in Five Acts', by the Rev. R. C. Maturin, with prefatory remarks. The only edition existing which is faithfully marked with the stage business and stage directions as performed at the Theatres Royal, W. Oxberry, Comedian, 1827.

9   *BL* 2, pp.193–4.

10  R. C. Maturin, op.cit., p.22.

11  *Letters of Charles and Mary Lamb*, ed. E. V. Lucas, 1935, vol. 2, p.187. J. D. Campbell, who quotes this letter (*JDC*, p.652), thinks that it proves that Coleridge wrote another play which has disappeared, but although the possibility cannot be ruled out, the reference to the acting is so like Coleridge's comment (*CL* 4, p.625) that *Zapolya* fits too well to justify a further supposed play.

12  Lord Byron, *Complete Works*, ed. E. H. Coleridge, 2nd edn., 1905, *Poetry*, vol. 4, p.337.

13  *CP* 2, p.495.

14  *CL* 1, p.106.

15  *CL* 1, pp.125–7, gives Coleridge's reply to George's criticism.

16  R. Southey, *New Letters*, ed. K. Curry, vol. 1, *1792–1810*, NY and London, 1965, p.73.

17  *CL* 1, p.318.

18  *CL* 1, p.325.

19  *CL* 1, pp.384–5.

20  *JDC*, p.646.

21  *CL* 3, p.179. As this was written in 1809, allowance should perhaps be made for Coleridge's adaptable memory.

22  P. Machule, 'Coleridge's Wallenstein-Übersetzung', *Englische Studien*, 31, 1902, pp.182–239, p.187.

23  J. L. Haney, *The German Influence on Samuel Taylor Coleridge*, 1902, p.20.

24  *Life and Correspondence of Robert Southey*, ed. C. C. Southey, 1850, vol. 5, p.142.

25  Macready's working papers are in the Forster Collection at the Victoria and Albert Museum. They consist of sheets of a published version of the play on which a thorough 'scissors and paste' job has been done. In the life of a busy actor-manager, this seems to indicate a serious intention to give the play a theatrical performance, but a diary entry of Macready suggests that 'though abounding with noble passages and beautiful scenes, it is spread over too much space to be contracted within reasonable dimensions.' W. Macready, *Reminiscences*, ed. F. Pollock, 1876, p.397.

26  *CN* 1, 869, 21.83 and n.; 871 1.11 and n. Also *CP* 2, Appendix 1, pp.1016–29.

27  *CL* 1, p.604.

28  *CL* 1, p.608.

29  *CL* 3, p.14.

30  *CL* 4, p.563n.

31  *CL* 4, p.617.

32  *CL* 4, p.620.

Notes

33   *TT*, p.25.
34   *CP* 2, pp.510-11.
35   *CP* 2, p.820. Coleridge changed most of the names in the revised version and in the comparison which follows I have used only the names in *Remorse*. The complete list of characters with both sets of names is as follows:

| *Remorse* | *Osorio* |
|---|---|
| Valdez | Velez |
| Alvar | Albert |
| Ordonio | Osorio |
| Monviedro (Inquisitor) | Francesco |
| Zulimez | Maurice |
| Isidore | Ferdinand |
| Naomi | Naomi |
| Teresa | Maria |
| Alhadra | Alhadra |

It is a curious thing that there is little discussion of the changes which Coleridge made for *Remorse*. Parallel texts are easy to find. E. H. Coleridge and J. D. Campbell print both plays in full and the 1873 anonymous edition of *Osorio* (its first publication) lists alterations which were made for *Remorse*, but there is no full-scale comparison of the two works.
36   *JDC*, p.650.
37   *CP* 2, p.555.
38   *CP* 2, p.255.
39   *CP* 2, p.856 and n.
40   *CL* 3, pp.523-4.
41   *JDC*, p.646.
42   *Westminster Review*, April-July 1850, vol. 53, no.2, pp.349-65, p.349.
43   P. Machule, op.cit., p.239.
44   B. Q. Morgan, 'What happened to Coleridge's *Wallenstein*', *MLJ*, 43, 1959, pp.195-201, p.201.
45   G. Wilson Knight, *The Starlit Dome*, 1959, p.171. There is an excellent discussion of the play in this book.
46   *CP* 2, p.950.
47   *CP* 2, p.883.
48   J. R. de J. Jackson, 'The Influence of the theatre on Coleridge's Shakespearean criticism', Princeton, 1961, gives useful details of Coleridge the playgoer and gives Coleridge's dramatic criticism its proper background in the theatre of his own time.
49   A. S. Downer, *The Eminent Tragedian, William Charles Macready*, Cambridge, Mass., 1966, p.253.

Chapter 3    Poetry

1  *CP* 2, pp.951-68.
2  *CL* 1, pp.656, 658, and *CL* 2, p.714.
3  *Letters of William and Dorothy Wordsworth*, vol. 1, ed. E. de Selincourt, 2nd edn., C. L. Shaver, Oxford, 1967, p.307.
4  *CL* 1, p.631.
5  *CL* 1, p.658.
6  *BL* 2, p.6.
7  *Monthly Review*, June 1976, pp.194-5. In J. R. de J. Jackson, *Coleridge: the Critical Heritage*, 1970, p.37.
8  *CP* 1, p.173n.
9  W. J. B. Owen, *Wordsworth and Coleridge, Lyrical Ballads 1798*, Oxford, 1967, introduction, pp.vii-xx.
10  *BL* 2, p.28.
11  W. J. B. Owen, op.cit., p.3.
12  G. Watson, *Coleridge the Poet*, 1966, p.64.
13  *JDC*, pp.607-8. G. Wilson Knight, *The Starlit Dome*, 1959, p.103, also thought 'France' 'one of his finest odes'.
14  *CP* 1, p.297.
15  *CP* 1, pp.71-2.
16  *CP* 1, p.91.
17  *CP* 1, p.93.
18  *BL* 1, p.5.
19  *JDC*, p.578.
20  *CP* 1, p.101.
21  *CP* 1, p.113.
22  *BL* 1, p.202.
23  *CP* 1, p.167 and n.
24  *CP* 1, p.245.
25  *CP* 1, pp.262-3.
26  *CP* 1, pp.259-60.
27  A. D. Snyder, *Coleridge on Logic and Learning*, 1929, p.76.
28  *CP* 1, p.242.
29  *CCLS*, p.30. Cf. L. C. Knights, 'Idea and symbol: some hints from Coleridge', *Metaphor and Symbol*, ed. L. C. Knights and B. Cottle. Proceedings of the 12th Symposium of the Colston Research Society, 1960; reprinted in *Further Explorations*, ed. L. C. Knights, 1965, and in *Coleridge: a Collection of Critical Essays*, ed. K. Coburn, 1967.
30  *CP* 1, pp.180-1.
31  *CP* 1, p.265.
32  *CP* 1, p.267.
33  W. J. B. Owen, op.cit., p.105.
34  *CP* 1, p.209.

35  *TT*, p.87.
36  H. House, *Coleridge*, 1953, pp.90–1.
37  *CN* 2, 2090, 15.56.
38  W. J. B. Owen, op.cit., p.105. However *Twentieth Century Interpretations of The Rime of the Ancient Mariner* ed. J. D. Boulger, New Jersey, 1969, gives some of the most seminal modern criticism of the poem.
39  *CP* 1, p.197.
40  *CP* 1, p.213n.
41  *MC*, p.373.
42  *CP* 1, p.224.
43  A. H. Nethercot, *The Road to Tryermaine*, Chicago, 1939.
44  E.g. A. J. Harding, *Coleridge and the Idea of Love*, 1974, pp.66–74.
45  G. Whalley, *Coleridge and Sara Hutchinson and the Asra Poems*, 1955, p.117.
46  First published in E. de Selincourt, *Wordsworthian and Other Studies*, Oxford, 1947, pp.67–76. Also found *CL* 2, pp.790–8.
47  B. F. Fields, *Reality's Dark Dream*, Chicago, 1967, emphasises this aspect of the poem.
48  *CL* 2, p.797.
49  *CP* 1, p.366.
50  *CP* 1, p.365.
51  *CP* 1, p.364.
52  *CL* 2, pp.864–5.
53  *CP* 1, p.374.
54  *CP* 1, p.391.
55  *CP* 1, pp.396–7.
56  N. Fruman, *Coleridge, the Damaged Archangel*, 1972, p.260.
57  *CP* 1, p.479.
58  *CP* 1, p.480.
59  *CP* 1, p.440.


Chapter 4   Literary Criticism

1  Cf. note 10 below.
2  J. R. de J. Jackson, *Method and Imagination in Coleridge's Criticism*, 1969, p.1.
3  *ShC* 2, pp.255–6. Raysor gives a valuable survey of Coleridge's lecture career, which I have briefly summarised.
4  *CL* 3, p.534.
5  T. Ashe, ed., *Miscellanies, Aesthetic and Literary*, 1885, pp.74–5.
6  *CL* 1, pp.277 and 279.

7    JDC, p.538.

8    BL 1, pp.173-4.

9    JDC, p.543.

10   J. R. de J. Jackson in a note in his *Method and Imagination in Coleridge's Criticism*, p.175, gives a useful summary of the various contributions to the debate and comments: 'The reviews so far identified show signs of Coleridge's characteristic trains of thought, something of his penchant for moral and theoretic implications, but little to my mind, of the sustained power which made him famous; I should attribute the marked difference in quality partly to the lack of an underlying philosophical structure in his early literary discussions.' While I agree about the lack of a philosophical dimension in the reviews, the presence of just such a quality in both the poetry and the prefaces of the period leads me to think that the exigencies of reviewing was the cause and not any philosophical deficiency in Coleridge.

11   CL 1, p.318.

12   MC, p.370.

13   CCF 1, pp.137-40.

14   MC, p.373.

15   BL 2, p.223.

16   Quoted in Jackson, op.cit., p.147.

17   CL 2, pp.811-12.

18   CL 2, p.830.

19   CL 4, p.923.

20   G. Whalley, 'The Integrity of *Biographia Literaria*', *Essays and Studies*, 1953, pp.87-101, perhaps led the field here.

21   Cf. Chapter 2, pp.39-40.

22   BL 1, p.1. Shawcross considers (p.203) that this was added after much of the work was written.

23   BL 1, pp.102-5.

24   CN 1, 921, 21.121.

25   BL 1, p.1.

26   BL 2, pp.38-9.

27   BL 1, pp.14-15. Coleridge's footnote illustrates the 'abstract meaning' by a quotation from a poem by a 'young tradesman':

     No more will I endure love's pleasing pain,
     Or round my heart's leg tie his galling chain.

28   BL 2, p.49.

29   BL 2, p.50.

30   BL 2, p.53.

31   CN 3, 3611, 24.23.

32   CN 3, 3970, 18.271.

33   BL 1, p.44.

34   *BL* 2, p.109. The coverage of Wordsworth's defects occupies pp.97-105.
35   *BL* 2, p.129.
36   S. M. Parrish, 'The Wordsworth-Coleridge controversy', *PMLA*, vol. 73, 1958, pp.367-74. Now incorporated in S. M. Parrish, *The Art of the Lyrical Ballads*, Cambridge, Mass., 1973.
37   *TT*, pp.171-2.
38   *BL* 2, p.12.
39   *BL* 2, p.124.
40   *BL* 1, pp.60-1.
41   *BL* 1, p.161.
42   *BL* 1, p.198.
43   *BL* 1, pp.200-1.
44   *BL* 1, p.202.
45   *BL* 1, p.62.
46   I. A. Richards, *Coleridge on Imagination*, 1934, p.94.
47   *CP* 1, pp.188 and 197.
48   *BL* 1, p.202.
49   *BL* 1, p.272.
50   *BL* 2, p.14.
51   *Letters of William and Dorothy Wordsworth*, vol. 2, pt.1, ed. E. de Selincourt, 2nd ed., M. Moorman, Oxford, 1969, pp.83-4.
52   *ShC* 2, p.28.
53   *ShC* 2, p.227.
54   *CN* 3, 4393, 22.60 and note.
55   *ShC* 2, p.14.
56   *ShC* 1, p.126.
57   *ShC* 1, p.223.
58   *Notes and Lectures upon Shakespeare*, ed. Sara Coleridge, 1849, vol. 1, notes, pp.338-40.
59   R. H. Fogle, *The Idea of Coleridge's Criticism*, Berkeley and Los Angeles, 1962, p.121.
60   *ShC* 2, p.145.
61   *ShC* 1, pp.127-30.
62   *ShC* 2, pp.278-9.
63   *ShC* 2, p.85.
64   *CL* 3, p.501.
65   Cf. Chapter 2, p.57.
66   *ShC* 2, p.136.
67   *TT*, p.47.
68   *ShC* 2, pp.192-3.
69   *ShC* 1, p.lvi.
70   *Works of Charles and Mary Lamb*, ed. E. V. Lucas, Vol. 2, p.26; quoted *CL* 3, p.55n.

71  C. C. Seronsky, 'Coleridge's Marginalia in Lamb's copy of Daniel's poetical works', *Harvard Library Bulletin*, vol. 7, 1953, pp.105-12.
72  *MC*, pp.133-4.
73  *MC*, p.220.
74  *BL* 1, pp.4-5.
75  *TT*, p.25.


Chapter 5   Political Journalism

1   *CCW*, p.5.
2   *CCL*, p.309.
3   *TT*, p.120.
4   C. Brinton, *The Political Ideas of the English Romanticists*, 1926, discusses the changing attitudes of the writers of the period.
5   R. Southey, *New Letters*, ed. K. Curry, vol. 2, *1811-38*, p.385.
6   *CL* 1, pp.179-80.
7   *CL*.1, p.397.
8   *CL* 2, p.1002.
9   *EOT* 1, p.223.
10  *CCL*, p.6.
11  *CN* 3, 3845, 18.249.
12  *CCL*, p.25.
13  D. Stuart, 'Anecdotes of the poet Coleridge', *Gentleman's Magazine*, vol. 9, May 1838, pp.485-92, p.486. The series continued: June 1838, pp.580-90; vol. 10, July 1838, pp.22-7 (this included a letter from H. N. Coleridge), and August 1838, pp.124-8.
14  *CCL*, p.xxxi.
15  *CL* 2, p.1001.
16  *CCL*, p.214.
17  *CCW*, p.5.
18  *CL* 1, p.194.
19  *CCW*, p.374.
20  *BL* 1, p.114.
21  *CL* 1, pp.268-9.
22  *CL* 1, p.556.
23  *CL* 1, pp.572-3.
24  *CL* 1, p.579.
25  D. Stuart, 'Anecdotes of the poet Coleridge', *Gentleman's Magazine*, vol. 9, May 1838, p.487.
26  *CL* 1, p.233n.
27  *CL* 3, p.320.

28  *BL* 1, p.145.
29  D. Stuart, op.cit., p.491.
30  *Two Addresses on Sir Robert Peel's Bill*, April 1818, printed privately, 1913, p.25.
31  *CP* 1, p.260.
32  *CCL*, p.45.
33  *CCL*, p.46.
34  *CCL*, pp.59-60.
35  *CCL*, pp.61-2.
36  *CCW*, p.271.
37  *CCW*, pp.272-3.
38  *CCW*, pp.131-2. The earlier lecture is in CCL, pp.232-51.
39  *CCW*, p.139.
40  *CCW*, p.138.
41  *Edinburgh Review*, vol. 12, July 1808, pp.355-79, p.356.
42  Ibid., p.357.
43  *CCW*, pp.54-5.
44  *EOT* 3, p.1010. J. Colmer, *Coleridge, Critic of Society*, 1959, says that this refers to a speech of 3 February 1800, but the letters prove that Coleridge was not awake throughout this speech.
45  *CL* 1, p.573 and pp.574-5.
46  *The Speeches of the Rt. Hon. William Pitt in the House of Commons*, ed. W. S. Hathaway, 1806, vol. 4, p.62.
47  *EOT* 2, p.295.
48  *The Speeches of the Rt. Hon. William Pitt in the House of Commons*, ed. W. S. Hathaway, 1806, vol. 4, p.46.
49  *EOT* 2, p.323.
50  *EOT* 2, pp.326-7.
51  *CCL*, p.63.
52  *EOT* 2, pp.649-50.
53  *EOT* 3, pp.811-12.
54  *EOT* 3, p.917.
55  *EOT* 3, p.862.
56  *EOT* 3, p.863.
57  *EOT* 3, p.871.
58  *EOT* 3, pp.919-20.
59  *EOT* 3, p.885.
60  *EOT* 3, pp.894-5.
61  *EOT* 3, p.925.
62  *EOT* 3, p.708.

Chapter 6   Political Theory

1   *CCL*, p.3. The quotation is from Mark Akenside's 'To the Right

Honourable Francis Earl of Huntingdon', with some Coleridgean variations.

2  *CL* 3, p.197.
3  *CL* 3, p.141.
4  *CCF* 1, xlix n. The introduction gives a useful account of the production of *The Friend*.
5  *Letters of William and Dorothy Wordsworth*, vol. 1, ed. E. de Selincourt, 2nd edn., C. L. Shaver, Oxford, 1967, p.322.
6  *CL* 3, pp.130-1.
7  *Letters of William and Dorothy Wordsworth*, vol. 1, ed. E. de Selincourt, 2nd edn., C. L. Shaver, Oxford, 1967, p.398.
8  *CCF* 2, pp.78-9
9  *CCF* 2, p.152.
10  *CCF* 1, p.209, for example.
11  *CL* 4, p.670.
12  *CCF* 1, p.210.
13  *CL* 4, p.695.
14  *CCLS*, p.31.
15  *CCLS*, pp.228-9. Following common practice, I shall refer to the first *Lay Sermon* as *The Statesman's Manual* and the second as the *Lay Sermon*.
16  *C&S*, pp.59-60.
17  D. P. Calleo, *Coleridge and the Idea of the Modern State*, 1966, p.3.
18  *CCF* 1, p.185.
19  *CCF* 1, pp.303-12.
20  *CCLS*, pp.28-9.
21  L. C. Knights, 'Idea and symbol: some hints from Coleridge', *Metaphor and Symbol*, ed. L. C. Knights and B. Cottle, Proceedings of the 12th Symposium of the Colston Research Society, 1960; reprinted in *Further Explorations*, ed. L. C. Knights, 1965, and in *Coleridge: a Collection of Critical Essays*, ed. K. Coburn, 1967.
22  *CCLS*, pp.31-2.
23  *CCLS*, pp.32-3.
24  *CCLS*, pp.49-50.
25  *CCLS*, p.39.
26  *CCLS*, pp.39-40.
27  *CCLS*, p.47.
28  *CCLS*, p.60.
29  *CCLS*, pp. 63-4.
30  *CCLS*, p.211.
31  *CCLS*, p.169.
32  *CCLS*, p.170.
33  *CCLS*, p.189.
34  *CCLS*, pp.205-7.

35  *CCLS*, pp.229-30.
36  *CCF* 1, p.16.
37  *CCF* 1, pp.148-9.
38  *CL* 4, p.639.
39  Cf. Chapter 5, p.125.
40  *CCF* 1, pp.38 and 39.
41  *CCF* 1, p.61.
42  *CCF* 1, p.77.
43  *CCF* 1, p.82.
44  *CCF* 1, pp.97-8.
45  *CCF* 1, p.125.
46  *CCF* 1, p.159.
47  *CCF* 1, p.175.
48  *CCF* 1, pp.199-200.
49  *CCF* 1, p.214.
50  *EOT* 2, pp.550ff.
51  *CCF* 1, p.223.
52  W. F. Kennedy, *Humanist versus Economist: The Economic Thought of S. T. Coleridge*, Berkeley and Los Angeles, 1958.
53  *CCF* 1, pp.251-3.
54  *CCF* 1, p.338.
55  *CCF* 1, p.336.
56  *CCF* 1, p.292.
57  *CCF* 1, p.301.
58  *C&S*, p.146.
59  *C&S*, p.24.
60  Useful studies of the political thought of the Romantic poets are A. Cobban, *Edmund Burke and the Revolt against the Eighteenth Century*, 1929, 2nd edn., 1960; C. Brinton, *The Political Ideas of the English Romanticists*, 1926.
61  *C&S*, pp.45-6.
62  *C&S*, p.71.
63  *C&S*, pp.124-5.
64  Cf. C. R. Sanders, *Coleridge and the Broad Church Movement*, Durham, N.C., 1942.
65  *CCF* 1, p.299.

Chapter 7   On Religion

1  *CL* 1, p.123.
2  *CL* 1, p.91.
3  *LR* 4, pp.50, 54 and 58, for example.

4   *CN* 3, 4005, M.7; also in *Omniana*, ed. R. Gittings Fontwell, 1969, p.357, and *TT*, p.429.
5   *BL* 1, p.10.
6   *CL* 1, p.372.
7   *CN* 2, 2448, 17.22.
8   *CL* 2, p.1189.
9   *CL* 2, p.1192.
10  *CL* 2, pp.1197-8.
11  *CL* 3, p.462.
12  *CL* 3, p.480.
13  *CL* 3, p.495-6.
14  *LR* 4, pp.437-8.
15  *CL* 5, p.290.
16  *AR*, p.ix.
17  *AR*, pp.xvi-xviii.
18  *CL* 5, p.434.
19  *LR* 4, pp.425 and 438.
20  *CIS*, p.38.
21  *CCL*, pp.86-7. These details are amplified in the footnotes to the lectures.
22  *CCL*, p.46, and cf. Chapter 5, p.128.
23  *CCL*, pp.162-3.
24  *CCL*, pp.106-7.
25  *CCL*, p.108.
26  *CCL*, pp.207-8.
27  *CCL*, pp.67-8n.
28  *CCL*, pp.210-11.
29  *CCL*, pp.224-5.
30  *CCL*, pp.228-9.
31  J. D. Boulger, *Coleridge as Religious Thinker*, New Haven, 1961. The book as a whole usefully sets Coleridge's ideas against a background of early nineteenth-century theological debate.
32  *AR*, pp.xvii-iii.
33  *AR*, pp.165-6.
34  *AR*, p.152n.
35  *AR*, p.15.
36  *AR*, p.40.
37  *AR*, p.41.
38  *AR*, pp.114-15.
39  *CL* 5, pp.137-8.
40  *AR*, p.121.
41  *AR*, p.122.
42  *AR*, p.66.
43  *AR*, p.140.

44  *CL* 5, p.92.
45  *CIS*, pp.30-1.
46  *CIS*, p.39.
47  *CIS*, p.43.
48  *CIS*, p.64.
49  *CIS*, p.75.
50  *TT*, p.153.
51  *CIS*, pp.57-8.
52  *TT*, pp.23-4.
53  *CN* 3, 3754, 18.67.
54  *CL* 6, p.895.
55  *CN* 2, 2983, 11.52.
56  *CN* 3, 4007, M.8.
57  *CIS*, p.79.


## Chapter 8  Philosophical Writings

1  *BL* 1, pp.91-2, 202, for example.
2  *CN* 1, 1515, 4.80.
3  *CN* 1, 1646, 21.392.
4  A. D. Snyder, *Coleridge on Logic and Learning*, New Haven and London, 1929, p.71.
5  *CL* 5, p.98.
6  *PhL*, p.39.
7  *CL* 2, p.699.
8  *CL* 2, pp.677-8.
9  *CL* 2, p.700.
10  O. Barfield, *What Coleridge Thought*, 1972, p.43.
11  *CL* 2, pp.947-8.
12  Cf. Chapter 4, p.89, and *JDC*, p.538.
13  This is the same plan as that of O. Barfield's *What Coleridge Thought*, a book which is invaluable to any attempt to extricate a body of thought from Coleridge's writings.
14  *CL* 4, pp.825-6.
15  *CL* 4, p.860.
16  *CL* 4, p.821.
17  A. D. Snyder, *Treatise on Method as Published in The Encyclopaedia Metropolitana*, 1934, p.xxv.
18  Ibid., p.6.
19  *CL* 4, p.917.
20  A. D. Snyder, *Coleridge on Logic and Learning*, pp.16-17.
21  *CL* 3, p.533.

22  *CL* 5, p.265.
23  *TT*, p.296.
24  *TT*, p.293.
25  *BL* 1, p.66.
26  *BL* 1, pp.85-6.
27  *BL* 1, pp.169-70.
28  *BL* 1, p.173.
29  *BL* 1, p.174.
30  *BL* 1, p.176.
31  *BL* 1, p.180.
32  *BL* 1, pp.187 and 185.
33  *BL* 1, p.187.
34  *BL* 1, pp.197-8.
35  *CCF* 1, p.449.
36  *CCF* 1, p.453.
37  *CCF* 1, p.457.
38  *CCF* 1, pp.484-5.
39  *CCF* 1, p.459.
40  *CCF* 1, p.463.
41  *CCF* 1, p.479.
42  *CCF* 1, p.492.
43  *CCF* 1, p.495.
44  *CCF* 1, p.524.
45  *CCF* 1, pp.520-2.
46  *CCF* 1, p.517.
47  *CCF* 1, p.519.
48  *PhL*, pp.32-3. Quotations from *PhL* do not include the various editorial markings.
49  *PhL*, p.67.
50  *PhL*, pp.125-9.
51  *PhL*, pp.111-12.
52  *PhL*, p.171.
53  *PhL*, p.226.
54  *PhL*, p.280.
55  *PhL*, p.132.
56  *PhL*, p.146.
57  *PhL*, p.369.
58  *PhL*, p.371.
59  *PhL*, p.320.
60  *CL* 4, p.807.
61  C. Miller, 'Coleridge's concept of nature', *Journal of the History of Ideas*, vol. 25, 1964, pp.77-96, p.86.
62  *TL*, p.42.
63  *TL*, p.49.

64    *TL*, p.50.
65    *TL*, p.51.
66    *TL*, pp.57-8.
67    *TL*, p.40n.
68    *TL*, p.81.
69    O. Barfield's book is particularly useful with respect to the *Theory of Life*.
70    A. D. Snyder, *Coleridge on Logic and Learning*, p.90.
71    Ibid., p.110.
72    J. Muirhead, *Coleridge as Philosopher*, 1930 and 1954, has some useful additional material.

## Conclusion

1    K. Coburn, 'Poet into public servant', *Transactions of the Royal Society of Canada*, 54, series 3, June 1960, section 2, pp.1-11, p.1.
2    *TT*, p.139.
3    *CCLS*, p.79.
4    *CCLS*, p.30.
5    *CN* 2, 2540, 17.98.
6    *BL* 1, p.202.
7    A. J. Harding, *Coleridge and the Idea of Love*, 1974, p.63.
8    *PhL*, pp.172-3.
9    J. H. Muirhead, *Coleridge as Philosopher*, 1954, p.225.
10   *TT*, p.274.
11   *CCF* 1, p.55.
12   *CL* 6, p.772.

# Bibliography

(Place of publication is London except where stated.)

The following list is highly selective and includes only a few of those books and articles which are interesting to a student of Coleridge. In making my choice I have been influenced by considerations of usefulness – hence the list is longer for more obscure aspects of Coleridge as I felt that the reader who wanted to read about the poetry would have no difficulty in finding books. Even so, I should like to re-iterate the comment I made in the Introduction; the best companion to Coleridge studies is Coleridge and accordingly the first section is headed:

Coleridge

S. T. Coleridge: *Collected Works:*
1 *Lectures 1795 On Politics and Religion,* ed. L. Patton and P. Mann, 1971.
2 *The Watchman,* ed. L. Patton, 1970.
3 *Essays on his Times,* ed. D. V. Erdman, 1978 (too late to be used in the preparation of this book).
4 *The Friend,* ed. B. Rooke in two volumes, 1969.
6 *Lay Sermons,* ed. R. J. White, 1972.
10 *On the Constitution of Church and State,* ed. J. A. Colmer, 1976 (too late to be used in the preparation of this book).
The notes in these editions as well as the way in which they are presented make them invaluable and as soon as other works appear in this series this edition will supersede the editions below for although many of them are excellent, the most recent is out of date and the oldest is over a century old.
*Aids to Reflection,* reprint of 1839 edition by H. N. Coleridge, Bohn Library, 1884.
*Biographia Literaria,* ed. J. Shawcross, Oxford, 1907.
*Collected Letters,* ed. E. L. Griggs, Oxford, 1956, 1959, 1971.
*Collected Notebooks,* ed. K. Coburn, New York, 1957 and 1962; Princeton, 1973.
*Confessions of an Inquiring Spirit,* ed. H. St J. Hart, 1956.

*Essays on his own Times*, ed S. Coleridge, 1850 (this is the edition referred to in the text, as the Collected Works edition did not appear until it was completed).

*Hints towards the Formation of a Theory of Life*, ed. S. B. Watson, 1848.

*Literary Remains*, ed. H. N. Coleridge, 1836-9.

*Miscellaneous Criticism*, ed T. M. Raysor, 1936.

*On the Constitution of Church and State*, ed. H. N. Coleridge, 1839 (this is the edition referred to in the text, as the Collected Works edition did not appear until it was completed).

*Philosophical Lectures*, ed. K. Coburn, 1949.

*Poetical Works*, ed. E. H. Coleridge, Oxford, 1912 (this and the Campbell edition include the plays).

*Poetical Works*, ed. J. D. Campbell, 1901 (especially useful nòtes).

*Shakespearean Criticism*, ed. T. M. Raysor, 1930.

*Table Talk and Omniana*, ed. T. Ashe, 1884.

*Treatise on Method as published in the Encyclopaedia Metropolitana*, ed. A. D. Snyder, 1934.

*The Political Thought of S. T. Coleridge*, ed. R. J. White, 1938.

*Inquiring Spirit*, ed. K. Coburn, 1951. (This and the above book provide useful introductory selections of published and unpublished material.)

## General Studies

*Background*

Briggs, A., *The Age of Improvement*, 1959.

Bryant, A., *The Years of Endurance*, 1942.

Bryant, A., *The Years of Victory*, 1945.

Bryant, A., *The Age of Elegance*, 1950.

Byatt, A. S., *Wordsworth and Coleridge in their Time*, 1970.

Willey, B., *Eighteenth Century Background*, 1940.

Willey, B., *Nineteenth Century Studies*, 1949.


*Coleridge*

Bate, W. J., *Coleridge*, 1968.

Beer, J. (ed.), *Coleridge's Variety*, 1974.

Coburn, K. (ed.), *Coleridge*, Englewood Cliffs, 1967.

Fruman, N., *Coleridge, the Damaged Archangel*, 1972.

House, H., *Coleridge*, 1953.

## Life

More or less contemporary studies offer a peculiar insight which more than compensates for the incompleteness, partiality and unscholarly nature of many of these books.

Allsop, T., *Letters, Conversations and Recollections of S. T. Coleridge*, New York, 1836.

Carlyle. T., 'Coleridge' in *Life of Sterling*, 1885.

Cottle, J., *Reminiscences of S. T. Coleridge and R. Southey*, 1847; Facsimile reprint, 1970.

de Quincey, T., *Reminiscences of the English Lake Poets*, ed. E. Jordan, 1961.

Gillman, J., *Life of S. T. Coleridge*, 1838

Hazlitt, W., 'My First Acquaintance with Poets' in *Complete Works*, ed. P. P. Howe, vol. 17, 1933, pp.106-22.

Lamb, C. and M., *Letters*, ed. E. V. Lucas, 1935.

Robinson, H. C., *On Books and their Writers*, ed. E. J. Morley, 1938.

Wordsworth, D., *Journals*, ed. E. de Selincourt, 1941.

Wordsworth, D. and W., *Letters*, ed. E. de Selincourt, vol. 1 revised C. L. Shaver, Oxford, 1967; vol. 2 pt 1 revised M. Moorman, Oxford, 1969; pt 2 revised M. Moorman and A. G. Hill, Oxford, 1970.

Of Coleridge's own works the following are particularly relevant: letters 174, 179, 208, 210, and 234 (autobiographical letters to Poole), and *Biographia Literaria* Chapters 1 and 10 and Satyrane's letters.

From among many studies of Coleridge the following should help to round out an acquaintance with the man:

Campbell, J. D., *Samuel Taylor Coleridge*, 1894

Coburn, K., 'Poet into Public Servant', *Transactions of the Royal Society of Canada*, 54, Series 3 June 1960, section 2, pp.1-11.

Griggs, E. L., 'Robert Southey's Estimate of Samuel Taylor Coleridge', *Huntington Library Quarterly*, vol. 9 November 1945, pp.61-94.

Griggs, E. L., 'Coleridge and his Friends', *Charles Lamb Society Bulletin*, 1956.

*Coleridge Fille* (a biography of Sara Coleridge), 1940.

Hanson, L., *The Life of Samuel Taylor Coleridge* (the early years), 1938.

Hayter, A., *A Voyage in Vain* (Coleridge's journey to Malta 1804), 1973.

Lefebure, M., *Samuel Taylor Coleridge: A Bondage of Opium*, 1974.

Margoliouth, H. M., *Wordsworth and Coleridge, 1795-1834*, 1953.

Potter, S. (ed.), *Minnow among Tritons* (Mrs S. T. Coleridge's letters to Thomas Poole 1799-1834), 1934.

Sultana, D., *Samuel Taylor Coleridge in Malta and Italy*, Oxford, 1969.

Whalley, G., *Coleridge and Sara Hutchinson and the Asra Poems*, 1955.

Plays and Poetry

Boulger, J. D. (ed.), *Twentieth Century Interpretations of The Rime of the Ancient Mariner: A Collection of Critical Essays*, Englewood Cliffs, 1969.

Donohue, J. W., *English Theatre in the Age of Kean*, Oxford, 1975.

Bibliography

Fletcher, R. M., *English Romantic Drama 1795-1843: A Critical History*, New York, 1966.

Knight, G. W., *The Starlit Dome*, 1959.

Langbaum, R., *The Poetry of Experience*, 1957.

Lowes, J. L., *The Road to Xanadu*, revised ed., Boston, 1931.

Nethercot, A. H., *The Road to Tryermaine*, Chicago, 1939.

Nicoll, A., *A History of the Early Nineteenth Century Drama 1800-50*, vol. 1, 1930.

Watson, G. G., *Coleridge the Poet*, 1966.

Yarlott, G., *Coleridge and the Abyssinian Maid*, 1967.

Literary Criticism

Abrams, M. H., *The Mirror and the Lamp*, 1953.

Appleyard, J. A., *Coleridge's Philosophy of Literature*, Cambridge, Mass., 1965.

Brett, R. L., 'Coleridge's Theory of Imagination', *English Studies*, 1949, pp. 75-90.

Fogle, R. H., *The Idea of Coleridge's Criticism*, Berkeley/Los Angeles, 1962.

Jackson, J. R. de J., 'The Influence of the Theatre on Coleridge's Shakespeare Criticism', unpublished Princeton University thesis, 1961.

Jackson, J. R. de J., *Method and Imagination in Coleridge's Criticism*, 1969.

Read, H., *Coleridge as Critic*, 1949.

Richards, I. A., *Coleridge on Imagination*, 1934.

Whalley, G., 'The Integrity of Biographia Literaria', *Essays and Studies*, 1953, pp.87-101.

The following articles all attempt to solve the problem of Coleridge's early work for the *Critical Review*:

Erdman, D. V., 'Immoral Acts of a Library Cormorant: the extent of Coleridge's contributions to the Critical Review', *New York Public Library Bulletin*, 1959, 63, pp.433-54.

Patterson, C. I., 'An Unidentified Criticism by Coleridge related to Christabel', *Proceedings of the Modern Language Association*, 67, 1952, pp. 973-88.

Patterson, C. I., 'The Authenticity of Coleridge's reviews of Gothic Romances', *Journal of English and Germanic Philology*, 50, 1951, pp. 517-21.

Roper, Derek, 'Coleridge and the Critical Review', *Modern Language Review*, 60, 1960, pp.11-16.

Whalley, G., 'Coleridge on Classical Prosody: an undentified review of 1797', *Review of English Studies*, n.s.2, 1951, pp.238-47.

Politics

Brinton, C., *The Political Ideas of the English Romanticists*, 1926.

Calleo, D. P., *Coleridge and the Idea of the Modern State*, New Haven/ London, 1966.

Cobban, A., *Edmund Burke and the Revolt against the Eighteenth Century* (A study of the political and social thinking of Burke, Wordsworth, Coleridge and Southey), 1929.

Colmer, J. A., *Coleridge, Critic of Society*, Oxford, 1959.

Erdman, D. V., 'Coleridge as Editorial Writer' in *Power and Consciousness*, ed. C. C. O'Brien and W. D. Vanech, London/New York, 1969, pp. 183-201.

Hindle, W. H., *The Morning Post*, 1937.

Kennedy, W. F., *Humanist versus Economist* (the economic thought of S. T. Coleridge), Berkeley/Los Angeles, 1958.

Mill, J. S. *Dissertations and Discussions*, 1859.

Stuart, D., 'Anecdotes of the poet Coleridge', *Gentleman's Magazine*, vol. 9, May 1838, pp.185-92; June 1838, pp.580-90; vol. 10, July 1838, pp.22-7; August 1838, pp.124-8.

Thompson, E. P., 'Disenchantment or Default' in *Power and Consciousness*, ed. C. C. O'Brien and W. D. Vanech, London/New York, 1969, pp. 149-81.

Woodring, C. R., *Politics in the Poetry of Coleridge*, Madison, 1961.

Religion and Philosophy

Barfield, O., *What Coleridge Thought*, Middletown, Conn., 1972.

Barth, J. R., *Coleridge and Christian Doctrine*, Cambridge, Mass., 1969.

Beer, J., *Coleridge the Visionary*, 1959.

Boulger, J. D., *Coleridge as Religious Thinker*, New Haven, 1961.

Harding, A. J., *Coleridge and the Idea of Love*, Cambridge, 1974.

James, D. G., *The Romantic Comedy*, Oxford, 1948.

Knights, L. C., 'Idea and Symbol: Some Hints from Coleridge' in *Metaphor and Symbol*, ed. L. C. Knights and B. Cottle, Proceedings of the Symposium of the Colston Research Society, 1960, in *Coleridge*, ed. K. Coburn, 1967 and Knights, L. C., *Further Explorations*, 1965.

Lockridge, L. S., *Coleridge the Moralist*, Ithaca/London, 1977.

McFarland, T., *Coleridge and the Pantheist Tradition*, Oxford, 1969.

Miller, C., 'Coleridge's Concept of Nature', *Journal of the History of Ideas*, vol. 25, 1964, pp. 77-96.

Muirhead, J. H., *Coleridge as Philosopher*, 1930.

Sanders, C. R., *Coleridge and the Broad Church Movement*, Durham, North Carolina, 1942.

Shaffer, E. S., *'Kubla Khan' and the Fall of Jerusalem*, Cambridge, 1975.

Snyder, A. D., *Coleridge on Logic and Learning*, New Haven, 1929.

Willey, B., *Samuel Taylor Coleridge*, 1972.

# Index

# Index

Gale and Fenner, 33; *see also* Rest Fenner
*Gentleman's Magazine*, 125
George III, 120, 142
Gillman, J., and Mrs, 15, 26, 33, 47, 59, 125, 149, 150, 208, 209, 228
Godwin, W., 14, 45, 58, 127-8, 168, 173, 183-4, 205, 210, 231
Goethe, J. W. von, 52
Green, J. H., 15, 34, 58, 194, 198, 201, 216
Griggs, E. L., 38, 124

Habeas Corpus Act, 14, 120, 129, 151
Harding, A. J., 234
Hardy, T., 14
Hartley, D., 13, 14, 94, 101, 127, 132, 150, 174, 176, 203, 204, 212, 236
Hazlitt, W., 2, 4, 9, 21, 38, 41, 115, 208
Hessey, J. A., 182
Hobbes, T., 101, 226
House, H., 75
House of Commons, 135, 138, 139
Hurwitz, H., 33, 194
Hutchinson, S., 9, 23, 27, 29, 30, 31, 59, 79, 93, 149, 179

Ireland forgeries, 131

Jackson, J. R. de J., 86, 103
Johnson, Dr S., 86, 112

Kant, I., 3, 25, 94, 101, 106, 191, 212, 216
Kean, E., 38, 39, 40, 44, 46, 47, 112
*Keepsake*, 65
Kemble, J. P., 39, 43, 108
Knight, G. W., 54
Knights, L. C., 154-5
Kosciusko, T., 118
Kotzebue, A. F. F., 41, 44

Lafayette, Marquis de, 118
Lamb, C., 11, 17, 21, 29, 31, 34, 38, 40, 41, 62, 73, 111, 202
Lamb, M., 17

Leibnitz, G. W., 25, 101
Leighton, Archbishop R., 181, 183
Liverpool, Lord, 152
Lloyd, C., 17, 20, 62
Locke, J., 25, 150, 204, 226
Longmans (Longman and Rees), 44, 60, 123
*Love a la Mode* (Macklin), 109
Lovell, R., 16, 41
Lowes, J. L., 74
Lully, R., 205
*Lyrical Ballads*, 17, 20, 21, 27, 43, 59, 60, 61, 62, 64, 73, 74, 75, 79, 91, 93

McFarland, T., 4
Machule, P., 53
Mackintosh, Sir J., 118-19
Macklin, C., 109
Macready, W. C., 38, 44, 57, 109
Mann, P., 127
Mathews, C., 47, 109
Maturin, C., 39-40, 94
Maurice, F. D., 171
Mill, J. S., 152, 171
Miller, C., 227
Milton, J., 11, 24, 86, 88, 96, 99, 100, 104, 105, 108, 164
*Monk, The*, 78, 90
Montagu, B., 30, 124, 149
*Monthly Magazine*, 62
Morgan, B. Q., 53
Morgan, J., 15, 31, 32, 59, 93
*Morning Chronicle*, 17, 61, 118, 119
*Morning Post*, 21, 23, 24, 25, 62, 64, 79, 117, 118-19, 123, 125, 126, 135, 140, 148-9, 160, 166
Muirhead, J. D., 235
Murray, J., 33, 52, 53

Napoleonic Wars, 19, 114, 128-9, 130, 135, 140, 149, 162
Necessarianism, 13, 132, 174, 229
Nethercot, A. H., 79

Occam, William of, 225
Otway, T., 102

264